D0652427

HONOR BOUND

HONOR BOUND

A Gay Naval Midshipman
Fights to Serve His Country

JOSEPH ★ STEFFAN

AVON BOOKS ◆ NEW YORK

For my parents, Charles and Margaret Steffan, and for three great friends and role models: Howard Bragman, Sandra Lowe, and Marc Wolinsky

Unless otherwise noted, all photos appear courtesy of Joe Steffan.

AVON BOOKS
A division of
The Hearst Corporation
1350 Avenue of the Americas
New York, New York 10019

Copyright © 1992 by Joseph Steffan
Front and back cover photos by Michael Britto
Published by arrangement with the author
Library of Congress Catalog Card Number: 92-53654
ISBN: 0-380-71501-5

Published in hardcover by Villard Books; for information address Villard Books, a division of Random House, Inc., 201 East 50th Street, New York, New York 10022.

The Villard Books edition contains the following Library of Congress Cataloging in Publication Data:

Steffan, Joseph
    Honor Bound / Joseph Steffan, III
      p.   cm.
1. United States. Navy—Gays. 2. Steffan, Joseph, 1964-
3. United States Naval Academy—Biography. 4. Seaman—United States—
Biography. I. Title
VB324.G38S74   1992
359'.008'6642—dc20   92-53654
[B]

First Avon Books Trade Printing: August 1993

AVON TRADEMARK REG. U.S. PAT. OFF. AND IN OTHER COUNTRIES, MARCA REGISTRADA, HECHO EN U.S.A.

Printed in the U.S.A.

OPM 10 9 8 7 6 5 4 3 2 1

Author's Note

Out of respect for the privacy of certain individuals mentioned in this book, the following pseudonyms have been used: Dan Sorenson, Jennifer Olsen, Kevin Johnson, Mr. Lyndstrom, Mrs. Jarvis, Mr. Pancio, Miss Stewart, Scott Davis, Miss Sanders, John and Anne Morrow, Rob Connor, Keith Stuart, Chaplain Owen, Tim Carson, Greg Brooks, Sarah, Pete Corcoran, Alan Kinney, Laura, Jack McCauley, Tom Olton, Brad Schmidt, and Christene.

Additionally, minor factual alterations have been made to some descriptions and events in order to protect the identities of gay midshipmen who have graduated and continue to serve in the military.

Acknowledgments

I would like to acknowledge Tom Stoddard, Paula Ettelbrick, Cal Steinmetz, Greg Craig, Leona Perreault, and the many other attorneys and staff members who have worked on our legal challenge to the military's policy, especially those at Lambda Legal Defense and Wachtell Lipton; Congressman Gerry Studds, Kate Dyer, and the public officials, advocates, and activists who have done so much to increase public awareness of the military's treatment of gay and lesbian service members; Copy Berg, for his encouragement and insight; Brad, Dorothy, and Phil Kimmelman, for their special friendship and support through the conception and writing of this book; my literary agent, Jed Mattes, and my editors, Doug Stumpf and David Highfill, for believing in me and for their invaluable guidance; my sisters, Cheryl, Cindy, and Connie, who have always been there for me; and Jerl Surratt, Barry Skovgaard, and John Strand, whose friendship and thoughtful advice have helped me to stay on an even keel.

CONTENTS

HONOR BOUND

1

⸻☆⸻

Warren

I sat at the kitchen table, pulling on my running shoes as I looked out the window onto a sunny July morning. This was going to be a great run, I thought, a great run on one of those rare northern Minnesota days when the temperature is actually above freezing. It seems that most of my memories of growing up in Warren are white ones: white Christmases, white Thanksgivings, white Halloweens, and an occasional white Easter. Summer in Minnesota is a strange time of year, that little hiccup of warmth between late winter and early winter. Today, I could enjoy my run without having to wear multiple layers of sweats, gloves, and hats.

As I began stretching, my mom walked in.

"So, how far are you running today?" she asked, pouring herself a cup of coffee.

"I run out to Luna and back on Saturdays," I answered. "It's about nine miles."

"You be careful out there on that highway," she said, taking her first sip. "Those semitrucks are dangerous, especially when they're passing."

It was a frequent motherly warning.

"Yes, Mother," I responded, using my best I'm-not-an-infant-anymore voice.

"I mean it, Joe," she answered in a stern but concerned voice. "You be careful out there."

"Yes, Mother," I echoed again, smirking at her until she finally smiled and sat down to read the paper.

If only she knew how many times I had almost been hit, I thought. Like most mothers, my mom had her overprotective streak. I remember one Christmas I begged myself blue in the face for a BB gun. She would answer me only with an endless litany of its inevitable harms, beginning with that parental classic: shooting my eye out. And although I was older now, practically a senior in high school, Mom still made a point of telling me to be careful about one thing or another. I guess it was her way of reminding me that she was still my mother. It was just frustrating that she so often turned out to be right.

Having finished stretching, I said good-bye and set out across our front lawn and down the street. Our house is on a street that dead-ends before the Snake River, a small stream that slowly winds its way through Warren and has a tendency to dry up during the summer. The beginning of my jog brought me through most of town, which was a diversion of only a few minutes.

Warren is the classic example of a rural midwestern farming community—a fast-disappearing piece of Americana. It was founded before the turn of the century by immigrants, primarily from Scandinavia, who were too poor to live anywhere else and too stubborn to give in to the brutality of winter. A century later, their descendants and those few crazy people who had joined them numbered nearly two thousand. Warren had grown to become the county seat and the largest town within nearly thirty miles.

Running through town, I could name most of the people who lived in the houses I passed along the way—a schoolteacher, the basketball coach, the newspaper editor. Each house was a reminder of someone or something. In a small town like ours, everything is interconnected. This level of familiarity has its benefits. People know and greet you on the street, and nearly every time you pass a car the driver waves. Sometimes, as you pass by, you realize it's someone you haven't seen for a while, so you both put on your brakes and back up to chat for a while. In an area with more traffic this might present a problem, but Warren doesn't have much traffic. In fact, Warren doesn't even have any traffic lights except for a couple of flashing yellow ones. Other drivers just drive around you, wave, or stop to join in. Honking your horn at someone would be considered the apex of rudeness.

Of course, familiarity can have its drawbacks as well. In any close-knit group, gossip is the mainstay of conversation. Any worthwhile small-town discussion is replete with various hushed and enticing tidbits. But even gossip in Warren is limited by politeness. Particularly juicy or shocking gossip is usually reserved for private conversation or the telephone. Still, it was certain that within a few hours of any significant event, everyone in town had heard about it from at least three people. I often wondered that the local telephone-switching station didn't overload and burst into flames under the burden of these rumorfeeding frenzies. But the telephone office never did ignite, and as I jogged through town, life in Warren moved along at its usual, leisurely pace.

Our town had a post office, two grocery stores, a couple of grain elevators, and seven churches. We also had a drugstore, where my father had started his first job as a pharmacist over thirty years earlier. He eventually became a partner in the business, later taking over the store when his partner retired. As the only pharmacy in our entire county, it enjoyed a limited monopoly. But in recent years, it was struggling, like most local businesses, to survive between the crunch of a perpetually depressed farm economy and increasing competition from chain stores in larger towns.

My mom worked as a secretary at one of the banks in town when she wasn't busy taking care of my sisters and me. I was the third of four children, and the only boy, which meant I got the luxury of my own room and never had to wear dreaded handme-downs. I think my youngest sister, Connie, was in her early teens before she actually got her first piece of new clothing.

Growing up in Warren was a pleasant and uncomplicated experience. My family was stable and loving, and my sisters and I never wondered if there would be food on the table when we got home. We grew up isolated from the pressures of drug use and violence that so many American children face daily, too young and naïve to consider our isolation or worry about what lay beyond the prairies. Even Minneapolis and Saint Paul were more than five hours away. It seemed as though our lives would always remain unchanged, with the "outside world" nothing more than a figment of our television's imagination.

As I continued to jog, I crossed a bridge over the river and made my way toward the edge of town and the stretch of highway pointing toward Canada, sixty miles north.

When people think of Minnesota, they usually envision thousands of crystal-clear lakes teeming with fish, and rivers intertwining beautiful pine-covered terrain. Although that's pretty much true of most of the state, Warren is, unfortunately, not in that part. It lies on the northwestern edge of the state, which marks the beginning of the Great Plains of the west. In other words, Warren is flat. Extremely flat. Everything around Warren is flat for as far as the eye can see in every direction, ground down by centuries of glaciation during the ice age. The terrain is broken only by an occasional row of trees or patch of forest between vast fields of wheat, sunflowers, and sugar beets. Which is not to say that the land doesn't have its own unique beauty; it just might look a little desolate to the untrained eye.

Of course, this made choosing jogging routes quite simple. I was not burdened with having to determine the relative scenic value of each route. Nor did I have to worry about annoying hills or other geographical features. I just picked a direction and ran.

Today's direction was north, and I passed the Laundromat and drive-in restaurant as I headed up Highway 75 toward the bowling alley just outside town. Warren's bowling alley was the town hangout for us high school kids. Not many of us liked to bowl; it was just the only place big enough to hold us all, and someplace where we could be fairly sure our parents wouldn't show up. After any home football or basketball game, it was packed to the rafters.

The highway started with a slow curve out of town and then lay perfectly straight to the horizon. My destination was a group of grain bins four and a half miles away. The pace of my movements and breathing was smooth and steady, and I could feel myself entering that trance-like state that would carry me through the distance.

I thought about how many times I had made this run over the past four years, ever since I began running with Dan Sorenson back in eighth grade. Although Dan was two years ahead of me in school, we had gotten to know each other through the student council and working on projects for the annual science fair. Aside from being extremely intelligent, he was a remarkable athlete. He was also completely dedicated, practically to the point of obsession. When he wasn't working on one of his many projects, Dan was either running or lifting weights to keep himself in peak physical condition. He was the quintessential wrestler, with a short, muscular frame and lightning reflexes.

My own athletic career to that point had been remarkably unimpressive, much to the chagrin of my father. From an early age, it was obvious that he wanted me to be good at sports. Around the time I started kindergarten, he also started me in Little League baseball. I begrudgingly endured eight years of baseball with little to show for my efforts besides an occasional bloody lip from not quite managing to catch the ball before it hit my face.

In elementary school, I attempted to play basketball, amassing a three-year-career scoring total of eight points. Through this time and into high school, my dad was always there to cheer me on, no matter how pitiful my performance or how long I sat on the bench. There were times when he would spend hours watching our games, just to see me play for a few minutes. But he was never discouraging, even after I dropped my first football kickoff return in junior high, and then managed to kick it back to the other team for their first touchdown of the game.

I had always been an excellent student, and it was never as though I felt my parents weren't proud of me. I was involved in many other activities, from choirs and band to student government. But as the years passed, no matter how well I did in school, I couldn't escape the feeling that I had somehow let my dad down.

By the time Dan and I got to know each other, I had pretty much given up on the idea of ever being good at sports. In fact, I had come to despise sports as the one thing that made me feel bad about myself. Even my father had seemingly come to accept the reality that he would never have an athlete son.

Later that year, Dan actually persuaded me to join him on one of his daily runs—a four-mile trip around the section of land south of town. The run proved far more difficult than I had anticipated. It especially wasn't helped by Dan's insistence that we stop at every telephone pole to do ten push-ups. I never realized just how many telephone poles could be crammed onto four miles of road.

By the time we neared the end, I was completely, utterly, and totally exhausted, and pissed off at Dan, the telephone company, and myself. I finally had to stop, walking the last half-mile into town and trying not to puke my guts out. Perhaps four miles was a bit ambitious for my first distance run, but I was still humiliated. More than anything, I didn't want Dan to think I was a wimp. He was not just a friend to me; he had also become a hero, a role model who I looked up to and was determined to emulate. This first run had shown me just how difficult that was going to be. But the more I thought and fumed about it, the more determined I was to finally overcome my athletic limitations.

Two days later, I got up early in the morning and set out alone for the same stretch of road. Now, for me, getting up in the morning is an accomplishment in itself. I had always hated getting up early—i.e., before ten o'clock. But humiliation is a great motivation, and I was feeling particularly motivated. This time I ran a little more slowly and skipped the push-ups, concentrating on my pace, the sound of my feet, anything to keep going. I simply wanted to make the distance without having to stop.

At the time, making it all the way home seemed like a small victory, but I look back on that morning as a real turning point in my life. It was the first time that I had proved something, not to please my father, or even Dan, but for myself. It was a powerful lesson. I had succeeded at something physical, and I had done it because I wanted to.

Through that summer and the following year, I continued to run, most of the time with Dan. After a while, I could keep up with him easily. We ran all over, sometimes for four miles, sometimes six or more, around sections of land, the town reservoir, or out to the airport and back. We even made a workout of running the grandstand stairs at the fair grounds—one hundred trips up the stairs and down, until our legs were practically numb. We would run at all hours, in the cold or rain, dodging skunks on gravel country roads at night, coming home soaked to the skin and covered with mud.

After a summer of running and working out, I was in good shape and thinking about taking one last shot at sports. Before the start of the school year, Dan convinced me to try out for the wrestling team, a decision that was especially surprising to my father. He was justifiably skeptical, but nonetheless encouraging as always.

Although my performance as a wrestler was not magnificent, I did manage to win a few matches, and wrestling practice was an incredible way to keep in shape. I had never worked so hard, run so much, or been as completely exhausted as after wrestling practice. In fact, I did so much running, both during the season and the summers, that I decided to try out as a distance runner for the track team the following year. It turned out to be the last step in my long search for an athletic niche.

After our first few practices, my track coach suggested that I compete in the mile run. My first race was against some tough competitors, but I actually managed to place third, much to the astonishment of everyone, including myself. At the next meet, I not only finished second, but also ran the mile in under five minutes (4:56.07), a time that was considered unusual for a sophomore in our part of the state.

Soon, I was not only placing in races but winning them—gold medals and all! I had finally stumbled onto something I was good at, and no one was more surprised or pleased than my dad. Whenever I won a race, his usual comment was "Not too bad," and a smile that revealed his pride. But as much as I enjoyed the fact that he was happy, it was also gratifying to know that I had taken up running on my own, and that my success was the result of self-motivation instead of subtle or overt pressure. I understood that if I had simply done it to please him, it wouldn't have been nearly as satisfying.

After my first few races, my coach asked me to expand my running to include the two-mile race as well. I was a little skeptical about the possibility of running the mile and two-mile back to back, but our team was small and we needed whatever points we could get. Even if I just managed to place, it would help out.

As it turned out, running both events wasn't as difficult as I imagined. There was enough time between them to relax, and I actually tended to do better in the two-mile, probably because few of the good milers were insane enough to run the two-mile as well.

By the end of the season, our team had managed to capture the district track championship. I had placed first in the two-mile and second in the mile, advancing in both events to the regional meet, one level below the state meet.

The regional meet was held that year in Walker, Minnesota, and my finishing times during the season put me about eighth in the mile, and about sixth in the two-mile going into the meet. I needed an unlikely first- or second-place finish in either event to make it to the state meet.

Before every race, I would settle back in the grass off to the side of the field away from everyone else, close my eyes, and listen to the *Chariots of Fire* sound track on my Walkman. I know it sounds corny, but no matter what the setting or competition, listening to the same music before each race relaxed me and cleared my mind.

I tried to think as little as possible about the other runners in the race, concentrating rather on the real opponents: time and pain. Our minds are remarkably effective at convincing us to avoid pain, which is usually a good thing. But any type of physical exertion involves a certain amount of pain, and winning required more than simply being in good physical shape; it meant recognizing and overcoming illusory pain in order to run faster than my body wanted to.

The mile race came first in the meet, and after a few warm-up sprints, I joined the other runners at the starting line. We all became silent as the starter poised his gun in the vacuum-like second before it shot us into the race.

As usual, I was not at the front of the pack out of the start. I never was a sprinter, so I didn't worry about jumping to the lead right away. Usually, the guys who sprinted the first lap of the mile were the ones who died well before the end. The strategy my coach and I had developed was to avoid the initial panic and simply run a consistent, even pace for the duration of the race.

By the end of the first lap, things had calmed down a little, and the other runners started slowing down. As they did, I began to move up in the pack. But this was not just another race. These runners had made it to the regional meet—they were the best milers in our part of the state, and it was obvious that they were not slowing down a great deal.

I continued to push through the second and third laps, trying to keep up my pace while slowly gaining on the small cluster of runners who had broken away to take the lead. By the time the gun sounded again to mark the final lap, I had moved up to sixth place.

With only one lap left, everyone began to pick up the pace as we pushed for the finish line. About halfway around the track, I passed the fifth runner as we broke into the final sprint. My legs were numb as I rounded the last curve and moved past the fourth runner. But the three lead runners were too far ahead, and I realized they could not be caught. I sprinted toward them, but crossed the finish line in fourth place.

In a way, I was happy to have done better than expected, but I couldn't help feeling disappointed. I had miscalculated my competition, and a slightly faster pace might have given me a better chance at the end. But I had done well, and the team points awarded for my fourth-place finish meant Warren was that much closer to winning the entire meet.

With the mile over, only one chance at the state meet remained. I began to rationalize to myself why I shouldn't expect to make it this year. The competition was tough, it was only my first year out, and several runners had significantly better times than I did. Even to come close to first or second place and a trip to the state meet, I would have to cut nearly fifteen seconds off my best time of the year, an unlikely accomplishment.

I tried to put these thoughts out of my mind as I recovered from the mile run and contemplated my strategy for the two-mile, only an hour away. If I was going to have a chance, I had to stick tighter to the leaders at the beginning of the race, push myself for a faster pace overall, and hope I had something left for the sprint to the line. After warming down, I sat back in the grass and started up my Walkman once again.

My parents were there, as they had been for almost all the

races I ran that year, to cheer me and our team on. The day was absolutely beautiful—sunny and warm, unlike so many bitterly cold and rainy meets we had endured that year. Walker had a fine track facility, situated on a hill overlooking Leech Lake. As I looked across the track to the sun bouncing off the waves in the distance, it struck me as so remarkable that I was even here at this meet. Only a year earlier, I had all but given up hope of being good at any sport. Now, it had all changed completely.

The encouragement of my teammates, my coaches, and especially my dad, had an immense impact on my own feeling of self-worth. It was as though I finally began to realize that we really have no limitations as individuals, other than our own self-imposed limitations. We accumulate and piece together an image of who we are from the people around us, and we eventually accept that image as our true identity. It's like the kids in elementary school who get picked on for being fat or not very good at schoolwork. Eventually they truly believe they're worthless. And because human nature is to avoid disappointment, they give up trying. They accept their place in life, and every day the dreams of childhood shrink to fit neatly, safely, within that place. If I had believed what people told me, I never would have bothered to try out for track. And I would have lost what has been the most important lesson of my life—to never believe the people who say, "You can't."

The time for the two-mile had finally arrived, and I joined the other runners on the starting line. At the gun, we shot off the line, and this time I pushed hard to stick with the leaders. After the first lap, I was still with the front of the pack, determined to keep within striking distance. As we moved into the remaining laps, the pace began to slow almost imperceptibly. By the start of the second mile, six of us had established a strong pace and were increasing our lead over the other runners. The pace was fast, and I pressed to keep up. There was nothing to lose—this could be my last race of the year, and I wanted to cross the finish line without an ounce of energy left to spare.

By the sixth lap, two more runners had dropped out of the pack and the crowd and my parents were on their feet. This was one of the last events of the day, and the outcome could well decide which team would claim the meet. Team members had lined the edge of the track as we moved into the seventh lap. We were engulfed in a shower of screams and shouts of encouragement, but I was oblivious as my own excitement started to build. With only one more lap left, I knew I had a chance.

As we passed over the starting line, and the gun sounded the final lap, I was running third of the four leaders. The pace started to quicken into the final sprint, and I could feel adrenaline rushing into my system. The crowd was wild, and my parents had moved down to the finish line. With only half a lap left, I made my move, passing the other runners and taking the lead.

As we neared the final curve, I could feel the other runners close behind, but I was pulling away from them. I hit the straightaway with the finish line only a hundred yards away. My legs churned as though the track was being pulled out from under me and I was simply trying to keep up. By now I was sprinting all out and no one was going to catch me. As I burst across the finish line, the screams of the crowd hit me.

In his excitement, my dad leapt across the track toward me, nearly knocking down the second-place finisher. I was surrounded by ecstatic teammates, my dad, and our coaches. I had cut nearly thirty seconds off my best time for a finish of 10:16.5—a new school record and a victory that helped our team capture first place in the regional meet. From that point on, I looked at life from a different perspective. I would no longer accept limitations or barriers, self-imposed or otherwise.

Continuing my jog, I neared the grain bins next to the highway. I could barely see the neighboring town of Argyle off in the distance. Over the years, Argyle had built up a friendly but distinct sports rivalry with Warren, especially when it came to basketball.

Every year during the district championships, our teams were inevitably pitted against each other. Our quiet towns were transformed into seething hordes of frenzied fans whose existence, it seemed, depended on victory on the basketball court. At least half the population of our towns would journey to the tournaments in vast car caravans that stretched far across the prairie.

I remember hearing a rumor that before a particularly crucial game, the mostly Catholic citizens of Argyle had gathered for Mass, during which a solemn benediction was held for the basketball to be used in the upcoming game.

To people in Warren, most of whom are Lutheran, this seemed downright pagan. Ours was one of the few Catholic families in town, and my Lutheran friends often commented that I must leave church exhausted from the constant standing, kneeling, genuflecting, and crossing.

I remember one time when my oldest sister, Cheryl, brought her boyfriend to Sunday Mass with us. As a good Lutheran, he had never been to a Catholic service, and actually seemed nervous about attending one. When the altar boys and priest marched in carrying huge candles and waving incense, he leaned over to me and said, "Wow, this is really strange." I leaned back and said, "Wait until they sacrifice the goat on the altar." He stared blankly back at me for a moment, countering with a quick chuckle of disbelief, but I noticed him closely monitoring the actions of the priest and listening intently for muffled bleating from the wings of the church.

The halfway point of my run was a sign that named the cluster of grain bins on the side of the road, in black letters on a white background spelling out L-U-N-A. I never understood why this place had a name, especially one as strange as Luna. I looked it up in the dictionary once, and it's the name of the Roman goddess of the moon. Although it might be a good place to get a look at the moon, it didn't provide a topographical advantage over any other portion of the county. I pondered this mystery, as I did every week for about ten seconds, then turned around and headed back into town.

Running was often my best time to think, maybe even better than the time I spent mowing our lawn. With nothing to distract me, my mind wandered from thought to thought. I generally spent a lot of time thinking, wondering about why things are the way they are. I had always been curious, wanting to know how things worked. Many an appliance had seen its demise at my hands, and even at a very young age I had a strange propensity for ripping open my stuffed animals to see what was inside.

Many of my thoughts were about the future, particularly

my own. I knew that I wanted to be successful in life, but I wrestled with the definition. What was success supposed to be? Like everyone, I had a fear of failure, but perhaps even more than failure, I was afraid of ending up doing something I didn't enjoy. I was afraid of mediocrity, of failing to reach my potential, or of trying my hardest and feeling indistinguishable from the crowd. If success meant anything to me, it meant doing something unique with my life, something challenging, and above all, something meaningful.

By the end of my sophomore year, I had taken my first concrete step toward the recognition of that goal. Earlier, when Dan and I were displaying our projects at the regional science fair, he was approached by a Navy officer, Captain Barry Prichard, about the possibility of attending the Naval Academy following his graduation from high school. It was an option that neither of us knew much about, other than the fact that the Naval Academy is one of the military service academies, along with West Point and the Air Force Academy.

As Dan learned more about the academy, he became increasingly interested in applying. It seemed like the perfect opportunity—a chance to attend a highly selective college that values not only academic ability but physical excellence and leadership ability as well. And if you can get in, it's not only free, they pay you for attending! Of course, after graduating you have to serve five years as an officer. But in 1980, at the dawning of the Reagan era and the rebuilding of America's military might, that didn't seem like such a bad idea.

Dan eventually applied to the academy, received the required congressional nomination, and was accepted. In the meantime, I had grown equally intrigued by the possibility of attending the Naval Academy. By the time Dan graduated and left for Annapolis, I had decided that I wanted to go there as well.

Five months later, Dan resigned from Annapolis. The academic and emotional stresses of the first year were more than he had bargained for, the pay wasn't much, and overall, he just didn't feel it was for him. In the weeks after his return to Warren, we spent time discussing the trials of the first, or plebe, year at Annapolis—memorizing vast amounts of useless information, being treated like scum, and generally feeling demoralized. It sounded like an extremely difficult experience, but I still wanted to try. Knowing about Dan's experiences prepared me and gave me a realistic understanding of what to expect.

After that, I spent a lot of time contemplating what this path in life might hold for me. This was not simply a two-year stint in the service; this involved four years at Annapolis, followed by five years of active duty as an officer in the Navy. At age seventeen, I was setting up the next nine years of my life! The world was at relative peace, but who knew what could happen in nine years? And I didn't know how my thoughts, goals, and perspective on life might change over those years.

Like many people, I did not necessarily view the military as a good thing. To me, the need for militaries represented the failure of our governments and our societies to deal in a logical and mature way with the problems that faced us. I felt that sheer hatred of violence and bloodshed should be enough motivation to make us seek a peaceful, diplomatic resolution to any situation. And yet, pragmatically, I understood that the world is not perfect. War is, unfortunately, as much a part of history as peace.

These concerns were tempered by my strong belief in the ideals of the United States, especially the understanding that all people deserve freedom—the freedom to simply be themselves, and to live their lives without fear or oppression. Few countries have embraced this ideal so explicitly. What can be better than allowing people to live their lives as they choose, to give them the freedom to take the limited time they have on earth and craft an existence that is uniquely theirs?

As much as I disliked the idea of war, I reasoned that if we are to assure the survival of these ideals in a world where war exists, then we must be the best at war—if for no other reason than to deter conflict. We must have the best equipment, and we must have the best people. And if I truly believed in our ideals, then I had to be willing to be one of those people. I had to be willing to risk my life for what I believed in, to enter the military of my own free will with the goal of not simply putting in my time, but working to improve the military as well.

Some of my reasons for wanting to attend Annapolis were

less idealistic. It was a very difficult institution to get in to, and mere acceptance, especially in my small town, represented an unusual and substantial accomplishment. Like the athlete who envisions the glory of victory, I wanted to feel the admiration of my friends and family. Perhaps I wanted also to prove to myself that I had the courage to succeed, to prove my own self-worth, and to survive something that even Dan had not been able to endure.

Such was the reasoning behind my decision. I had no concrete answers, only a youthful, idealistic vision and the willingness to try something I hoped I could accomplish. It was a mixed bag of idealism, reality, and naïveté—and not without some conflicts. Like anyone setting goals in life, I looked ahead with both optimism and fear.

Determined to burn my bridges behind me, I applied only to Annapolis. This was not about making a choice between one fine college and another, because to me the academy was much more than just a school. It represented a commitment, a way of life, and a challenge that no civilian school could replicate.

I was interviewed by my congressman's appointment panel, and before that, I had visited Annapolis to attend its annual high school science seminar. My family didn't travel much, so I had never been outside the Midwest before. This was my first trip to the East Coast, and my first time on an airplane. I remember looking out the window for what must have been close to an hour, marveling at the tops of the clouds spread out below like a surreal polar landscape.

Everything was so impressive to me, the city of Annapolis as well as the academy itself, that I must have walked around with my mouth open half the time. The academic facilities were amazing, a mixture of modern and historic buildings filled with nautical testing tanks, wind tunnels, and computers. The academy's domed chapel was awe-inspiring, with its beautiful Tiffany stained-glass windows and massive pipe organ.

On the day I was to return to Warren, I sat on a bench in the middle of the academy grounds listening to music from the chapel's carillon and looking out across the yard. It was one of those rare moments in my life when I've stopped consciously to impress my thoughts and feelings upon my memory. Today that moment is vivid in my mind. I can still feel the warmth of the sun on my face and the sense of profound calm that washed over me. Whatever fear and anxiety I had harbored about my decision to attend Annapolis dissolved on that day. Somehow I could feel deep in my soul that I belonged there.

With my senior year of high school now only a month away, I was already growing impatient to hear the results of my appointment hearing. If I got the nomination, only the final hurdle of acceptance by Annapolis would remain.

Heading back home on my run, as I looked down the highway toward Warren, I felt the subtle poignancy that had haunted me since my return from Annapolis. As much as I loved my hometown, its people, and my family, I was beginning to sense the transition that lay ahead. I knew that this would be my last summer in Warren, my last summer at home.

For the first time, I had seen beyond the prairies to the outside world, beyond the quiet isolation and comfort I had known all my life. From the beginning, this place had molded me; its ideals and values had formed an integral part of who I am. I knew that as long as I remembered this place, as long as I knew my roots, I would be ready for anything the world had in store.

2

—☆—

"An Ideal Candidate"

My sister Connie and I bounded up the stairs into school, our shoes crunching the thin layer of snow left after the janitor's shoveling. The icy cold air of a bright December morning bit at our faces as we rushed toward the doors. "God, I hate getting up in the morning," I muttered under my breath.

As usual, we were none too early for our 7 A.M. stage-band practice, arriving just in time to take out our instruments, grab our music, and walk into the practice room. I played first trombone in our jazz band, a small specialty group made up of members of the high school band. Connie played trumpet. It was a morning pretty much like most mornings that year. If I wasn't arriving early for stage band, it was an early practice for one of the choirs, or a meeting for some other organization. But no matter how often I had to get up early, I never quite seemed to adjust to it.

I took my seat next to Kevin Johnson, the other first trombone player and one of my best friends in school. Like most of my classmates, I had known Kevin for what seemed like forever. Nearly all of us had started kindergarten together in the elementary school next door.

Kevin and I had a lot in common, starting with our minimal baseball skills. We probably first got to know each other sitting on the bench during those early Little League days. In school, we were always competing against each other for grades and had a running bet over which one of us would graduate first in our class. Our mutual interest in science had led to a series of impromptu experiments, designed more to satisfy our own pyromaniacal tendencies than to test any particular scientific hypothesis.

One of our most memorable experiments took place on a Saturday afternoon during seventh grade. We set up an elaborate series of flasks, tubing, and glass pipe on my bedroom floor, taking care to protect the carpet with carefully placed sheets of aluminum foil. The experimental fluid in this case, as in almost all of our experiments, was rubbing alcohol. Although I had never quite grasped its medicinal value, or why people would want to rub it on their bodies, I knew that it burned with a vengeance. And because my dad was the local pharmacist, we always had an ample supply in the house.

Alcohol in one flask was heated by a Bunsen burner powered by a small butane torch tank. The alcohol vapors from the flask flowed through tubing submerged in ice water, where they condensed and dripped into another flask heated by a second Bunsen burner. The alcohol vapors from the second flask then flowed up a glass tube and ignited into a huge blue-and-orange flame, which blazed like a miniature offshore oil rig.

Kevin and I stood back in awe. As we were congratulating each other on our success, we were suddenly startled by a loud POP! We watched in horror as the rubber stopper from the first flask sailed across the room, taking the tubing with it and knocking over the remaining apparatus. I gasped in horror as burning alcohol poured onto my bedroom carpet. I momentarily contemplated running down the hall to get the fire extinguisher, but decided that would be too hard to hide from my parents. Kevin and I dropped to the floor, blowing wildly at the spots of flame scattered across the room. In a few seconds, the fire was out. I surveyed the room, my heart beating wildly. There was remarkably little damage to the carpet, except for a few melted spots here and there, but they were easily covered up by a strategic rearranging of furniture.

After the Great Distillery Explosion, or GDE, as it was henceforth known, our interests moved from home combustibles to low-level explosives. One formula particularly intrigued us, because once it dried it would explode on the slightest contact. Unfortunately, it included iodine crystals as a component, and these proved difficult to obtain. Despite repeated pleas to the high school chemistry teacher that our need for iodine crystals was scientifically justifiable, we were denied access to the mysterious amber bottle that housed them in the lab's chemical storeroom.

Not to be discouraged, Kevin and I decided that we could probably make our own iodine crystals at home by boiling down iodine in a test tube. Wary of a possible reoccurrence of the GDE, we decided to use my mom's kitchen stove as our heat source. After several minutes of heating over the stove flame, the iodine stubbornly refused to boil. Unaware of iodine's unusual boiling characteristics, I cranked up the heat. Suddenly, in one gigantic, violent boil, all of the iodine shot straight up out of the test tube, splattering a grotesque, reddish-brown blotch across my mom's textured white kitchen ceiling. Despite my desperate attempts to remove the stain, it remained completely unaffected. I finally gave up, and located a can of white paint in the basement to cover the stain. My mom has since been mystified by the strange spot on the kitchen ceiling that eventually seeps through each new coat of paint.

Since those days, Kevin and I had outgrown most of our self-destructive tendencies, devoting more and more time to other things. I had become involved in sports, and now he seemed to spend most of his free time with his girlfriend. After stage-band practice, we talked for a few minutes while we packed up our instruments. Although we had almost all the same classes and were in both bands together, it seemed that we rarely had any time to catch up with each other. This pattern had come to characterize most of the friendships I had developed in school.

I liked my classmates and had always been able to get along with just about anyone. In fact, I had been elected class president at the beginning of the school year. But no matter how many friendships I developed, I never felt particularly close to any one person. In a way, I figured that was what girlfriends were for, but I had never really had a girlfriend. All through high school, my relationships with girls had always been more friendships than anything else.

When some of my friends started dating girls early in high
school, I didn't really understand what was happening. To me,
they were the same girls I had known since we teased each other
on the elementary school playground. And although we had
become a little more courteous toward each other over the years,
I didn't sense any particular change in my feelings toward them
or how we related to each other.

At first, I attributed the actions of my friends to adolescent
role-playing, which we are all supposed to undertake. From our
earliest years, we learn that boys and girls eventually grow up
and feel something special toward one another called love. They
get married, have kids, and everyone lives happily ever after. All
around us this ideal is reinforced—from the shows we watch on
television, to couples holding hands in the park, to the Bible
stories we hear in church, to the wedding announcements
printed every week in the newspapers.

Every child knows these principles long before we even
begin to grasp what love is. Society provides a complete framework for our sexuality that is reinforced every day through the
subtle influence of our families, our community, advertising,
and the media. All around us, there is an implicit understanding
of who we are and who we are expected to become when we
grow up.

Along with my friends, I started dating girls in high school.
We would go out, have pizza, see a movie, and then I would
take the girl home, kiss her good night, and go home. It was
simple enough, and like most adolescents, I didn't date girls
because I was overcome by some intense, burning desire to do
so. I simply knew it was expected, it was normal. To not do it
would be to stick out, to be abnormal, and if there is one thing
adolescents don't want, it's to be different.

During the summer before my junior year of high school,
I developed a friendship with Jennifer Olsen, a girl a year ahead
of me in school. She was the upcoming president of our student
council, and I was the upcoming vice president. That summer,
we drove down to the Twin Cities for a student-council leadership seminar. It was a five-hour drive each way, so we had
plenty of time to get to know each other. She was very friendly
and one of the most popular girls in school, with a ready smile

and a quick sense of humor. I had always felt insecure around girls, but Jennifer was somehow different. Her warmth and humor made me comfortable, and I was glad to spend time with her.

We spent nearly the whole trip joking and laughing ourselves nearly to the brink of unconsciousness. By the time we got back to Warren, we were inseparable. We spent almost all of the remaining summer together. I would often drive the twelve miles out to her family's farm to spend the afternoon talking with her about our grand schemes for the upcoming school year, or just watching television or working in the yard. I felt closer to Jennifer than to any girl I had ever known. I wondered, and even hoped, that Jennifer might finally be the right girl for me, the one who would make me feel what the other guys were feeling.

At about the same time, I became very involved in a Christian youth organization called Teens Encounter Christ. Although I had never really considered myself very religious, I was very moved by my first TEC weekend retreat, which followed many of the same self-disclosure, self-realization principles as adult programs such as est, but in a religious context.

I would number this experience among my most formative, not because it enhanced my religious beliefs, but because it reinforced a very basic ideal not only of Christianity, but of humanity—that is, to accept and care for people unconditionally, regardless of what we perceive to be their faults or limitations, and to start that acceptance with ourselves.

Jennifer eventually became involved in TEC as well, and we spent most of our free time and weekends with the friends we made there, traveling to events and reunions. This experience and its religious overtones served to reinforce my already conservative beliefs. Throughout high school, I never took one sip of alcohol, and the thought of premarital sex was out of the question, even if I had felt some urge to engage in it.

When I was with Jennifer, I never felt any pressure to make our relationship more serious than it was, and the nature of the relationship was always one of friendship. For me, this was a comfortable and convenient arrangement because I was still not feeling much of an attraction to girls. I hoped that if Jennifer and I spent enough time together, I might begin to develop that attraction to her. I figured that maybe I was too involved in other things, or that the right hormones just hadn't kicked in yet.

We continued to date through the school year. Jennifer was voted homecoming queen, and I was her date for the homecoming dance and the prom that year. It seemed like we were always together, but my feelings for Jennifer never changed. We were very close, but even on those rare occasions when I kissed her, I never felt anything. And that made me feel bad, even guilty. Every time I kissed her and felt nothing, I felt like I was lying to her, deceiving her into believing there was something there that just wasn't.

She was becoming increasingly emotionally invested in the relationship, but it just wasn't clicking for me. I wanted more than anything to feel something special toward her, but I didn't know what it was I was supposed to feel. Maybe she wasn't the right girl, or maybe I really wasn't supposed to feel anything special. How was I supposed to know when I was feeling love? Maybe no one really felt love, maybe it was all role-playing and this was as intense as it got, or maybe I just wasn't ready yet, for whatever reason.

During the summer after her graduation from high school, we still hung around together, but I could feel myself pulling away. Being around Jennifer was becoming less enjoyable, not because of her, but because of what I was feeling or, more accurately, wasn't feeling. Spending more time with her seemed like simply adding insult to injury. I didn't want to hurt her anymore. Although I saw her a few times during my senior year of high school, our friendship eventually faded.

Despite the failure of our relationship, a part of me continued to believe, to hope that someday I would feel toward Jennifer what had been missing all along. Someday I would return to Warren, where she would be waiting faithfully for me, we would get married, have kids, and live happily ever after. Until that time, I decided, I wasn't going to worry about it.

In retrospect, it is so clear to me that I was avoiding something, reacting with denial and avoidance to my own growing fear that there was more to my sexual confusion than simply a lack of attraction to women. It was something I didn't want to think about, that I couldn't think about because it was too foreign to everything I knew, too threatening to my most basic sense of right and wrong.

My only reaction was to do what I had always done. I immersed myself in so many activities that I wouldn't even have time to think about anything else. I would be too busy, too involved, too distracted to deal with what was going on inside my own head.

And that is exactly what I did. I was in two bands and two choirs, president of the student council and senior class, a captain of the wrestling team. My summers had been spent at all-state choir, Boys State, the Naval Academy science seminar, and a high school "United Nations" program in Canada. I had continued my religious involvement as president of our local Catholic Youth Organization and youth representative on our bishop's pastoral council. Every moment of my day was filled with school, practices, and meetings. My fears about not having a girlfriend had been eliminated by removing any free time I could possibly spend with one.

After putting away my trombone, I headed to my locker to grab the books for my first class. The members of each class had their own particular area of lockers lining the hallways between classrooms. Our lockers didn't actually have locks on them, but that was just one more thing we took for granted in our small school.

In the few minutes before the bell rang, I joined in with some girls from my class who were talking and laughing about some memories from elementary school. Since starting our senior year, we seemed to spend nearly all of our time reminiscing about growing up together. We shared memories and anecdotes about classes and teachers, playing together on the playground, swimming at the pool in the summers. It was a sign that we recognized our time together as a class was ending after nearly twelve years.

Most of us were going off to college, and we knew that after we left, this town would never again be quite the same for us. Little would change physically, maybe a few new houses or a new grain elevator might be added, but we knew our place here would never be the same. Other kids would sing in the musicals and play sports. They would live their time in the spotlight.

Later in the day, I got a message to stop by the office of our high school guidance counselor, Mr. Lyndstrom. He had been helping me with my application to the Naval Academy, and I was anxious to hear any news he might have about the congressional appointment results. If I got a nomination and everything went well, I would know sometime in the spring that the academy had accepted me.

As I walked into his office, Mr. Lyndstrom greeted me with his usual broad smile. To my surprise, he stood up and shook my hand, smiling even more broadly than before. "Congratulations," he said, "you're in."

I was puzzled. "What do you mean? In what?"

"The Naval Academy. You got the nomination, and you've been accepted by the academy."

I was stunned. "Already?" I asked. "I thought it was supposed to take longer than this. I thought we weren't supposed to hear until spring."

"Nope," he answered. "You got the nomination and the academy granted you early acceptance as an ideal candidate."

I thanked him and practically ran out of his office in my exuberance. Finally, after two years of waiting, filling out endless forms, writing essays, and intense anticipation, my greatest dream was coming true.

That afternoon, as I told my friends and later my parents the great news, the realization of my acceptance began to take hold. There was nothing in my life for which I had hoped and longed more. No victory could have felt more incredible, more profound, than my acceptance to Annapolis. I can't imagine how devastated I would have been if I had not been accepted—or if I had known then how my dream of graduating from Annapolis would end.

After receiving the news of my acceptance, the rest of senior year seemed to fly by. The wrestling season was pretty much a bust. Our team finished with a rather undistinguished zero wins and twelve losses. I sang the part of Curly in *Oklahoma!* that spring for our annual musical, just as track season was starting. With only one season left, I held the school records for both the mile and the two-mile, but I had been unable to come even close to my goal of breaking a ten-minute two-mile.

As graduation approached, Kevin and I heard a rumor that someone else had clinched the spot for class valedictorian. We decided there was only one thing to do. We went to the principal's office and asked him if there was anyone besides Kevin and me in contention for second place in the class. He said there wasn't. We knew that our averages were practically the same, which the principal verified, so we made two requests: first, that neither of us ever find out who finished with higher grades, and second, that we share second place as co-salutatorians. He was happy to agree. After our neck-and-neck competition throughout school, the question of who had won no longer seemed important. The bottom line was that we were friends and we respected each other.

Of course, our decision also meant that we both had to speak at graduation. Thankfully, I had sung in our musicals, so the thought of speaking in front of a crowd wasn't that terrifying for me. A few weeks before graduation, we were asked to preview our speeches to Mrs. Jarvis, one of the English teachers who was also a good friend of my mom's. I figured this was the perfect time for a little practical joke. After preparing a serious speech for the real graduation, I set to work preparing a fake one for the preview session.

On the day of our presentation, I showed my fake speech to Kevin and the valedictorian before we entered the auditorium, which was empty except for Mrs. Jarvis sitting in the middle of the seats. We took our places on the stage, and Kevin started his speech. After he was done, Mrs. Jarvis made a few comments, and then it was my turn. With Kevin and the valedictorian sitting with straight faces behind me, I launched into my speech. My voice was somber and pensive:

> Graduation is a time for reflection. When we reach this great turnpike in the road of life, this great wave in the surf of life, this large cherry in the fruit salad of life, this big chunk of meat in the Alpo of life . . .

A bloodcurdling "STOP!" echoed through the auditorium as we all broke into uncontrolled laughter on the stage. Finally, Mrs. Jarvis began to laugh as well.

"I should have expected something like this from you, Steffan," she shouted from her seat in the auditorium.

I finished the rest of the joke speech just for fun, and then gave my real speech, of which she was significantly more approving.

Finally, graduation night arrived. The evening went pretty much as planned. The senior choir members sang, and everyone cried. The band played, and everyone cried. We gave our speeches, and—you get the picture. During the awards part of graduation, I was presented with my certificate of appointment to the Naval Academy by a Navy representative. I could feel the circle closing. Two years ago, I had seen the same presentation when Dan graduated, and now it was my turn, my chance to try.

After graduation, there was only one task to complete before I left for Annapolis. I had to run the last two races of my track career at the state meet. The mile run was held on the first day, and I did relatively poorly. I finished about fifth to last, and ran nearly ten seconds slower than my best time.

The two-mile was held the next day. I knew this would be my last competitive race, and I pushed so hard I thought my lungs would explode. When I finally crossed the finish line, I was nowhere near placing, but from the times being called out, I knew I had finished close to ten minutes. My coach had been clocking the race, so I ran up to him to get my time. He looked at me and smiled. "Nine minutes, fifty-eight seconds," he said. I had finally broken the ten-minute barrier, on my very last race. There couldn't have been a better way to end my unexpected high school track career.

I was due to report to Annapolis on July 6, only about a month away. I knew I wouldn't be back to Warren until Christmas, the longest I would ever have been away from home. There would be many trials between now and then, and I tried not to think about how tough this year was going to be. I spent time driving around with friends, going out to movies, and slowly saying my good-byes.

I left Warren on July 5, 1983. That morning I packed only a few things. The instructions that the academy had sent said not to bring any civilian clothes. During our first year we would be allowed to wear only our uniforms.

As my parents and I drove out of Warren, I felt an urge to look back, to burn that last image into my memory so deeply that I could never forget. I had lived my whole life there. That place was safety, warmth, and security. And I was scared— excited and scared, but mostly scared. I wanted to turn back time and try it again, to take what I had learned growing up and have the chance to grow up again, to not make any mistakes, to have more fun, to simply live it over.

But I didn't look back. I kept my eyes fixed on the horizon, staring out the front window until Warren was gone. A door had closed behind me, and I knew it was time to take my next step.

3

"Maggot!"

My plane landed at Baltimore-Washington International Airport, and I took a cab to the Holiday Inn in Bowie, Maryland, about ten minutes outside Annapolis. Getting to sleep was nearly impossible as my mind incessantly wandered to thoughts about tomorrow—Induction Day.

The next morning I awoke early and took a cab into Annapolis's historic district, arriving about an hour before my scheduled reporting time. I wasn't going to take any chances on showing up late on my first day. I spent the extra time soaking in the morning sun at the Annapolis city dock only a few blocks outside the academy's main gate. Lined with colorful boats, the narrow inlet jutted into the edge of the historic district, with its beautiful Colonial buildings and an array of shops and seafood restaurants.

To the northeast, the green-copper-and-gold dome of the Naval Academy chapel towered against the clear blue sky. Unchanged for a century and a half, the academy's high brick wall stood like the boundary of a different time—when courage, duty, and honor meant something more pure than we outside the wall could grasp. The distant, countless voices of the past echoed through the stone buildings, across marching fields and bricked courtyards.

As I picked up my duffel bag and walked down the narrow, cobbled street toward the academy, I felt surprisingly calm and relaxed. My growing anticipation had given way to a peaceful acceptance that this would be a long and difficult journey. And it would be a marvelous journey. I wanted a challenge—something tough, rewarding, and unique—and this was my chance. The outcome would depend on how completely I was willing to devote myself to this goal.

I passed through the academy's main entrance, with its imposing iron gates. The center of each gate bore a bronze seal of the Naval Academy—a sailing ship above an open book, with the hand of Neptune grasping a trident rising above it all. A flowing ribbon surrounded the scene reading, U.S. NAVAL ACADEMY—EX SCIENTIA TRIDENS, the Latin meaning, "From knowledge, sea power."

My destination was Halsey Field House, which lay off to the right as I entered the grounds. This would be my first stop in the transformation from civilian to "plebe," the less-than-complimentary term for midshipman fourth class. A vast series of tables and blue partitions filled the huge enclosure, like a giant rat maze channeling streams of confused new plebes. Herding the plebes and sitting at the various tables were first-class midshipmen, impressive in their white uniforms with gold-striped black shoulder boards.

The term "midshipman" is a vestige from the days when young officers in training held their formations in the center of the ship, called the midship. Midshipmen are often called mids, but they despise the oft-used term "middies" because it sounds too cutesy. Even more despised is the misnomer "cadet," because it is properly used only at Annapolis's rival academy, West Point.

At Annapolis, the classes are not referred to as freshman, sophomore, junior, and senior; they are referred to by rank—midshipmen fourth class, third class, second class, and first class. Among midshipmen, slang terms are commonly substituted for these ranks. The fourth class are called plebes, the third class are youngsters, the second class are just called second class, and the first class, firsties.

I approached the registration table and stated my name to a firsty seated behind a box full of small brown-paper envelopes. Each envelope was bulging, the flap pinned shut by a rectangular black plastic name tag. The firsty quickly located my packet

and handed it to me. On the tag STEFFAN '87 was etched through
the black plastic, revealing the yellow layer below. I opened the
envelope to find three more identical name tags inside. "Move to
the next station," he said, pointing to a nearby set of tables
surrounded by boxes.

I walked to the next table, and the next, accumulating item
after item: booklets, forms, bags, and boxes. The process went
quickly. We were told what to do, and we did it. There was little
talking as my new classmates and I flowed through this human
pipeline. I moved between stations in a kind of solemn awe, like
an outside observer peeking through the bushes at the very beginning of a secret tribal ceremony. I wondered when the tribal
frenzy would begin, the screaming and abuse that Dan had described. Up to now, everyone had been calm and polite, even
cordial, to us, the new members of the class of 1987. It seemed
like such a strange phrase, the class of '87. "The class of '87," I
repeated silently to myself, as if trying to reinforce its reality. I
was here. I was really here, and it was beginning.

I was measured and given a set of loose white uniforms. I
changed into one, packing my civilian clothes in my duffel bag.
The uniform was simple, a pair of drawstring pants, white can-
vas Keds, and a pullover jumper covering an academy T-shirt.
The uniform also included a white sailor's hat with a blue rim
called a dixie cup, which is worn only by plebes during plebe
summer.

At the end of the pipeline we flowed into an open area of
the field house and were segregated into groups by firsties reading names from clipboard lists. A tall, dark-haired midshipman
with two gold stripes and a star on his shoulder boards finally
called my name.

"That's me," I responded, and he glanced at me. I only
caught his eyes for a moment, but they were dark icy blue. His
red name tag read PANCIO in thin, white letters.

"You're with me, Mr. Steffan—Delta Company, Eleventh
Platoon." His voice was stern, and mirrored the coldness of his
eyes. After calling about ten of us, he led us out of the field
house to the concrete sidewalk.

"From now on, we're going to march," he said. "Form two
rows and follow me. No talking, no looking around." Each of
us had slung over our shoulders a huge laundry bag packed with

old and newly accumulated items. As Mr. Pancio called a cadence, we did our best to follow and stay in step. Luckily, I had had some practice from marching band back home.

Our first stop was a courtyard where we dropped off our civilian clothes. As plebes, we were not allowed to wear civilian clothes or even have them in our rooms. They were packed in cardboard boxes and shipped home. The only thing I had left was the shaving kit my parents had given me before I left Warren.

Our next stop was the barbershop. I knew that midshipmen had to wear their hair short, which didn't bother me because I had worn mine short for years. It had a tendency to curl if I didn't. But in anticipation of induction, I had had it cut extra short before leaving Warren. I was hoping the barber would just look at me and say, "Yours is short enough. Next." But as I watched my classmates emerge one by one through the glass doors of the barbershop, their heads shaved clean down to a fine stubble, I gave up hope of escaping the shears.

The line of dazed plebes worked its way slowly into the barbershop. As I passed through the doors and leaned against the wall, I was caught in a kind of trance, watching the row of barbers at work. Their hands moved quickly, a comb in one and powerful, industrial-looking electric shears in the other, as they shaved the heads. Piles of hair collected like autumn leaves at the barbers' feet, and the deep, hypnotic buzzing of the shears filled the room.

As the new plebes watched their physical transformation in the long mirror that stretched across the room, I noticed how deeply they seemed to be affected. With each sweep of the shears, their youthful self-assuredness spilled out. I marveled at how different they seemed from before, when they had been waiting in line. It was as though, in addition to their appearance, their whole demeanor had changed. That hair had been a part of them, a physical anchor to their identity. Every time they had looked in the mirror, it had reminded them of who they were. Now, like the clothes we had packed away, another reminder was gone. The physical components of identity were slowly being erased.

When my turn arrived, I sat down in the chair. In the mirror, I saw the empty faces watching me, their lips slightly parted, eyes transfixed. The metal of the shears was cool and smooth as it cut, vibrating across my scalp. I looked in the mirror at my own reflection, the new white uniform, and the emerging stubbly head. Things were definitely moving fast. In only a few hours I had changed so much already. I wondered how much change was still to come, what would be next.

I looked in the mirror but I could barely recognize myself. What would I be like in a month, or a year? Would I know myself? But it didn't seem to matter. I would become who I would become, who the academy would make me. I was ready to be changed. I welcomed it.

We were led next to Bancroft Hall, the academy's huge dormitory complex, the largest in the world. It is composed of eight separate five-story wings enclosing nearly five miles of hallways. During the academic year it houses the entire Brigade of Midshipmen, all 4,500 students. We entered the fourth wing through large metal doors and walked through a maze of bleak hallways. All the hallways were identical, their floors covered with shining waxed tiles, the walls with pale ceramic blocks. The walls were broken intermittently by identical wooden doors with metal slots for nameplates. Men had black nameplates with white lettering; women had white nameplates with black lettering.

At the center of every turn in a hallway, a smooth metal plate lay in place of the floor tiles. I remembered Dan's telling me about these plates. He had said that plebes were required to run or "chop" through the center of the hallways, executing a quick military turn at each corner while sounding off with a "Go Navy, sir," "Beat Army, sir," or some other appropriate phrase. The tiles at these turns had worn out so often that they could not be repaired fast enough and had been replaced with metal plates.

We followed Mr. Pancio noisily up a set of metal stairs. The runners were embedded with chunks of grit, like sandpaper, for traction, but the front edge of each stair had been ground away, polished shiny by years of wear. We continued winding up the stairs, flight after flight until we finally reached our company area on the fifth floor. Great, I thought, top floor—so far, so bad. This will be like doing the grandstand drill every day.

I was assigned a room with one roommate, a tall, dark-haired fellow, a high school football player from a small town in

Ohio. Our room was fairly large, with two beds and two large desks. We each had a closet for uniforms and storage, and each room also had its own shower area complete with a sink and medicine cabinet. As we began putting away some of our things, a female firsty walked in. She was short, with straight dark hair, and her shoulder boards each bore one gold stripe and a star.

She introduced herself as Miss Stewart, our squad leader. She was the antithesis of Mr. Pancio, almost cheery in her demeanor. She spoke to us casually, but with a sense of formality, as if she were unaccustomed to her role. I felt awkward standing there as she explained what we were to do next, wondering if I should be standing at attention or calling her "ma'am." Everything seemed so much more relaxed than I had expected.

She told us to put away as many of our things as we could before lunch. The swearing-in ceremony would begin afterward, and we were to memorize the oath of office printed in a small book we had received called *Reef Points*—the plebe's bible. It contained most of the information, or "rates," we would have to memorize during the summer about ships, aircraft and submarines, weapons, ranks and insignia, and countless other bits of military minutiae.

Later, Miss Stewart called our whole squad into the hallway to go over some papers we were to sign before the ceremony and introduce us to one another. A squad is the smallest component of the organizational system at Annapolis, and there were thirteen plebes in our squad. Two more squads along with ours made up a platoon and three platoons made up Delta Company, our plebe-summer company.

My fellow squad members and I introduced ourselves, talking briefly about our backgrounds. It was a surprisingly diverse group. Two of our squad members were women, two were Asian Americans. Our hometowns spanned the country, from California to Iowa, Georgia, New York, and New Jersey. There was even another Minnesotan, a former enlisted Marine sergeant named Scott Davis from Grand Rapids. Scott had come from enlisted service straight to the academy, as a certain percentage of each class does. His military experience and advice would prove helpful to all of us as we made the transition into plebe summer.

After this meeting we marched down to lunch in King Hall, the academy's huge dining hall. Each squad ate together at its own table in areas grouped by company. Delta Company was one of a dozen companies making up the entire plebe-summer group, which is called the Plebe Summer Regiment. This regiment is divided into two battalions, the Port and Starboard battalions, of six companies each. Altogether, I was in the Plebe Summer Regiment, Port Battalion, Delta Company, 11th Platoon, 3rd Squad. This complexity was later exacerbated by our having to memorize the leaders of each level.

Once we were seated, each table was quickly served by a large crew of mess attendants. Lunch was strangely quiet, with everyone caught up in his own thoughts and anticipation. The hall was filled with an almost electric tension. It seemed as though days had passed since I stepped through the academy's main gate, but it had been only hours. Six weeks would pass before I could step through that gate again, and at this pace those six weeks were going to be an eternity.

After lunch it was time for the swearing-in ceremony. We were marched to the center of the academy grounds, where a field of metal folding chairs had been arranged. They faced the elevated courtyard between two large science buildings, Michelson and Chauvanet halls. At the top of the steps leading to the courtyard, a podium stood before a row of black-and-gold wooden chairs, the back of each marked with a gold academy seal.

Gathered around the area were hundreds of civilians—friends, family, and anxious parents. They had traveled here to see their sons and daughters take their first military step. As we drew near, I could see their mixed expressions of pride, excitement, and sadness. They seemed surprised at how quickly we had already transformed, how similar we all looked. They strained to pick out their children in the blinding sea of white uniforms and dixie cups. But there were no clues—no familiar sweatshirts or baseball caps, not even hair—only a single, unique face floating among fourteen hundred others.

All around us were monuments to the bravery and sacrifice of those who had served before us. They, too, had once stood here, looking not much different than we did now, wondering what lay ahead. They probably wondered if they would have the strength to do what was right, the courage to risk everything—their hopes and dreams, perhaps even their lives. It was as though I could feel them here with us. Their voices cheered us onward, tempered by a wistful regret for lost youth—and lost innocence.

The ceremony began with the procession of the colors, the flags of the United States, Naval Academy, Navy, and Marine Corps. After the obligatory speeches, the entire class was called to attention. Along with my classmates, I raised my right hand as the superintendent, the academy's highest-ranking officer, led us in the oath of office:

I, Joseph Steffan, having been appointed a midshipman in the United States Navy, do solemnly swear that I will protect and defend the Constitution of the United States against all enemies, foreign and domestic; that I will bear true faith and allegiance to the same; that I take this obligation freely, without any mental reservation or purpose of evasion; and that I will well and faithfully discharge the duties of the office on which I am about to enter; so help me God.

When I had first read the oath, I was surprised that it focused entirely on the Constitution. I had always assumed that our duty was somehow bound to the government or the president. It was reassuring to know that our duty was to the constitution, something above political whims. Within the space of that brief invocation we had crossed the line between civilian and military. I was now, officially, a midshipman in the United States Navy. Although my parents weren't here, they made hotel reservations in Annapolis that afternoon—reservations for my graduation, nearly four years away.

After the ceremony, many of my classmates sought out their families and friends in the crowd. It was their last chance to say good-bye before the summer, and there were many tears on both sides. It was too depressing to hang around and watch, so I started walking back toward Bancroft Hall to return to my company area. As I approached, I heard a strange sound, as though a football game were being played on the other side of

the hall, the shouts and screams of the fans carrying across the
yard.

But as I drew nearer, it became clear that there was no
football game. The shouts were coming from the hall itself.
They were the shouts and screaming of firsties and of my classmates. Their voices bounced across the huge brick courtyard
between the wings, echoing off stone walls like a vocal racquet-
ball game. I realized now that we truly had crossed the line. The
gauntlet had begun.

I ran into the hall and up the winding flights of stairs toward my company area. On every floor I heard the screams of
firsties and the unfortunate plebes they had cornered. After
reaching the top of the stairs, I walked quickly down the hall,
looking straight ahead. Few people from our company had returned from the swearing-in, so I miraculously made it all the
way to my room without being stopped. I stepped through
the door breathing a heavy sigh of relief and waited tensely as
the volume of the screams steadily increased outside.

A few minutes later, my roommate popped through the
door, his eyes wide with fear. He had also managed to make it
through the halls unscathed. Just then, one of the firsties from
our company kicked open our door and ordered us into the
hallway. Lined up against the wall with the rest of our company,
we were swarmed over by firsties suddenly transformed into
raving, screaming lunatics.

Although there was little we were required to know at that
point, the firsties were able to trip up everyone. It was nearly
impossible to repeat something like the entire oath of office from
memory, word for word without pausing, or glancing away, or
simply going blank. Even if you knew it cold, the sheer stress of
the onslaught was paralyzing. There was just too much going
on, with my classmates screaming answers and the firsties
screaming "Faster!" "Start over!" or "Louder!" just inches in
front of your face.

As plebes, we had only five basic responses: "Yes, sir,"
"No, sir," "Aye, aye, sir," which is the affirmative response to
any order, "No excuse, sir," and "I'll find out, sir." If
you didn't know the answer to a question, even if you were
simply uncertain about one part, there was only one answer:

"I'll find out, sir." Absolutely, under no circumstances, would you ever say, "I don't know," or try to repeat as much as you knew. That would be an open invitation for an even more vicious attack.

The evening meal was even more overwhelming than the afternoon. The dining hall echoed with deafening screaming. At each table, we were immersed in a battle for survival, and we learned quickly that there was no escape from failure. Each of us was grilled until we forgot, or paused.

The same treatment continued through the evening, broken only by a few short meetings and training sessions, a whirlwind of continuous activity. By the time my head hit my pillow that night, I was utterly drained. If this was any indication of the days to come, the summer was going to be even longer and tougher than I had anticipated.

My roommate and I awoke the following morning at 5:00 to finish putting away all of our things and clean our room. With our first formal room inspection only a short time away, we needed every spare moment to get our room into shape.

The day officially started with a 6 A.M. formation followed by a quick march to PEP, an acronym for the Physical Excellence Program. It was an hour-long series of rigorous calisthenics, from sit-ups to push-ups to wind sprints. PEP was ruled by Coach Heinz Lenz, a legendary figure at the academy who, despite his advancing age, was incredibly fit. He was one of those people who got up in the morning to run ten miles as a warm-up for his daily workout. Coach Lenz stood on a tall platform overlooking the practice football field where PEP was held, barking out commands over a P.A. in his heavy German accent.

The firsties stood on the field supervising, pushing everyone to keep up. They would sometimes challenge us to cheer by screaming "Eighty-four!," the year of their graduation. Our class would all scream back in unison, "Eighty-seven, sir!" The cheering would continue back and forth until one side gave in. By the end of the hour, we were drenched with sweat and nearing exhaustion. I was particularly grateful for having kept in shape through the wrestling and track seasons that year.

Those plebes who demonstrated outstanding physical stamina during PEP were eventually awarded the honor of wearing colored company T-shirts and the title "super." Scott Davis, our former Marine, was chosen as a super after the first few PEP sessions. Those who were out of shape or who could not keep up with the pack were ordered to wear their academy T-shirts inside out. They were denied the privilege of wearing the academy crest on the chest. These poor unfortunates inherited the name "subs" and additional derision from the firsties. After a few of these grueling morning sessions, my classmates and I had adopted a new definition for PEP: the Plebe Elimination Program.

PEP was a lesson in survival, like so many lessons of that summer. We quickly learned that the most important goal was simply making it from one moment to the next. By concentrating on the task at hand, surviving each new assault on our stamina, dignity, and pride, we survived for hours and days, and then weeks.

Much of the summer focused on memorizing and recalling rates. Every day, the list of information we were required to know grew, and any spare moment was usually dedicated to memorization. Within a short time we were to have memorized the names and ranks of all the firsties in our company, as well as those of the other company commanders and of those above them. We also had to memorize the hometowns of every one of our company mates, information about monuments and buildings in the yard, the menus for each meal, famous naval sayings, ranks and insignia of the enlisted men, and officer ranks of each branch of the military—the list went on and on.

Some of the information was practical, relating to ships and aircraft, navigation and weapons systems. Other memorization was inane, the remnants of long-standing tradition. For example, if a plebe forgot to say "Sir," the firsty would ask the magic question, "Why didn't you say 'Sir'?"

Instead of responding "I'll find out, sir," the plebe was required to give the following answer, exactly and at high speed:

Sir, "sir" is a subservient word surviving from the surly days in old Serbia when certain serfs, too ignorant to remember their lords' names, yet too servile to blaspheme them, circumvented the situation by surrogating the subservient word "sir," by which I now belatedly address a certain senior cirriped, who correctly surmised that I was syrupy enough to say "sir" after every word I said, sir!

Even more difficult than the memorization was learning to concentrate and respond under the assault of the firsties. We were to answer every question in a loud, confident voice without hesitation. The slightest pause or error, an omission of a "the" or "an," was met with a screaming "Start over!" No matter what the rate, there was only one correct answer, and the firsties knew it cold. We had to keep reminding ourselves that they had actually gone through this once themselves. Whether we were repeating the menu for the day or a long quotation, every word had to be exact, verbatim, in order.

We were constantly reminded that, in the Navy, there is no room for indecision or excuses. Every question had an answer, and every situation a response. I recall Mr. Pancio once preaching, "Never apologize. Either you accomplished your mission or you failed. Saying you're sorry isn't going to change a thing." During every day of plebe summer that truism was drilled into us. The firsties would say, "What are you going to say when you're the officer of the deck on a destroyer, and three missiles are headed right at you? Are you going to say, 'I don't know' and get your ass blown off, along with everyone else on the ship?" The firsties had an uncanny ability for boiling everything down to life and death. Whether we were late for a formation or forgot an item on the menu, it was always a matter of life and death.

Every day, from PEP to lights-out, was scheduled down to the minute. Between formations and meals, we were constantly marching between training lectures, squad meetings, picking up more boxes of stuff, and getting measured for an endless array of uniforms. We were trained on everything from wearing our uniforms, marching with a rifle, and proper saluting to folding our shirts and socks and preparing our rooms for inspection. Everything we did had one precise method. Our uniforms hung in one direction on their hangers, grouped by colors; our T-shirts were folded to leave the academy crest exposed; towels were folded in threes, mirrors spotless, chrome polished, name tags centered and a quarter inch above the pocket. There was only one way for everything—the Navy way.

The two worst times during the day were meals and "come-arounds." A come-around is a time for "instruction," when an upperclassman orders you to come around to his room and get screamed at for a while. During the summer, come-arounds were usually done en masse, the hallways packed with plebes and screaming firsties. Meals were equally intense as we sat at attention, looking straight ahead throughout the meal. Any looking around would summon a scorching "Eyes in the boat pleber!" from firsties who seemed to have eyes in the back of their heads. Only when answering a rate would we look them in the eye.

The meal was served family style. The food was brought to the table and we passed it around, firsties first. When eating, we took one bite of food, put down our silverware, put our hands in our laps, and chewed. A favorite trick of the more sadistic firsties was to ask for a rate immediately after a plebe had taken a bite of food, forcing him to gag it down as quickly as possible before answering. Needless to say, we soon learned to take very small bites.

Between answering rates and an occasional bite of food, we were ordered to stand on our seats and give "cheers" to show our spirit for Navy. With a thousand plebes in King Hall constantly yelling cheers and screaming answers to rates, it sounded as though we were dining at the Super Bowl.

My squad and I were particularly grateful to have been assigned Miss Stewart as our leader. She was definitely the most mellow squad leader in our company and made clear from the start that she didn't like to yell. Unfortunately, the firsties who were not squad leaders rotated from one table to another for meals and made up for Miss Stewart's lack of screaming.

One of our most frequent and least enjoyable table guests was the cold-eyed Mr. Pancio. He was moody and unpredictable, calm one moment and brutal the next. Having him at our table was like waiting for a time bomb to go off, and the tension was more unbearable than being yelled at. Sometimes, if one of us screwed up a rate, he would react calmly and just go on to someone else. On other occasions he would snap, exploding into a rage and dragging us through rate hell. During these times, there was nothing worse than looking into his piercing scowl, with his lips drawn back, nearly white, and those ice-cold eyes staring right through you.

During both meals and come-arounds, we discovered that one of the first lessons of plebe summer is teamwork. Part of the underlying purpose of this training is to teach the new plebes to stick together, to support each other as a way of surviving the onslaught of the firsties. One of the cardinal sins of plebehood was making one of your classmates look bad, however unintentionally. Assume a firsty asked one of your classmates a rate, like "How many stars does a lieutenant general in the Army wear?" If your classmate could not answer, and you were asked next, the correct response was not "Three." It was "Request permission to help my classmate, sir." Then, if you were granted permission to help, you could state the answer. Neglecting this courtesy was known as bilging your classmate, a reference to bilge pumps used to pump oily residue and leakage out of the bilges of ships.

In the first few days of the summer, almost everyone forgot, at one time or another, to request permission to assist, much to the amusement of the firsties. The only thing worse than not knowing a rate was bilging a classmate with a correct response. In order to rub in the lesson of this omission, firsties would often sentence the offending plebe to spend the remainder of the day squaring his corners by sounding off "I'm a bilge pump, sir," instead of "Go Navy" or "Beat Army." This public announcement served not only to embarrass the offender, but to attract the attention of any nearby firsties who would perhaps otherwise allow the plebe to pass unmolested. The firsty would most likely stop the plebe, and an interchange similar to the following would occur:

Firsty: "Plebe halt." (The standard order to stop a plebe from chopping down the hallway. The plebe would stop dead, execute a military about-face to face the firsty, standing at attention, looking straight ahead.) "So, you're a bilger?"

Plebe: "Yes, sir."

"How did you bilge your classmate?"

"Sir, I gave the correct answer to a question without requesting permission to correct my classmate."

"What was the question?"

"Sir, the question was 'How many stars does a lieutenant
general in the Army wear?' "

"And your classmate couldn't answer the question?"

"No, sir."

"And so you bilged him?"

"Yes, sir."

"Do you like your classmate?"

"Yes, sir."

"So, you're a faggot?"

"No, sir."

"How much do you like your classmate?"

"I'll find out, sir."

"So, you know all your rates?"

"I'll find out, sir."

"What do you mean, 'I'll find out'? Either you do or you
don't!"

"Yes, sir."

"So you do know all your rates?"

"Yes, sir."

"OK, maggot, you can start by telling me all the ranks in
the Marine Corps, officer and enlisted in reverse order from
general down!"

"Sir, the ranks of the Marine Corps in reverse order are:
general, lieutenant general, major general . . ."

"Stop! Start over, and give me the insignia for each rank."

"Sir, the ranks and insignia of the Marine Corps in reverse
order are: general, four silver stars; lieutenant general, three
silver stars . . ."

"OK. What color is a mid-channel buoy?"

"Sir, a mid-channel buoy is black and white, vertically
striped."

"What color is a junction buoy?"

"Sir, [pause] I'll find out, sir."

"What do you mean? I thought you said you knew all your
rates? Were you lying to me? Should I put you up for an honor
offense?"

"No, sir."

"So, what's your problem?"

"I'll find out, sir."

"Damn right you'll find out, and you'll do it by evening meal because you're coming to my room for come-around. Got it?"

"Aye, aye, Sir."

"Who is your classmate that didn't know his ranks?"

"Sir, request permission to not bilge my classmate."

"No way maggot, you blew it. Bilge away."

"Sir, my classmate is Midshipman Fourth Class Smith."

"Well, you've earned the pleasure of telling Mr. Smith that he's going to join us as well."

"Aye, aye, sir."

"Shove off."

"Aye, aye, sir."

And so life would continue, until the next corner, and the next, and the next.

Almost any organization develops its own special language of terms and slang, and the military stands at the forefront when it comes to arcane terminology. Part of acclimating to the academy meant learning military terminology and a seemingly endless list of slang terms peculiar to the academy.

In addition to terms like "chopping," "bilging," "come-around," and "rates," we quickly learned that a lazy midshipman is a "bagit," a brownnoser is a "smack," and any easy task was "cake." A high-ranking firsty with lots of stripes was a "striper," a tough upperclassman who yelled a lot was a "flamer," and getting yelled at was to get "flamed." This was not to be confused, however, with getting "fried," which meant being placed on report for a conduct violation.

We learned these terms from context. Our formal training sessions explained the myriad rules, regulations, and traditions that made up the fabric of academy life. One of the first things we discussed during these sessions was the Honor Concept. Like the other service academies, the Naval Academy is a highly idealistic institution. Midshipmen are trained to adhere to a code of ethical behavior that exceeds what society expects of its citizens.

The Honor Concept lies at the heart of this idealism and is simply defined: "A midshipman will not lie, cheat, or steal." It differs slightly from West Point's Honor Code, which states, "A cadet will not lie, cheat, or steal, or tolerate those who do." At West Point, if a cadet observes an honor violation and fails to turn in the offending cadet, he may also be separated. At Annapolis, a midshipman observing an honor violation has the option of either turning in the individual or counseling him. After discussing the offense and counseling the offender, the midshipman has the personal choice of whether or not to report the incident.

The honor system at Annapolis is run entirely by midshipmen, and any offense is adjudicated by an honor board made up of midshipmen. After reviewing the evidence, the board votes to recommend separation or retention. From there, the recommendation is passed through the commandant of midshipmen, to the superintendent of the academy and, ultimately, to the Secretary of the Navy. The honor board's recommendation is rarely overturned by any of these officials.

The Honor Concept was not simply a goal or a nicety to us. It was the ultimate reflection of what it meant to be a midshipman. Breaking the Honor Concept was not like breaking a conduct rule, like staying out after taps. It was a denial of everything we believed and respected. Those without respect for honor, for the truth, were simply unworthy of being midshipmen.

Despite the difficulty of the first few weeks of plebe summer, there was something incredibly exciting about it. It was a piece of history, an age-old process of which we had now become a part. Despite the almost constant humiliation that we endured, my classmates and I were becoming deeply bound together by the experience. After the first few shocking days, we had begun to adjust, to adapt and grow; and now we were becoming stronger.

At the end of each day we lined the dark halls of our company area, dressed in identical blue-and-gold Naval Academy bathrobes and slippers. As our final act of the day, we sang together the Naval Academy's school song:

Now college men from sea to sea
May sing of colors true,
But who has better right than we
To hoist a symbol hue?
For sailor men in battle fair
Since fighting days of old
Have proved the sailor's right to wear
The Navy Blue and Gold.

It was a small celebration, an announcement of belonging, of unity, and most importantly, of victory. We had survived another day. Each night, as I crawled between the sheets of my bed, it felt as though a month had passed since morning, since being shocked out of deep and peaceful sleep by the reveille bells.

I had long before learned to avoid thinking about the day to come, to simply appreciate a moment of peace and solitude, as I had learned to cherish each moment of calm these days. This summer had few constants, except for the oppressive heat and humidity that followed us through the day. I heard rumors that we were enduring the hottest plebe summer in twenty years, although I wondered if every class heard that. It was definitely the hottest summer of my life. Every day was a repeat of the one before, with temperatures and humidity in the high nineties. You couldn't even think without breaking a sweat, and as we marched, the heat of the pavement seeped through our shoes, baking the soles of our feet.

Our only respite from the heat was the air-conditioned coolness of the academic buildings in which many of our training sessions were held. But after a few weeks of constant transition between the stifling heat of the outdoors and the frigid climate indoors, most of my class had come down with severe summer colds. We were like a pack of invalids, coughing and hacking constantly.

I recall one afternoon when our entire class was assembled in an auditorium for a training lecture given by a high-ranking academy officer. The sound of coughing was so constant and distracting that the officer in charge stopped the lecture and gave us all a fifteen-minute sermon on how our constant coughing was disrespectful and how we were jeopardizing the reputation of our class. We all sat there in disbelief, wondering how he could order us to instantly become well, but we were especially afraid of officers and tried to suppress our coughing, with little success. After that incident, the firsties ordered us to sleep with our windows closed at night because they felt the cool night air was the cause of our colds. Of course, that didn't make getting to sleep any easier.

After only a few days into the summer, several of our classmates gave in to the strain, leaving to seek another path in life. But as I fell asleep at night with the strange feeling of my short, stubbly hair on the pillow, I knew that I would endure this ordeal. If I could survive one day, I could survive them all, one at a time.

Thanks to my conversations with Dan, I felt prepared for plebe summer and managed to do a good job during my first few weeks. I knew my rates and was a "squared away" plebe. In fact, everything was going quite well—until one particularly fateful afternoon. Our platoon was returning to company area and had just entered Bancroft Hall. We had passed through a set of doors adjacent to our most feared of all areas—the small section of hallway where the regimental staff, the highest-ranking firsties, had their rooms.

Entering that forbidding area was especially tense for me that morning because this was the day we were supposed to have memorized the names of the regimental staff members, and I had not memorized them. The thought of simply passing through their area lacking this knowledge was enough to make me nervous. It may have been the tension of this hidden deficiency that caused me to break my concentration because, as I walked into Bancroft Hall, I did something that would have been normal upon entering any building—any building that is, *except* Bancroft Hall. I removed my hat.

As a matter of etiquette, a midshipman removes his hat, or "cover," as it is called in the Navy, upon entering any building. However, Bancroft Hall is not treated like an ordinary building. It is treated like a ship, and covers are not removed upon boarding a ship.

Although I immediately recognized my mistake and quickly moved to replace my cover, it was too late. As luck would have it, half of the entire regimental staff was walking down the hall just as I made my blunder, and in seconds they were upon me.

I was snatched from my platoon and engulfed in a flurry of screaming uniforms, all questioning me as to why I had so blatantly committed an act of such sheer and utter stupidity, seemingly unequaled in the history of the academy. The speed and force of the attack were so overwhelming that I was momentarily stunned, unable to respond with much more than a look of bland puzzlement. I had never seen so many high-ranking firsties, so many gold stripes, gathered in one spot, and now I was at the center, the blazing focus of a striper inferno.

Within seconds of my capture, my worst fear became reality. One of the firsties, a woman, covered her name tag, told me her position on the staff, and asked me what her name was.

I had absolutely no idea, not even an inkling of who she was. I issued the required response: "I'll find out, sir."

"SIR??!!!!!!!!!!," she screamed, her face red with fury. "Do I look like a SIR to you?!!!!!" This was an unfortunate mistake, for I had neatly transformed a horrible situation into a situation so completely, totally grotesque that it transcended comprehension. Another staffer, a woman standing next to her, repeated the same question to me.

"I'll find out, ma'am" was my response.

They were incredulous, screaming in total disbelief that one person could be the recipient of such a huge share of stupidity.

The two female firsties screamed at me simultaneously, their faces pressed to within an inch of my own. I had not yet discovered the technique of focusing beyond the face of the attacker, and all I could see were the distortions of disbelief on their faces.

And then something incredible happened. It lasted only a second, perhaps a fraction of a second, but I saw it, clear and unmistakable. One of them smirked. The smile crossed her face like the blink of an eye, and she forced it down instantly, expertly. But I had seen it, a momentary recognition that this frenzy of abuse was partly a facade, an image like the Wizard of Oz's mighty projection. She had revealed her underlying amusement at my situation, the totality of my helplessness amid this horde of midshipmen Furies.

And as remarkable as it sounds, I knew in that instant that I was going to start to laugh. It was like sitting in church during the most solemn and silent of moments, and you suddenly think of something so funny, so completely absurd, that you have to bite your lip, close your eyes and look down, forcing yourself to think of dead puppies to keep from breaking out in laughter. Somehow, the firsty's smile had triggered that same reaction, but I could not look down or close my eyes. I could only look ahead, and looking ahead I could only see the distorted, screaming faces of the firsties and the absurdity of the situation into which I had landed. I bit my lip, heaps of dead puppies piling up in my head, but it was too late—I started laughing.

The firsties were stunned. They couldn't believe what was happening, but it became very clear to me that they no longer appreciated the humor of the situation. The two women were especially enraged because they felt I was laughing at them, challenging their authority.

Nearly an hour later, I wasn't laughing anymore. I had endured a come-around hell, having listed every bit of plebe knowledge, every single rate I was supposed to know, forward, backward, and upside down. The firsties had pulled out the *Plebe Indoctrination Manual* and exhausted the complete list of required knowledge, one by one, systematically revealing those areas I had not memorized.

I had stumbled often, the stress of the situation thwarting my ability to recall information, adding to my already anxious state. When I was finally dismissed, I chopped out of regimental area, drenched in my own sweat. I felt as though every muscle in my body had been held in a tight contraction for that hour. I was physically, emotionally, and mentally exhausted by the ordeal. And now they knew me. The entire regimental staff knew who I was, and the two women I had unwittingly insulted swore that I would live to regret the day I had set foot on their academy's soil.

I was in trouble—big trouble. After only a few weeks, I saw my academy career flashing before my eyes. That evening, the two female firsties visited me in my company area, pulling me away from a company-wide come-around for their own private session. I had spent every free second of the day trying to memorize my rates and honing what I already knew. But they found every weakness, every deficiency, and played on every pause and uncertainty. At the end of another hour I had performed miserably again, allowing myself to become flustered, to pause when I knew the answer or forget what I knew.

When they were finally finished, they explained that this night had been strike one, and that they would visit me for two more nights. "Three strikes," they said, "and you're out." And with that, they left. I wondered what their threat meant. Did they actually have the power to kick me out if I didn't meet their expectations? In any case, I wasn't going to give them a reason. I was going to show them I could take the heat.

During every spare moment I studied my rates, and the new rates that were added to the list each day. Every time I glanced at my watch, the dread of another evening of hell made my stomach churn. What amazed me was how little time we had to study. It was rare to have any type of break between events, even a few minutes, and it wasn't as though we could wander around the grounds studying. We were marched everywhere, carrying with us at all times our small, plastic-covered copies of *Reef Points*.

The second night started off much better, but ended up almost as badly as the night before. I knew almost every rate I was asked, my delivery was quick and precise. But they worked me over until they found every flaw, every omission. It was incredibly frustrating. There was no way anyone could ever memorize everything we were supposed to know—and they realized that. But reality wasn't part of what was being taught here—it was about survival. Regardless of the odds, we were supposed to keep trying, keep fighting.

Since there was no way we could succeed if someone really wanted to screw with us, it was tolerance that we were really learning—frustration tolerance. This would be one of the great lessons of the academy, learning to accept how little control I had over my own life, part of what it has traditionally meant to serve in the military. Everything in the military is uniform, the guns, the ships, the tanks, and the people. The people are meant to be as interchangeable as any other piece of equipment, to respond uniformly to any given situation.

The firsties were testing me—forcing me to prove how much I wanted to stay at the academy. Some of my classmates had come here with no understanding of what they were up against. Some came only to please their parents and their families, or for the glory of attending an elite institution. But each of us quickly learned that for plebes there truly is no glory. It's a tough, oppressive life, and those without the genuine desire to stay, those who weren't here for the right reasons, didn't last through the summer.

That was part of what this summer was all about—it was a test of stamina, willpower, and desire. Now my own desire was being tested. I knew I wanted to stay at the academy more than anything, to survive and to succeed. Now I had to prove it beyond a shadow of a doubt. When the stripers believed my own desire to succeed, to become a leader, to perform not simply because of pressure but because I had the desire to do my best, then they would let me off the hook.

On the final evening back in regimental area, my back against the wall, I answered every rate quickly and precisely. I thought faster, more efficiently than ever before. I had finally overcome the fear that had made me falter earlier. I was focused and confident, and I succeeded. What I had thought was impossible only a few days before was possible, and I had done it. The sheer desire to succeed had pushed me to realize that I had more inside me than I myself knew. As I chopped back up to my own company area that evening, I felt a pride in myself and a pride in the academy I had never felt before. I had passed an important test and learned a little more about myself in the process.

Even in situations as intense as this one, the firsties are bound, at least in theory, by rules and limitations. In the early years at Annapolis, "hazing" was a common part of indoctrination, and plebes were subject to physical punishment at the whim of the upperclassmen. Hazing was eventually phased out because it was dangerous and because it didn't really teach anything. It was more like fraternity initiation than training for young officers. Strict regulations now exist against hazing, and anyone caught hazing a plebe can be punished severely or even separated from the academy.

My plebe summer was free of hazing except for one incident that sticks very clearly in my mind. One morning our platoon lost a PEP tug-of-war contest, and the firsties threatened us with an especially tough group come-around because of our failure. By that afternoon, the temperature was 100 degrees with characteristically stifling humidity. Before the come-around, we were all ordered to put on our sweat gear with our rain gear on top. We were also ordered to bring our rifles—old, heavy non-firing M-1 rifles that we had been issued for marching and drill. The firsties gathered us in one end of the hallway and then closed all the windows and doors around us.

We were ordered to start jogging in place, and with about forty of us in this "sweat box," the temperature in the hallway began to soar. Within minutes the heat was like a sauna, and sweat poured from my face and soaked my sweat gear. As we jogged, we were ordered to hold our rifles straight out in front of us, until we couldn't hold them out any longer. Then we would be ordered to bring them in, and finally to hold them out again. As this torturous cycle continued, the muscles in my arms and back began to burn with pain. Eventually they became numb, responding to the orders as if I no longer had any control over them.

After thirty minutes, the air in my lungs felt like water. I struggled to breathe and my mind began to drift, as it sometimes did when I was running a race, when I wanted to shut off the pain. I focused on anything but the present, on images of calm and coolness. I thought about playing in the snow when I was a kid back in Warren. The winter blizzards would create huge snowdrifts in the narrow, frozen river channel behind our house. My friends and I used to spend hours digging elaborate tunnels and caves in the hard-packed snow. As the winter light began to fade in the late afternoon, we would light candles we had smuggled out of our houses, propping them in depressions in the cave walls. We huddled together in our snowmobile suits, our hats, scarves, and gloves soaked through with melted snow.

A noisy clattering snapped me back to reality as the person behind me collapsed, falling unconscious with his rifle to the smooth tile floor. I dropped down to help him as firsties swarmed over us. He was all right and already coming around, but I glanced at one of the firsties and saw the fear in his eyes.

It was the first time I really questioned what was happening. In many ways, I had trusted the firsties—not to be kind, but to at least know what they were doing—to put us through this abuse because there was some underlying meaning or lesson to it. I was enduring the harsh treatment of the summer in the hope that I would somehow be made better because of it. I hoped to someday understand and appreciate the value of the difficult lessons of plebe summer and the long year to follow. But now I wondered if there was really any lesson at all to be learned here, or if we were simply the victims of dubious tradition—a tradition so ingrained in this institution that no one even thought to question it.

From that day on, I noticed things. They were things that would otherwise have slipped by, but now I had started to question, not simply to accept what was happening around me. I had come here believing that this was a perfect institution creating perfect leaders. But I had begun to notice the cracks in this image.

The firsties had endured their own plebe summer. Three summers before this one, they were in the sweatbox and on the PEP field. They were the survivors. One fourth of their class had not lasted, and now a select group of them had been chosen to work plebe-summer detail. They were revisiting their past, reliving their oppression in reverse. With every order and command, every come-around, their own power and achievements were affirmed. Now they owned it all—this place was theirs and we were their plebes. They were determined to maintain the sanctity of the academy by making our plebe summer at least as tough as their own.

Some were motivated by the desire to maintain a standard of excellence, to weed out those people who didn't really want to be here. They believed in the academy and what it stood for, and although they had felt much frustration during their underclass years, they had accepted the academy's limitations and moved on, trying to leave some mark of improvement in their wake.

Others had been destroyed by the academy. They had sur-

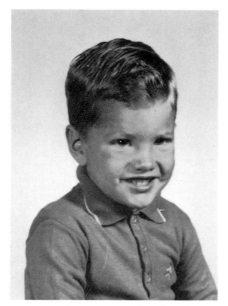

The gratuitous infant shot.

Displaying one of the many stuffed animals I destroyed during my childhood.

Waiting to march in Warren's summer parade in August 1969. The kids from our block did a tribute to the Apollo moon landing, complete with a tinfoil rocket led by a kitchen-utensil band. I was apparently part of the cymbal section.

A picture from my confirmation with our local priest and the bishop from our diocese. "David" was my chosen confirmation name.

Receiving the first-place medal after my surprise two-mile victory at the regional meet during my sophomore year.

The final race of my high school track career, the two-mile at the state track meet in 1983, where I finally broke ten minutes.

High school graduation with my three sisters, left to right, Cheryl, Connie, and Cindy, and my niece Jaimie.

My parents and me on the day of my graduation from high school.

Posing with my date at my high school senior prom.

My parents, me, and my sister Connie on the Academy grounds during plebe summer parents' weekend.

"Borrowing" the F-4 Phantom jet on display during Army Week my plebe year. We were discovered only moments after this picture was taken.

The Academy arranged a weekend exchange program with West Point during my second-class year, and I'm here with my weekend host in his room at West Point.

On my youngster-year sub cruise. My hands are on the "chicken valves," used to rapidly surface the sub during an emergency.

Setting up a movie in the officers' mess during the last weeks of my sub cruise. We wore blue jumpsuits instead of our regular uniforms and deck shoes to keep down the noise. Notice also the small square radiation meter hooked to my belt.

A formal Christmas dinner was held each year before we returned home on leave. This was taken during my youngster year, as my company mates and I posed with our traditional after-dinner cigars.

vived the years since plebe summer, but for all the wrong reasons. They had survived not because they believed in the academy, not because they truly wanted to serve their country, but out of fear. They were deathly afraid of failing or even giving the impression of failure.

If there is one thing midshipmen had in common, it was that we had never failed at anything. If we had one blemish on our record, we wouldn't have made it to the academy. Leaving the academy meant admitting a mistake, in a way, admitting failure and defeat. They were concepts both unfamiliar and frightening, perhaps even more so than the stresses of academy life themselves.

I was beginning to realize that no institution, not even one as rigid and controlling as the Naval Academy, could produce uniformly good leaders. Even the firsties on summer duty spanned the spectrum. The academy was not going to mold me into a leader; it was not going to "produce" leadership skills. The most it could do would be to provide examples, both good and bad. It was going to be up to me to choose, to decide what to emulate and what to avoid.

Plebe-summer duty is divided between two "sets" of firsties, the first set taking the first three weeks and the second set the remaining three weeks. As the halfway point of the summer approached, we began to anticipate the changeover and to worry about our new squad leader. After three weeks with the mellow Miss Stewart, we knew that any change was going to mean a tougher life for all of us.

Before the changeover, we were introduced to another constant of military life: performance evaluations. Midshipmen were constantly evaluated, graded and ranked, in both academics and military performance. These evaluations were used not only for class rank but also to determine who would eventually be selected to interview for leadership positions in the brigade.

To say that the academy is competitive would be a pretty dramatic understatement. The year my class was inducted, Annapolis was the most selective college in the country, with only one in eleven applicants chosen. During the same year, Harvard had selected one in six applicants. Half of my class had graduated either first or second from their high schools, and nearly 90 percent held at least one varsity letter. Obviously, none of us enjoyed losing, even if that meant coming in second. So the thought that one person in our squad was going to be ranked first and one was going to be thirteenth made everyone a little tense.

I was surprised when Miss Stewart told me during my review that she had ranked me first in the squad. I was certain that our squared-away Marine Scott Davis would get it, especially after my run-in with the regimental staff. But apparently I was doing something right, and I wasn't in any position to argue. The ranking was a great lift after three arduous weeks of the summer, an affirmation that I was on the right track.

As the day of changeover approached, our new squad leaders were announced and we were assigned another female squad leader, Miss Sanders. Some of our firsties, notably male firsties, were quick to inform us that we would find her "one of the academy's finest." Their tone of voice and laughter were more than a subtle indication of their sarcasm. It was a scene I would see repeated more often than I care to remember at Annapolis, an indication of two of the academy's most pervasive problems.

The first was the backbiting and undermining that can be an almost inevitable result of such an intensely competitive atmosphere. The firsties, even during plebe summer, often made remarks about other firsties that revealed hidden animosities.

The other problem was an often vicious opposition to women at the academy. Women had been admitted to all the service academies since 1976, and the first academy class with women had graduated only three years earlier in 1980. Although I believe most men accepted women at the academy, those who did not went out of their way to let us know. They were constantly bad-mouthing women midshipmen behind their backs and pressuring us to join in. They asserted that the academy was here to train "military leaders for combat, not female supply officers."

At that point, women weren't allowed in any combat situations, and it wouldn't be until after the Persian Gulf War that those restrictions would be relaxed, allowing female pilots to fly combat missions. The restrictions on women in combat only made it more difficult for them to earn the respect they deserved at the academy. These attitudes not only undermined the efforts of female leaders at the academy, they also set a tone of unprofessionalism and elitism. In an organization where mission accomplishment was supposed to be the ultimate goal, it bothered me that so many people were more concerned about maintaining their own personal visions of the military's "purity."

When the day of changeover arrived, it was like a step back to Induction Day, with the new firsties raring to take their first bite out of us. My platoon spent most of the day qualifying for pistol marksmanship at the naval station firing range across the Severn River from the academy. Although I had fired a pistol only a few times before, I was one of only two plebes in my platoon to qualify as "expert," the highest rating. It earned me my first and only military medal, for expert marksmanship. That day also happened to be my birthday, July 29, so it was a nice birthday present to help offset the gloom of changeover. I was particularly thankful that none of the new firsties found out it was my birthday. One of the tenets of plebe survival is invisibility, and the last thing I needed on this day was attention.

The new firsties were tougher than ever, and our new squad leader, Miss Sanders, was definitely a change. She was short and stocky, which is probably why she took so much heat from the male firsties. From what we overheard and were sometimes told outright, she had gone through a tough plebe year herself. The years following had probably been almost as difficult.

Despite what we had been told about her, she wasn't a bad squad leader. She was definitely tougher than Miss Stewart, grinding on rates almost constantly at the dinner table. But she lacked the bitterness that seemed to motivate other firsties who had gone through difficult years. Mr. Pancio was a prime example. He was also heavy, and we had learned from backbiting chatter that he had barely survived plebe year. The difference was that when Mr. Pancio screamed at us, I felt that he was venting his own anger and frustration.

Unfortunately, Miss Sanders never really had a chance to prove herself. The first-set firsties had done their damage, and the second-set firsties picked up where they left off. Only a week into second set, a couple of male firsties convinced some plebes in our company to crawl across the roof into Miss Sanders's room while she was out. They locked the door from the inside and on their way out hung one of her bras from a mop handle out her window.

At the time, it seemed almost funny, but I also felt sorry for her. This was much more than a simple prank against a firsty, it was sexual harassment and a sickening display of male arrogance. Of course, no one involved was really punished. The plebes got a public slap on the wrist from the firsties and a private pat on the back.

The remainder of the summer continued much as before, a constant cycle of PEP, training, meals, come-arounds and an ever-increasing list of rates. As the summer wound down, we received our second set of performance appraisals and I was again ranked first in our squad. It was gratifying to know that the first ranking wasn't an anomaly, and I was encouraged and excited to be doing so well.

The last weekend of plebe summer is parents' weekend, when parents are invited to join their plebes for their first liberty of the year. My parents and my youngest sister, Connie, flew out for the weekend. It was also on that weekend that I met my "sponsor family," a local family volunteering as part of an academy program to provide a "home away from home" for new midshipmen. My sponsors, John and Anne Morrow, lived on the edge of Annapolis on an inlet lake just off Chesapeake Bay. They had two children, a boy and a girl, who were both in high school, and a beautiful home complete with a swimming pool.

John was a retired naval officer, a 1962 graduate of the Naval Academy, and Anne was a nurse at the local hospital. My real family and I spent a wonderfully relaxing afternoon at the Morrows' house, getting to know them. Although the thought of being "adopted" by a local family had seemed a little strange initially, in only a short time I felt comfortable with them. John and Anne were great, and their hospitality, understanding, and compassion would prove to be a tremendous source of strength for me through the years.

As the weekend ended, it was especially hard to say goodbye to Connie and my parents. They seemed so proud of me and excited about how well I had done during the summer. It was great having them here, sharing in what I was doing and learning about my new life. The parting was also difficult because of what it represented. The summer was over. It had been grueling, much more so than I had anticipated. But it had only been six weeks.

The rest of the brigade was already returning from their summer cruises, and we would soon be transferring to our academic-year companies. Plebe summer had been only a first, short step. Now we had nearly ten months ahead of us. It was all too hard to face the reality that plebe year was only just beginning.

4

★

Plebe Year

As the academic year began, the twelve plebe-summer companies dissolved, and the thirty-six platoons in those companies transferred to each of the thirty-six companies that made up the regular Brigade of Midshipmen. The plebes in our platoon were now the plebes of 11th Company, along with members of each of the other three classes returning from the summer. From the top floor of the fourth wing of Bancroft Hall, we moved to our regular company area in third wing. We were now only on the second floor.

On the night of the return of the brigade, there was a company-wide come-around held to "acquaint" us with the rest of the company. This was much like the come-arounds of plebe summer, except that now we were outnumbered three to one. Even after plebe summer, it was quite a shock to be inundated by so many upperclassmen.

Within a few days, though, things had calmed down somewhat. With the onset of classes, everyone was distracted with school and their other activities. Although we were still under a lot of pressure, it wasn't nearly as intense as plebe summer, except that now we had a new taskmaster—academics.

As the academic year unfolded, each of the groups began to fall into distinct roles. The firsties became much calmer than during plebe summer. This was their last year, a chance for them to kick back, take advantage of their new rank and privileges, and count down the days until graduation. They ran the brigade

and were in charge overall, but now the task of tormenting the
plebes and the responsibility for our performance fell squarely
upon the second class. It was their job to pick up where the
firsties left off, to mold us in their image.

The youngsters only a year ahead of us were by far the most
relaxed of the upper classes. Their job was not so much to
torment us as to help us learn our rates, to test our knowledge
before we had to deal with the second class at come-arounds.
There was still a division between us plebes and the youngsters,
as there was between us and all the upper classes. Youngsters,
second class, and firsties all called each other by their first names
and interacted very casually, but plebes were different. We were
never called by our first names and never called anyone by his or
her first name. I was always Mr. Steffan, and the upperclass
were always addressed as Mr. or Miss or by their rank—for
example, Midshipman Second Class Jones—when being referred
to in conversation.

Any upperclassman who failed to maintain this formal distinction between the ranks was subject to being placed on record
for "fraternization," which is a serious offense. This is a term
that also refers to an unprofessional relationship between officers and enlisted personnel in the Navy, and the plebe distinction is somewhat parallel to that system.

Our daily lives as plebes, as with all midshipmen, were
ruled by a continuous series of bells. Bells woke us up in the
morning, announced the end of classes, called us to formations,
and marked the beginning of the evening study period called
study hour. The first bell of the day rang at seven in the morning, but we plebes were up before then, preparing for the day.
Our first formation was held at 6:30. We would get up about
five minutes early, throw on our regulation blue-and-gold academy bathrobes and slippers, and line up in the hallway outside
our rooms for an informal once-over.

After formation, we went back to our rooms, changed into
our black daily uniforms, and prepared for morning come-
arounds with our youngsters, "chow calls," and morning
formation. A chow call is a sort of verbal alarm clock, sounded
for the upperclassmen ten and five minutes before each formation. Morning-quarters formation was held at 7:30. Each section

of hallway had its own chow call station, a place where an assigned plebe stood, watching the hallway clock and waiting for the minute hand to click into place. At that moment, all of Bancroft Hall, the entire 4.8 miles of hallway, burst into the echoing of a thousand voices screaming in unison:

> Sir, you now have ten minutes to morning-quarters formation! The uniform for morning-quarters formation is: working uniform blue delta! The menu for morning meal is: scrambled eggs, bacon and sausage, biscuits, assorted cereals, juice, toast, and milk! The officers of the water are: the officer of the watch is Lieutenant Smith, Company officer; the assistant officer of the watch is Ensign Jackson, movement officer; the midshipman officer of the watch is Midshipman Lieutenant McKinney, Tenth Company commander!
> Special events in the yard include: Forrestal Lecture at 1930!
> Time, tide and formation wait for no man! I am now shoving off! You have ten minutes, sir!

After the first chow call, we would quickly chop back to our rooms, anxious to escape the vulnerability of the hallways. In our rooms, we were relatively safe, but in the open hallway, we were open game for any interested upperclassman. The key to chow calls was a quick, powerful, unblemished delivery and a quick escape. This was not always easy. Some chow call stations were particularly dreaded because of tough upperclassmen whose rooms surrounded the station. Being assigned one of these stations meant a good chance of being pounced on, regardless of how well the chow call came off. With no chance for a quick escape, you would be forced to remain, answering all the new rates you were supposed to know for the day. If an upperclassman really wanted to screw with you, he would come out just before the chow call to watch you, so you could see him out of the corner of your eye. Sometimes he would just come right up to you, staring at your face but saying nothing, waiting for the clock to strike.

After all the chow calls were over, the entire company would assemble for morning formation. As during plebe summer, the company is made up of nine squads of about a dozen midshipmen of all classes. The squad is led by a firsty, the squad

leader. The remaining squad members might typically consist of
another firsty, three second class, three youngsters, and four
plebes. The squad leader was responsible for each member of the
squad. If problems arose, from academics to military performance, it was the responsibility of the squad leader to deal with
them. The squad leader was also the first link in any squad
member's "chain of command." Any special requests, such as
asking permission to eat evening meal with visiting relatives off
the academy grounds, started with submission of a form to the
squad leader. From there, it was routed up the chain of command to higher authority for ultimate approval or denial.

Because the squad leader holds a position of responsibility
and is a member of the chain of command, he is not simply
called a midshipman first class. The squad leader holds the rank
of midshipman ensign and wears a single gold stripe and a gold
star on his shoulder boards or the sleeve of his uniform. The
next step in the chain of command is the platoon commander,
who wears two gold stripes and a star on his uniform and holds
the rank of midshipman lieutenant junior grade. And above the
platoon commander is the company commander, with three gold
stripes and a star, and the rank of midshipman lieutenant. The
company commander leads the entire company—all three platoons, all nine squads.

When the company gathers for any formation, the three
platoons line up, with the first squad in the front row, the
second and third squads behind. The platoon commander stands
in front of each platoon, and the company commander faces the
company, calling everyone to attention, making announcements, and dismissing the company.

Formations are a constant in academy life. Every day, three
times a day, the company gathers for formation. Missing formation is a serious offense—Absent Without Authority. As the
chow caller says, "Time, tide, and formation wait for no man."
If you were not in formation when the company was called to
attention, you were absent. It wasn't as though your squad
leader could just report "all present." That would clearly be an
honor offense.

After morning formation we had about forty-five minutes
to get ready for classes or eat breakfast. Unlike our other meals,

breakfast was served buffet style, and everyone who wanted to eat did so either before or immediately after formation. There were no squad tables, and everyone just filled in one table after another. We plebes, of course, were still required to eat at attention. Because we had so little free time, I rarely ate breakfast; instead I used the precious moments to prepare for class or brush up on rates. Even as an upperclassman I rarely ate breakfast, primarily because I hated getting up early to go down before formation. And unless my first class period was free, there usually wasn't enough time to wait in line and eat breakfast after formation.

The academic day consisted of six periods, four before lunch and two after. Attendance was required in all classes— there was no such thing as taking the afternoon off to cram for a test. After all, the taxpayers were paying for it. Although attendance at all of the service academies is "free," we had a saying among midshipmen: The academy is a hundred-thousand-dollar education shoved up your ass a nickel at a time.

Part of our duty as midshipmen was to learn, and that meant attending every class for which we were scheduled. This only added to our stress level, as we tried to memorize the next menu, prepare for the next come-around, and take notes for chemistry, all at the same time.

Although we chose majors like students at any regular college, the curriculum at Annapolis included a core of courses in naval science and engineering that everyone was required to take. This meant that even history and economics majors had to take electrical engineering, thermodynamics, differential equations, celestial navigation, and a host of other courses in addition to their major courses.

One of our most dreaded courses was first-year chemistry. Many a plebe survived the summer with flying colors, only to fall prey to chemistry or other difficult academic classes. Any midshipman who failed to maintain at least a 2.0 grade-point average on the four-point scale could be discharged for academic deficiency. And anyone who failed to keep up with military requirements or who repeatedly violated academy rules could be discharged for military-performance deficiency. We also had to pass three physical tests each semester—the mile run, obstacle course, and applied-strength test. Failure to meet these requirements could also end in discharge.

It was under this threat that we lived our days at Annapolis, watching our friends and classmates fall one at a time, slowly being weeded out. We knew when we were sworn in on Induction Day that we would not all last, but it was a hard thing to see people go. They had come with the same dreams we had, the same goals and desires.

Every day at Annapolis, I shared the fear of all midshipmen—the fear that any of us could fail, and in failing lose all that we had worked so hard to attain. No one can make it through the Naval Academy until he is handed that diploma—not one second earlier. With every test, every come-around, every day, the fear of failure haunted us. It drove us blindly toward the goal that was so far away, so many grueling days away that we forced ourselves not to think about it.

The noon formation and lunch followed morning classes and was generally the most difficult part of the day. Before chow calls and noon meal formation, we had come-arounds with our second class and were routinely put through the wringer. Each plebe usually was assigned to one youngster and one second class in the squad, and my second class that semester was notoriously tough. He was a complete stickler about uniform appearance, and he usually covered almost every rate during come-around. At first I hated his guts, but eventually I came to admire his tough, consistent style. He was demanding but fair. If I looked good and knew my rates, he would always congratulate and encourage me, and he rarely flamed on me just because he was in a bad mood.

In addition to our regular rates, we also completed a professional knowledge assignment each week, learning detailed information about military organization, ships, and weapons systems. Noon meal was just as tough, and in addition to answering rates, we were often required by our second class to research and prepare short, memorized presentations on various professional topics. As during plebe summer, we were often ordered to stand on our chairs and give cheers during the meal.

During the academic year, meals at Annapolis are something that must be seen to be fully appreciated. First of all, the entire brigade of 4,500 men and women eats simultaneously in King Hall. The enormous T-shaped room is filled with rows of hundreds of tables, each table seating a squad, as during plebe summer. No one is allowed to sit down until the brigade commander, the highest-ranking firsty, calls everyone to attention, reads announcements, and finally issues the order "Brigade, seats." Although meals are not as raucous as during plebe summer, nearly four times as many people packed into the space makes it seem just as noisy, with everyone talking amid a constant stream of orders, singing, and screaming from plebes standing on their chairs.

With noon meal over, the afternoon was completed by the last two periods of classes, followed by the mandatory sports period. Every midshipman is required to be involved in sports, whether as a member of a varsity or an intramural team. I started my first semester with junior varsity track, which was out of season, but I practiced every afternoon on the academy's running track.

After the sports period, it was back to the hall to shower and get ready for chow calls, more come-arounds, and our final formation, evening meal formation. We often had meetings or events scheduled after evening meal, followed by study hour. Study hour was sacred time set aside from 8 P.M. to midnight. Come-arounds and other interruptions were not allowed during study hour, and we were free to study in our rooms or in the library or academic buildings on the grounds. We were not required to chop through the halls, only walk quickly while remaining in the center of the hallway and squaring corners without shouting. The only requirement was that we be back in our rooms by taps.

After taps, we had one hour before lights-out at 1 A.M. Plebes were not allowed up past lights-out, which forced us to use study hour efficiently. If you didn't have that first period term paper finished by then, there was no all-nighter option. The earliest we were allowed to get up in the morning was 5:30, but few plebes had the energy to get up much before our 6:30 plebe muster. Such was the cycle of a midshipman's life. I would repeat this cycle, from formation and meals to classes, sports, and study hour nearly 1,400 times during my years at Annapolis.

One important respite from this cycle was my involvement in the choirs at Annapolis. During plebe summer, I had auditioned as a tenor in the Catholic choir as well as the academy's men's glee club, considered one of America's outstanding male choirs. I had been accepted to both, and also became the cantor, or song leader, for Catholic services at the academy. I eventually joined the Protestant chapel choir as well, spending every Sunday morning when we weren't traveling singing in the academy's magnificent chapel.

Although my involvement in the choirs took up a lot of precious time, it provided me with a crucial escape from the oppressive drudgery of daily academy life. The choirs also practiced during evening meal, which meant that I didn't have to eat evening meal with my squad. The choir ate early, immediately after the sports period and before the regular evening meal. At this early meal, we sat with other choir members at our tables and were allowed to eat and converse normally, and the distinctions between the classes were basically disregarded.

This was the standard for extracurricular activities or sports teams. When the group was together, there were no real class distinctions, and we called each other by our first names—even plebes. This look behind the class facade was especially important to me, because it allowed me to relate to upperclassmen as human beings for a while, which made the plebe system easier to bear. It helped me to see it for what it really was, a system of tradition. But after practice, back in the hall, we were plebes again. The upperclassmen we called Dave and Tim in choir were again Mr. Anderson and Mr. Smith, just as before. To carry that relaxed standard outside the choir would be fraternization.

In addition to providing a daily escape, the choirs also traveled extensively during the year. The glee club was especially busy, with about seventy performances a year, including several television appearances and performances before high-level dignitaries, including the president. These trips, usually over the weekend, were a chance to spend time away from the academy, something many plebes never have the chance to do. It also gave me the chance to get to know some of my classmates and other midshipmen away from the confines of academy life.

It was during this first year that I got to know some of my best friends at the academy. One of those friends was Rob Con-

nor, a classmate who sang in both the glee club and the Protestant choir. Rob was a tall, red-haired fellow from southern
California with a ready laugh, an incredibly quick wit, and a
racy mouth. Rob could swear the paint off a car, and he never
missed an opportunity to pass along his limitless repertoire of
ribald jokes and stories.

At first, Rob and I hated each other. He thought I was a
puritanical asshole, and I thought he was an obnoxious jerk.
But the more time we spent together at practices and trips, the
better I got to know and like him. He could always make me
laugh, even when I didn't want to, and I began to realize that
under his macho exterior was a genuinely caring and compassionate person.

Rob's tough facade was like other midshipmen's, a kind of
male posturing in response to intense competition and peer pressure. People were constantly trying to prove how tough they
were. I once asked one of my professors at Annapolis what he
disliked most about the Naval Academy. I never forgot his response. He said that midshipmen are under such intense pressure to conform, to not stick out as individuals, that no one risks
being themselves. They are afraid that if they stick out, if they
seem different from the crowd, their classmates will resent them.
He said this destroyed part of the true essence of being human—
the fact that we are all unique individuals, each of us having
special talents, experiences, and perceptions of the world around
us. By suppressing individuality, the academy and the military
was robbing itself of the strength of this diversity.

On those weekends when I wasn't traveling with one of the
choirs, I spent every possible moment of my liberty off the
academy grounds. Of course, there were many restrictions on
what we plebes could do on liberty. We couldn't travel farther
than fifty miles from the academy on weekends, which was
really irrelevant because we were also not allowed to drive
cars. We were also not allowed to even be seen walking with
a civilian member of the opposite sex in Annapolis or on the
academy grounds. Plebe life was designed to keep us focused
on school and our transition into and acceptance of military
life, and that life began with the realization of sacrifice. Part of
what we learned as plebes was how to endure that sacrifice, a

token of how much we might later be asked to sacrifice for our country.

We were allowed liberty, or the privilege of leaving campus, only on Saturdays, between noon meal formation and taps, but we had to return to the academy for evening meal formation. Meals on weekends were usually quite relaxed. We weren't required to eat at the academy, but since most of the upperclass was gone on weekend liberty, our chances of being harassed at the tables were minimal. Like most plebes, I cherished the few moments of freedom we were allowed, and I rarely ate at the academy on weekends or spent any more time on the grounds than absolutely necessary.

My typical Saturday schedule included leaving the academy after noon meal formation and heading out with a few of my classmates to the Burger King, which had just opened in the middle of the historic district. I never figured out how they managed to convince the historical society, which my sponsor John often referred to as the "hysterical society," to allow the construction of this blasphemous structure smack in the middle of such sacred turf. But we plebes didn't care—it was a place to go. On any Saturday afternoon the place was packed with plebes lined up to eat in civilian comfort, free from the screaming second class.

After lunch, we would walk around town, stopping by the ice-cream shop to wolf down a couple of pints of ice cream and wandering around the city dock or into the stores. If we were feeling particularly adventurous, we would hop a bus to the Annapolis Mall and wander around there, making sure to leave in plenty of time to catch evening meal formation. After formation, it was off to a movie and back in time for taps.

I also spent as much time as I could on weekends at the home of my sponsor family. John and Anne treated me like one of their own, and John's experience as an academy graduate and naval officer was a valuable source of education for me. Whenever I was feeling down, John would tell me about his own academy experiences. As he was fond of saying, "Back when they had a *real* plebe year at Annapolis!"

He told me about the days when hazing was allowed, and about the tricks he and his classmates played on the academy's officers. He shared one story about the two cannon that flank the entrance to Tecumseh Court, the brick courtyard in front of Bancroft Hall. Although the cannon are war relics, long since out of action, according to academy legend they will fire a salute if a true virgin ever passes between them. One of John's classmates seized upon this legend and, on the night before a particularly important academy event, loaded the cannon with remote-controlled charges. The following day, in the midst of high-flung naval pageantry, the superintendent of the Naval Academy escorted his wife toward Bancroft Hall. John's classmate was watching closely from a window in the hall. As the superintendent and his wife passed between the cannon, he detonated the charges, firing a thunderous salute from the cannon, much to the surprise of onlookers and to the amusement of the brigade. By the time John was done weaving his tales of the academy, I had forgotten my own troubles and was ready to handle another week of plebedom.

Many of my plebe weekends were spent away from Annapolis on choir or glee club trips. This was a great break from plebe life. On long glee club tours we could even wear civilian clothes when we weren't performing and experience a sense of freedom that had become almost foreign to us.

We also had the chance to meet women on glee club trips. Often, when we sang at colleges, a party would be held in our honor, usually by a group of sororities. Despite the straight-laced image of the academy, mixing one hundred sex- and fun-starved midshipmen, a lot of alcohol, and a batch of collegiate women produces a pretty consistent result. These parties inevitably ended up with a lot of drunk, horny midshipmen chasing women, followed by a day of explicit stories of sexual conquests recounted on the bus to our next stop on the tour.

Although as plebes we were not allowed to drink, even away from the academy, on glee club trips there was no ban on chasing women. As a matter of fact, it was encouraged. No, it was practically required. This was all sort of overwhelming to me. I was completely naïve, not only about sex, but about everything, including drinking. I had never had a drink in my life, not even a sip, except for wine at church. Drinking in my high school was something that just wasn't done if you wanted to be considered a good kid, and I had always wanted to be a good kid.

Back home, my conservative environment and involvement in the church shielded me from sex and alcohol. But now there was nothing to shield me, and the pressure to conform was on. Peer pressure can be a powerful thing, but it is probably stronger at a military academy, where it is amplified by training designed to produce complete uniformity.

But there was another force at work as well. The peer pressure I was feeling was enhanced by growing confusion about my sexuality. Or, I should say, my growing lack of confusion. When I had applied to the Naval Academy three years earlier, there was a question on a security questionnaire that read something like "Are you a homosexual?" At the time, I had checked "no" without even pausing to think about it. The possibility had never even entered my mind.

Homosexuality was a topic I had rarely heard mentioned when I was growing up, and even then only in disgust. I grew up thinking that a homosexual was a man who wanted to be a woman. He wanted to have sex with other men, or with young boys if he could get them. Homosexuals all talked with a lisp and swung their hips when they walked, trying to act woman-like, and I hated them. I had hated them all my life, for as long as I could remember. No one had taught me to hate them; no one had ever explained it. As a child I had learned from context, like I learned the meaning of new words from hearing people talk. I didn't have to look it up in a dictionary—I knew everyone hated "homos," and so did I.

But I had begun to slowly recognize that my apathy toward dating women had a flip side. I was beginning to feel an attraction to other men, or perhaps simply to realize that the attraction had always been there, only now it was stronger. Each time I felt the attraction, I was overcome with a deep sense of shame. I felt guilty, as though I had done something terribly wrong. Everything about this seemed wrong; it defied every sense of normalcy and propriety I had ever known.

These thoughts terrified me, and I tried to shut them out, consciously ignoring and denying them. I focused even harder on school, singing, my plebe duties—anything to keep my mind off them. I just wanted to feel normal, to escape the fear, guilt, and shame that were shadowing me. I knew I couldn't be a homosexual, I just couldn't. I didn't want to be a homosexual; I had never wanted to be a homosexual.

After all, I hated homosexuals—everyone hated homosexuals and I couldn't possibly be a homosexual. I didn't want to be woman—I was a man and I liked being a man. I didn't talk with a lisp, and nothing about me was like a homosexual. I was in a military academy, and homosexuals aren't allowed in the military. It was that thought that scared me the most—the thought of losing everything I was investing in Annapolis and my future as an officer.

As the first semester of my plebe year began to wind down, I started to anticipate Christmas leave and my first trip back to Warren since entering the academy. But there was plenty to keep me busy before then. The high point of the year was Army Week, the week before the annual Army-Navy football game in early December. Every year, this game between the Naval Academy and West Point is nationally televised and broadcast by radio around the world to American service members stationed overseas. It is a rivalry that practically overwhelms the academy during the week before the event.

That year's game was also a first in the tradition, because it would be played in the Rose Bowl in Pasadena, California, the first game not held on the East Coast. The entire brigades of both schools would be flown to California for the event, and the anticipation of this trip added to the frenzy of enthusiasm surrounding the event.

During this week, the dining hall was deafened with the constant screaming cheers of plebes demonstrating their Navy spirit for the upperclass. Plebes would sometimes be sent on covert missions carrying pies, pitchers of water, or full cartons of milk. The upperclass at one table would send these plebes to attack an upperclassman at another table, promising special privileges if they could deliver their payload and escape without being caught. Although this was obviously against the rules, it was rare that—even if the plebe was caught—he would be punished very severely because it was in the name of "spirit." Although these types of attacks happened intermittently during the year, during Army Week they were common. On one such occasion, a successful attack met with a reprisal of food bombardment so violent that the entire dining hall launched into an all-out food fight with nearly four thousand participants. The dining hall staff was so outraged that the plebes were called in to help clean it all up. But Army Week spirit was a tradition, sacred like all Navy traditions.

Another tradition of Army Week was executing pranks late at night on "recon raids." It was not uncommon for a company officer to return to the hall to find his office filled to the ceiling with newspapers or to find it completely empty, the contents transferred into a nearby bathroom and perfectly arranged. The academy grounds and buildings are a virtual museum of weaponry, from colonial cannon to torpedoes and missiles to Navy jets mounted on permanent display. The academy also has one of the country's largest collections of ship models, intricate and very expensive replicas of sailing ships, submarines, and aircraft carriers. These objects were a common target of recon raids and were often transferred to company officers' offices. One company officer opened his door to find a torpedo weighing several hundred pounds in the middle of his desk, nearly crushing it. On another occasion, much to the displeasure of the administration, several priceless ship models were found one morning floating in the academy's indoor diving pool.

One night early in Army Week, some firsties in our company enlisted our help with another recon raid. That evening, while the brigade was assembled for a mandatory lecture, two of the firsties snuck over to a Navy F-4 jet airplane on display behind Mahan Hall, the English and history building. They hacksawed through the retaining rods that held the jet in place. At three the following morning, a few firsties and about thirty plebes from several companies slipped from the hall, carefully avoiding detection by the academy police, irreverently referred to as "jimmylegs" by the mids. We pushed frantically on the jet, trying to roll it out onto the street with the goal of pushing it all the way back to Bancroft Hall and leaving it in Tecumseh Court. Our efforts were hampered by wet ground, into which the front landing gear was digging deeper and deeper. Every few minutes someone would whisper, "Jimmylegs!" and we would drop to the muddy ground, lying flat until the police were out of sight.

Finally, with the aid of a board gleaned from a nearby

building site, we got the front gear loose, wheeled the jet onto the street, and began pushing it toward the hall. Suddenly, a flurry of shrieking sirens and lights surrounded us as if from nowhere. In seconds the road was blocked by police vehicles from both sides, and we were showered in spotlights. A quiet murmur of "Oh, shit" came in unison from the group, and for a moment we all stood there, dumbfounded. Realizing we weren't caught yet, one of my classmates screamed, "Run!" and we instantly scattered in all directions. The jimmylegs didn't even try to catch us, and we all returned to the hall undetected.

The following morning, the brigade awoke to the order for plebes to get their sweat gear on and go help move the F-4 jet back to its spot on the grass. No one could believe it had actually been moved, and it wasn't long before the rumor leaked that it had been our company that was behind it. Although some of our classmates were upset over having to go out and move it back, which was not an easy task, most of them were pretty impressed that we had actually managed to pull the stunt off.

The glee club flew out early to California for some concerts, and later the brigade arrived to see Navy beat Army in an exciting and memorable game. On our return to Annapolis, the plebe class was granted "carry-on" privileges for the remaining weeks of the semester because of the victory. That meant we didn't have to chop through the halls; we just walked quickly down the center. We were also allowed to eat at ease and could even put our elbows on the table. This took some getting used to, and after so much conditioning at the dinner table, the upperclass practically had to order us to relax.

After finishing finals, I sat on the airplane home, wondering how it would feel to be back in Warren again, if things had changed. When I transferred planes in Minneapolis on the way to Grand Forks, I overheard a weather announcement. The windchill factor had reached a hundred below zero! Things couldn't have changed too much—this was definitely Minnesota.

My parents picked me up at the airport and the quiet, dark ride back to Warren through the moonlit snow touched me deeply, like an unexpected, clear memory. I felt as though I had

never left, that my parents had just turned around on the way to
dropping me off.

As we entered the streets of Warren, with a familiar red
plastic banner reading SEASON'S GREETINGS hanging over the road,
I felt very much at home. I guess your hometown is always your
hometown, no matter what. It continues to exist, even if only in
your own memory, holding the past in crystalline suspension
and providing a sense of place, of belonging, that is always
comforting.

By the time my two weeks of leave were over, I was anxious to get back to the academy. I had spent my time at home,
I had seen friends and family, but I had one more semester of
plebehood ahead of me, and I wanted to get it over with.

My second semester was tough. Even tougher than the first.
The weather was miserable, constantly overcast, cold and rainy.
These last winter months are known as the Dark Ages at Annapolis, and with good reason. They were depressing. All the
squads had been changed around, as they are each semester, and
I had a very tough second class, who got great pleasure out of
making my life miserable. His big kick was abusing me over my
lack of sports trivia knowledge, which was his great claim to
fame. He decided that because I was a Minnesotan, I should
learn more about hockey. He made me keep track of everything
related to hockey and give him a rundown at lunch of the prior
evening's scores and hockey-related news. At our come-
arounds, he was never interested in professional knowledge, but
would ask me inane questions about sports records and order
me to give a response even if I didn't know the answer. So I
would just pick any name I knew from sports, and he and his
roommates would laugh about what an idiotic answer I'd given.

In retrospect, it's kind of funny, but it really screwed me up
at the time. I was trying to do my best, to learn what I was
supposed to know to become an officer, and this guy was giving
me shit about nothing. At first I just chalked it up to frustration
tolerance and played along. I used to think there was some
meaning or lesson in what he was trying to do, but I finally
decided there was none. He was a generally miserable guy who
got his kicks out of making other people miserable.

Many plebes suffered from the same kind of misguided

authority from their upperclass; it was all part of the imperfect lessons of the academy in which idealism and reality stumble over each other. And it's one of the hazards of the military—every service member is at the mercy of his or her commander. If the commander wants to destroy your career, for good reasons or bad, it's not too tough to do so. Selections for promotion can become highly competitive, and a single negative performance review can make the difference between promotion and stagnation. The military, and especially the academy, teaches midshipmen that a good officer does what is right, regardless of the consequences. But the reality is somewhat different. In order to succeed and advance in the military, you almost always have to do what is popular, especially with your commander.

By the time spring had rolled around, life was starting to calm down. The onset of warmer weather and more sunshine made everyone lighten up a little, even the second class. I was spending a lot of time singing, and had joined the academy's Protestant chapel choir after returning from Christmas leave. Now, after cantoring at Sunday mass, I stuck around to sing at the Protestant services as well.

Plebe year had provided an ideal means of avoiding the issues of my sexuality, which had continued to bother me. The pace and burden were more than enough to fill my daily thoughts and keep my attentions focused on simply surviving. Not long into second semester, however, I had an experience that would bring those questions back in full force.

The glee club was on one of its many weekend trips, and we had completed a full day of concerts, followed, of course, by a full night of partying. About five of us who didn't or couldn't drink had ended up watching a movie in one of the hotel rooms shared by two second class. One of the second class, Keith Stuart, was watching the movie with us while his roommate was out partying with some other mids. When the movie finished about midnight, everyone got up and started heading back to their own rooms. I was the last to leave, and as I got up Keith said he was going to stay up and watch part of the next movie and that I could stick around for a while if I wanted to.

Although Keith and I didn't spend a lot of time together,

we got along well and sometimes joked around during rehearsals and trips. He was a good-looking guy, and I was definitely attracted to him, which made the present situation a little tense for me. As I sat back down on the foot of the bed, Keith lay down next to me. There were times when I had sensed a sexual tension between us, but I had tried to ignore it. I wasn't sure if what I was feeling was mutual or simply of my own making, but either way, it made me uncomfortable.

Keith and I talked for a while during the movie, and he eventually sat up next to me on the end of the bed. We were sitting close together, and when his leg drifted over and pressed against mine, I thought I was going to hit the ceiling. My heart was pounding, but I acted as though nothing was happening. As much as I wanted to deny what I was feeling, I couldn't ignore the reality that I wanted something to happen.

We looked at each other and we both realized exactly what was happening. Suddenly, it all seemed too overwhelming, and I began to panic. I just wasn't able to deal with it, and I immediately stood up and said, "I've gotta go."

Keith looked worried and asked, "What's the matter?"

"Nothing," I said. "I just have to get back to my room. We have an early morning tomorrow."

He looked at me for a few seconds and then answered, "Yeah, I guess we do."

"So we'll catch you tomorrow, OK?" I asked, finally calming down a little and smiling.

"OK," he said, realizing that I wasn't upset. "We'll catch you tomorrow—bright and early."

And with that I returned to my room.

Nothing ever happened between Keith and me, and we never discussed or even acknowledged that night on tour. Although the incident was far from torrid, it nonetheless convinced me that my feelings toward other men were real and significant. I wasn't going to be able to ignore and evade them forever, and I needed to start considering the possibility that I might be gay.

Near the end of the year, I decided to talk to someone about my feelings. I had gotten to know one of the chaplains, Chaplain Owen, quite well from my song leading at Sunday services and felt he would be approachable and understanding. The thought of actually telling someone about my feelings was incredibly frightening, and it took several trips by his office before I finally built up the nerve to knock on his door. When I did, I heard him ask me to come in. I opened the door and peeked my head in. Chaplain Owen was with one of my classmates, a guy named Tim Carson I knew fairly well from an intramural sports team we had both played on. Although I only glanced at him for a second, Tim's eyes were red, and it was obvious that he had been crying.

I asked Chaplain Owen if he would have time to speak with me later on, and he suggested I try back in a little while. After waiting nearby for about twenty minutes, I saw Tim leave the chaplain's office. I waited a few more minutes and then knocked again. Chaplain Owen asked me in and I took a seat.

I was quite uncomfortable, but I knew and trusted Chaplain Owen. His warm demeanor made me feel at ease, even though I was on the verge of revealing something so troubling. After seeing Tim, I thought about how much of his time must be devoted to moments just like this, with midshipmen coming to him with their problems and concerns.

We talked casually for a while, before I built up to why I was really there. I finally told him I needed to discuss something very important, but that I was worried about how it might affect my future at the academy. Even as a chaplain, I knew, Chaplain Owen had a duty as a naval officer to report all violations of regulations, although I seriously doubted that he would turn me in. I also questioned whether I was actually in violation of any regulations. Surely I could be punished for doing something, but could I be punished for simply "being" who I was?

He didn't seem surprised at all by my concern, and simply said that he would hold anything I told him in strict confidence. After a little stammering, I finally told him that I was feeling attracted to other men, and that I thought I might be a homosexual. I will never forget his first words. He looked me straight in the eye and said, "You're not alone, Joe."

"In fact," he continued, "the last person to sit in that chair told me exactly the same thing." Now this really took me by surprise, because I knew who that person was. But Chaplain

Owen would never have revealed something so personal about
someone else, even if he assumed I didn't know him. The only
explanation I could figure was that he had simply forgotten that
I had poked my head through the door earlier and had seen Tim
sitting there.

I told him that I was concerned about my feelings and
afraid of the threat they represented to my career. In a way, I
was expecting him to try and convince me that homosexuality
was wrong, to pressure me to change. Perhaps that's what I was
hoping for, an outside means of helping suppress what I knew I
could not suppress any longer on my own. But he did nothing
of the sort. We continued to talk for nearly an hour, and he was
completely supportive, neither preaching nor suggesting that
homosexuality was wrong. He acknowledged that my decision
to stay at the academy and live a double life would be a difficult
one, but he said only I could make that decision.

As I left to return to my company area, I felt both relieved
and sad. Although it had felt good to open up and talk to him,
I was still faced with the feelings and emotions I had been working so hard to avoid. Chaplain Owen had only underscored the
reality that I would eventually have to come to terms with my
feelings and with who I was. I could continue to run away, but
I simply couldn't run forever.

As for Tim, we continued to associate through sports and
later through leadership positions in the brigade. He eventually
became one of the highest-ranking midshipmen in our class,
both militarily and academically. Chaplain Owen eventually
transferred to another duty station, and I never told Tim what
had inadvertently been revealed to me that night. As much as I
needed someone to talk to, as he must have, I didn't have the
courage to tell him about myself. It was simply enough to know,
as Chaplain Owen had said, that I was not alone.

The beginning of spring meant the arrival of another of the
academy's time-honored traditions. "Hundreds Night" is held
on the evening of the one hundredth day before graduation. On
this night, the entire plebe class and the firsties trade places for
an annual and humorous role reversal.

Before evening-meal formation, my classmates and I
switched uniform insignia with the firsties. Before formation,

they showed up for come-arounds outside our doors and gave chow calls. Although it sounded like a free-for-all for us plebes, the firsties played their part to the hilt. Many of them showed up with their uniforms messed up and responded to every question with "I'll find out, sir," or just "Huh?"

Some of the firsties actually tried to perform, but either way, they ended up getting screamed at. The second class and youngsters gathered in the halls to watch, laughing at the firsties' antics and our transformation from timid plebes to full-fledged flamers. The evening meal was equally wild, with the firsties cheering and screaming through the meal. Some of them kept up their idiot-plebe routine by spilling food all over their plebe squad leaders. One of my classmates ordered a firsty to pass the milk and ended up with the whole carton in his lap, followed by a "Gee, sir, I'm sorry."

Hundreds Night was one of the very few lighthearted moments in an otherwise oppressive year. It was a chance for everyone to let off some steam and mellow out. After that night, the tension slipped another notch. In only a few more weeks, we would be gearing up for finals and then Herndon, the ceremony before graduation that would end our plebe year for good.

Every summer between academic years, midshipmen serve aboard active-duty naval vessels as part of their training. We each had the opportunity to sign up for these summer cruises based on merit and our areas of interest. Even before coming to the academy, I had been intrigued by submarines, by their technical complexity and the shroud of mystery surrounding them. I had spoken to several upperclassmen who had served on subs and was encouraged by their stories. Many of them had earned their "dolphins," a uniform pin awarded for completion of a rigorous technical training program while on patrol.

I decided to go all out on my cruise and signed up to serve aboard a nuclear missile submarine. It was the longest type of cruise available, and while most of my classmates would spend about a month or so on their cruises, my patrol would last nearly two and a half months. Essentially all of this time would be spent under water. As I was planning on going into subs after graduation, I figured this would be the best way to find out whether I would enjoy it. It would also give me time to earn my dolphins, something normally not possible on shorter attack-submarine cruises.

In the race through plebe year, Herndon marks the finish line. The ceremony, like plebe year itself, is based on both struggle and cooperation. The Herndon Monument, a twenty-one-foot granite obelisk, stands tucked away like a dark sentinel on the academy grounds across from the chapel, waiting for the one day every year when it is immersed in a screaming, sweating sea of half-clad bodies.

The monument is covered with a thick coating of white lard and topped with a dixie-cup plebe hat at its peak. The entire plebe class, clad only in gym trunks, tennis shoes, and T-shirts, attacks the monument. The goal: to replace the plebe hat with a regular, black-brimmed midshipman's hat called a combination cover. Once the hats are switched, the long plebe year officially ends.

Although it all sounds fairly straightforward, there are few events I have ever participated in that were more difficult or frustrating. We swarmed around the monument's base, sweating in the heat as thousands of onlookers—civilians, television crews, upperclassmen, and officers—packed the yard around the monument. Tiers of my classmates slowly approached the peak, only to collapse and crush the mids below. Those of us struggling near the base were smashed like sardines, pressed in by the hundreds surrounding us. Those around the outside were under the unfortunate misconception that if they all pushed in hard enough, a few of us would simply squirt to the top. Barely able to breathe and struggling to escape the crush, we screamed for everyone to stop pushing, carefully on the lookout for bodies falling toward us from the tiers above. Barefoot classmates clambered across our shoulders on their way up the monument.

A little organization would have gone a long way, but switching the hats was a high honor, and the person who made it to the top was destined, according to legend, to become the first admiral in our class. Before Herndon, the class had actually voted on whether a few of our classmates would be chosen to organize a quick, efficient assault on the monument or whether we would simply attack en masse. Unwilling to tempt fate and tradition, we had voted to attack, and after more than an hour of sweat, bruises, and frustration, we were cursing that decision, each other, and most of all, the damn plebe hat still poised untouched above us.

By now, nearly everyone had taken off their shoes and soaked shirts, throwing them at the hat in a vain attempt to knock it down. Several hits were right on target, but the hat refused to budge.

Finally, after what seemed an eternity, one of our smaller and more nimble classmates scaled the tiers to the top, pulling down the hat before the whole thing collapsed again. By now I had moved out to the edge of the crowd, battered and bruised by climbing feet and falling bodies. As the hat came down, a loud cheer went up from the crowd, and we renewed our attack with added determination.

Tier after tier approached the peak, only to collapse as the tension and excitement built up. Finally, the tiers were holding, and a lightweight classmate scaled the pack and stretched toward the peak, his fingers falling only inches short. A combination cover was passed up, and he tossed it lightly upward. It hooked on the peak and stuck. For a split second we all stared in awe, suddenly exploding in a shower of screams and cheers, jumping up and down in wild excitement, our arms raised in victory.

It was a moment to remember: We had burst through the bubble of plebehood, and the accumulated tension and frustration of the entire year erupted in one grimy, sweaty, bruised, incredibly glorious moment. The most difficult year I had ever hoped to endure had finally come to an end.

5

✦

Coming to Terms

On the morning following Herndon, I joined up with the other mids on my cruise. There were five of us from the academy assigned to the same sub, which was fairly unusual. Although technically the classes didn't advance in rank until graduation, still a few days away, we all switched shoulder boards on the way out the main gate toward the airport. As incredible as Herndon had been, there was something especially satisfying about replacing my plain black shoulder boards and seeing that first diagonal gold stripe of a midshipman third class.

Of the five mids on cruise, three of us were now youngsters and the other two, new firsties. The firsties switched from their second-class shoulder boards, with two diagonal gold stripes, to first-class shoulder boards, with a single horizontal stripe. The firsties made a point of reminding us that, according to tradition, we could not officially claim the title of youngsters until we returned from summer cruise and sighted the dome of the academy chapel.

After a long flight over the Atlantic Ocean, we switched planes at Heathrow Airport in London, flying north through Glasgow to Holy Loch. As I looked out the window of the plane over Scotland, I was amazed by the strange patterns etched out by the farmland below. The farmland in America is a nearly perfect patchwork of squares, neatly laid out sections like the ones I used to jog around. But over Scotland, I saw a maze of amorphous, seemingly unorganized fields spreading out below

like a pack of amoebas. They were separated by thin lines that I
imagined must have been the low, stone walls I had seen in
pictures of the Scottish countryside.

In Holy Loch, we took a cab to the pier where a tugboat
was waiting to bring us to the sub. The day was overcast and
dreary, a light rain sprinkling through the thin mist that hung in
the air. I had expected the sub to be docked, but we could see its
outline moving slowly through the bay far off in the distance.
The tug brought us out into the bay, eventually pulling up
alongside the submarine and matching its slow pace.

The sub was an awesome sight, a gigantic slab of black
metal moving effortlessly, silently, through the water. Its size
was remarkable—longer than a football field and four stories
tall, most of which were hidden below the waterline. A metal
gangplank was positioned across to the sub's missile deck, the
long, flat surface behind the sail lined with hatches covering the
missile tubes. Several enlisted men in life vests held the gangplank in place as we each walked across to the sub carrying our
seabags.

A small hatch was open on the deck, the only break in the
sub's smooth black surface, which shone like the glossy skin of
a huge sea creature. We each climbed down, tightly gripping the
cool, metal rungs that led to the deck below. It was a strange
feeling walking through the narrow corridors of this vast machine. Every surface was covered with pipes, valves, instrument
panels, and strange pieces of equipment whose functions I did
not know. It was like I was rooting through the innards of the
leviathan, its warm, sterile-smelling breath surrounding us.

Apparently, our arrival had been scheduled without a
minute to spare, and the sub was on its last turn out of the bay.
A little while longer and we would have been left behind. We
assembled in the officers' mess, the small dining room where the
ship's officers met and ate their meals. Although the room wasn't
large, it was one of the few spaces on board where it was possible to turn around with your arms out and not hit something.

After our initial briefing, we were each given small, yellow
plastic radiometers that hooked to our belts. They would record
our exposure to radiation during the cruise, and we were to wear
them at all times. Finding this thought less than comforting, I

asked how much radiation we could expect to be exposed to. The medical officer explained that U.S. nuclear submarines are designed to be extremely safe and have excellent shielding around the nuclear power plant and missile warheads. In fact, during the two-month cruise, he said we could expect significantly less exposure to radiation than people on the surface exposed to such normal radiation sources as the sun and color televisions.

The two firsties, who would serve as junior officers during the cruise, were assigned their bunks in officer berthing. As youngsters, we three remaining mids would serve on this cruise as enlisted personnel, and were assigned bunks in enlisted berthing. The berthing area consisted of rows of narrow bunks placed three high from the floor to ceiling. Each bunk had a curtain that could be drawn, a small fluorescent reading light, and a locking storage compartment with about two cubic feet of storage space.

We were not expected to make a port call during the cruise, so I had brought only a few things—two uniforms, a change of civilian clothes, my shaving kit, some cash, and my Walkman. I pulled each of the items out of my seabag, arranging them neatly in my locker. When I reached the bottom of the bag, I was dismayed to find that I had brought only one cassette tape— Beethoven's Ninth Symphony.

In only a few hours we were already busy getting familiar with the sub, helping prepare for the patrol, and training to stand watch. Because this was a full-length submarine patrol, we had not been assigned as extra crew. We were taking the place of crew members not on board, and that meant we each had jobs to do.

For us youngsters, that meant standing the helmsman and planesman watches, or basically, steering the ship. A submarine's depth and course are directly controlled by these two watch standers under the orders of the officer in charge, called the officer of the deck. The helmsman and planesman sit side-by-side at a large control panel with two steering columns, similar to those on a jet airplane. In fact, a submarine is similar to an airplane in that it moves three-dimensionally through space and is turned by a set of steering surfaces. The helmsman moves the huge rudder and stern planes at the rear of the sub, control-

ling its direction, or heading, and its angle in the water. The
planesman basically controls the submarine's depth through the
wing-like "fairwater planes" mounted on the sub's conning
tower, or "sail."

This seemed like a simple enough task at first, but it required a bit of practice. First of all, a submarine is quite a bit
heavier than, say, a car, and doesn't stop turning when you do.
As helmsman, I found my first few tries at changing course
overshooting by at least ten degrees. This difficulty was coupled
with the fact that I was also responsible for controlling the stern
planes that kept the ship level. I had to watch the compass
heading and the level indicator, or "bubble," at the same time,
and changing one inevitably affected the other. The constant
concentration this required was tiring, so the helmsman and
planesman switched places about every half hour to break the
monotony.

Planesman was generally an easier job, because there was
only one gauge to watch. But if the helmsman wasn't keeping
the bubble level, the sub would climb or dive, and the planesman would have to compensate to get us back on depth. Until
we got the hang of it, we were constantly compensating for each
other and sort of wobbling our way through the sea.

Within a few days the routine of shipboard life was established. The watch cycle was usually divided into three six-hour
shifts. Each shift would work for six hours, then have twelve
off. The only way I could tell if it was night or day was to check
my watch, and even then I wasn't always sure. For us mids, our
off time was spent studying and working with the crew on our
submarine qualification. This was a very difficult process, one
that normally takes an enlisted crew member two patrols to
complete. But each of us was determined to finish this cruise
with our dolphins, and we spent as much time as possible learning about every system on the submarine, from hydraulics to
weapons to sonar and communications.

This meant learning not only the principles behind how
these systems worked but also the exact location of valves, gen-
erators, power panels, and switches. Learning a system like hydraulics meant being able to discuss the operation of every key
component, its location, power source, and how to activate it or

shut it down in emergency situations. We were required to memorize and reproduce schematic diagrams of each system, noting flow directions, dozens of valves, and the systems that controlled them.

To become qualified, we had to memorize about fifty different systems and secure a signature from an enlisted watch stander for each system. Getting signatures was not a minor endeavor, because these enlisted men already had their dolphins, and they weren't keen on a bunch of mids waltzing through with an easy qualification. If anything, we were even more closely scrutinized than the junior enlisted men working on their quals.

There were no books to study for this information; we had to get it from someone standing watch on that system. After several hours of instruction and note taking, we would go off to study and memorize the system, perhaps come back for more instruction, and eventually ask one of the watch standers for a checkoff. Sometimes he would be too busy, or just wouldn't want to do it, so we would have to come back later or wait for another watch stander.

Eventually, someone would have time and would rattle off a series of questions: Where is this valve? Explain how this system works. If this pipe broke what would you do? Draw this schematic. In order to get a signature, you had to answer all the questions correctly. If you missed maybe one or two and the guy was nice, he'd let you go find out the answer and come back for the signature. If you missed any more than that, or it was clear you were trying to get by without knowing the system, you'd end up with no signature and a pissed-off watchstander who would tell his buddies you weren't prepared for the checkoff.

It was crucial for us mids to earn the respect of the crew. If we tried to act like we were better than they because we were eventually going to be officers, we could count on a tough time. At Annapolis there is a tendency to be elitist, to look down on enlisted people and expect that they will do what we say simply because we are almost officers. Youngster cruise is supposed to help break that arrogance by placing the mid in an enlisted role so he can better understand what it's like. On our sub I found the enlisted men and officers to be intelligent, capable people who were generally quite easy to get along with.

Between standing watch and working on my quals, I got very little sleep during the first few weeks of the cruise, only about four or five hours every twenty-four hours.

The pace took my mind off the monotony of the cruise. The basic mission of a ballistic missile submarine is to avoid detection. This meant that we spent most of our time cruising around the Atlantic Ocean at less than five miles per hour (or Mach .003 as we sometimes joked). If sonar picked up anything interesting, we usually ended up running away from it.

When I tell people about serving on a submarine, they usually ask two questions: "Didn't you get claustrophobic," and, "Do submarines have windows?" The answer to both is no. When most people think of submarines, they immediately conjure up images from movies like *Das Boot*, a German film about life aboard a sub during World War II. They imagine minuscule diesel subs crammed full of sweaty men turning valves while depth charges explode outside and water sprays from broken pipes. Nowadays, submarines are gigantic, especially missile subs, and nearly all of them are nuclear powered.

The sub I served on was a Lafayette class, built in the 1960s. Despite its immense size, it was considerably smaller than the newer Ohio-class missile subs. But even the Ohios were dwarfed by the then Soviet Union's Typhoon-class missile sub, depicted in *The Hunt for Red October*, which is as large as two Ohios strapped side by side.

Inside the sub, it's almost impossible to tell that you're moving or even in the water. At a few hundred feet below the surface we could have driven under a hurricane without even noticing. The only time the sub's motion was perceptible was when we were close to the surface during rough weather. Even then, the sub only rolled a little from side to side. Most of the time, for all we knew, we could have been sitting in dry dock.

On board a submarine, especially on a long, submerged patrol, life can become boring. Without the sun, and away from friends and family, it's easy to become depressed. The Navy recognizes this and tries to enhance morale as much as possible. The first and most important component of morale on a sub is food. From made-to-order omelets for breakfast, to homemade pizza for lunch, and steak and baked potatoes for dinner, the sub's cooks served up wonderful meals. On the day that marked the midpoint of the cruise, we were all treated to a celebratory meal of steak and lobster, with strawberry shortcake for dessert. There was even a soft-serve ice-cream machine on the sub for snacking between meals.

After a few days out, however, we ran out of food that didn't keep, like milk, fresh fruit, and vegetables. I'm a big milk fan, so I was a little concerned that the only things to drink were water, coffee, and a Kool-Aid–like substance everyone called bug juice. The water was on the flat side, tasting a little too reminiscent of its origins in the engine room's distilling plant. After gagging on some bug juice, which tasted like a mixture of Pledge and powdered alum, I decided it was time to start drinking coffee.

The sub also had a stockpile of movies, which were stored between the missile tubes and shown in the crew's mess. After the first few weeks, I was well enough along on my quals to risk watching a movie and would sometimes head to the crew's mess for a break. Six hours of watching the bubble is enough to make anyone crave entertainment, and my Beethoven's Ninth tape was wearing a little thin. But there weren't that many movies, and the crew could never agree on what to watch, so we usually ended up watching *Das Boot*. After about six showings of *Das Boot* I was ready to slit my wrists. But what else was there? I knew the officers also ran a movie every night in the officers' mess, which was off-limits to the crew, but I figured that as a mid I could get away with it, and anyway, at this point I was desperate.

I caught up with one of the firsties and asked him about it, and he said he didn't think the officers would care if I watched with them. He said he'd bring me in with him for the next movie. So the following night I slipped into the officers' mess with the firsty and sat down at the table just as the lights were being dimmed. The room was packed—even the captain was there, which made me a little nervous, but no one said anything about my presence. As the screen began to flicker, the firsty asked, "So what are we watching?" One of the officers responded, "*Das Boot*. We finally got it away from the crew."

I didn't want to blow my chance to start watching movies

with the officers, so I just sat there and tried to act interested. From then on, I was free to watch movies with the officers, and within a few days two other youngsters joined us as well. We were far enough into the cruise that no one really cared; we were getting along with the crew and getting our quals done, and things on the sub were really relaxed all around.

A few days later the ice-cream machine broke. When the cooks declared it irreparable, I thought there was going to be a mutiny. How could we keep a billion-dollar submarine in perfect working order and not be able to repair a stinking ice-cream machine? But it was probably a blessing, because confinement to a sub does not dramatically enhance your physical condition, especially with lots of good food and little opportunity for exercise. It wasn't like I could run laps around the missile tubes to keep in shape. First, there wasn't room, and second, the little radioactivity warning signs dramatically reduced my desire to linger in the area.

A few days later, an incident occurred that would limit my running options permanently. After working on my quals one night, I was asked by one of the officers if I wanted to play a game of chess. We set up the board in a small crew lounge area, but the room was too noisy, so we decided to move into the laundry room next door. In the short passageway into the laundry room, there was a hatch in the floor that led to a narrow space between some storage tanks below. The space was filled with pipes and valves, and one of the watch standers had to take readings there every half hour or so. In order to prevent anyone from falling into the hatch, a square bar could be folded down across the passageway.

Because the chessboard was already set up, I carefully picked up the whole board for the short trip. The bar was down across the passageway, but the watch stander was just coming out of the hatch and lifted up the bar for me. Because the chessboard completely blocked my view of the floor, I didn't notice that he had not closed the hatch. I stepped squarely into thin air and dropped eight feet through the hatch into the maze of pipes below.

My concentration had been so fixed on the chessboard that I had no idea what had happened until I hit the steel floor plates.

The officer later told me it was a miracle that I fell straight through the hatch, which was only sixteen inches wide. If I had reacted and moved my arms away from my sides, I would have broken at least one, and probably smashed my jaw on the metal hatch rim. He said I had fallen so smoothly that the chessboard was left on the floor above, many of the pieces still standing in place.

The compartment wasn't wide enough for me to fall to the floor. Stunned, I was sort of half-standing at the bottom, pressed between the ladder leading up and a metal wall behind. People came running to see what the hell had happened to make such a racket. Everyone was asking, "Are you all right?" I couldn't believe I hadn't been seriously injured, but everything seemed OK except for a few bruises. But as I tried to climb back up the ladder, I felt warm blood streaming from my right knee down my leg. Someone gave me a hand up the ladder and back into the lounge. One of the enlisted men rolled up my bloody pant leg to look at my knee. It didn't seem to hurt that badly, but when he got to the knee, I saw the people behind him cringe. My leg was cut just below the knee, clean down to the bone. Apparently, most of the fall was broken by my knee hitting one of the metal steps at the bottom of the compartment.

I was brought back to the medical officer's compartment, where he examined the cut. "You're lucky," he said, "a quarter inch higher and it probably would have severed your patellar tendon. It looks like the cut just nicked the bottom of it." He stitched me up, gave me some Motrin, and sent me hobbling off to bed. He said a crutch wasn't necessary—there were plenty of pipes and rails to hold on to.

I tried to get some rest, but was too bored to sleep. In an hour, I was up working on my quals, and I stood watch later that day. I kept off my knee, and it eventually healed to the point where I could walk on it without much pain. But the swelling left so much scar tissue in the area that it was years before I could run more than a couple feet without pain, and I still suffer from chronic tendonitis in my right knee.

We were nearing the halfway point in the cruise, and a rumor was going around the ship that we were going to make a port call. This was hard to believe because missile subs rarely make port calls in the middle of a cruise. In fact, one of the crew told me that our sub hadn't made a port call in nearly ten years. But sure enough, the next day the port call was announced, and a few days later we surfaced and were on our way into a port in southern England.

After we were docked and port call was announced, I left the sub and called home from the nearest pay phone. My mom was surprised to hear my voice. "What are you doing off the sub?" she said. "Did they get sick of you and kick you off?" We both laughed, and I told her about the port call and that some guys from the sub and I were heading to London for a day. I was calling collect, so we made it short, but it was good to hear her voice again.

Three of the crew and I rented a little red car and drove through the English countryside north to London. It was beautiful; everything was so incredibly green and lush, and the people were friendly. The only tough part was driving on the other side of the road, and we were nearly killed several times before the guy driving got the hang of it.

By the time we got to London, it was starting to get late and we were all so broke that we spent two hours searching for the cheapest hotel we could find. Rooms were more expensive than we had anticipated, and we finally gave in to paying more than we had planned. By that time, we were so exhausted that we crashed for the night.

The following morning we were up early, walking the streets in search of touristy stuff to see. We overheard some people talking about President Reagan being in town to meet with the Queen, so we decided to head to Buckingham Palace. When we arrived, there was a large crowd lining the gate. Apparently, the meeting was due to be over soon, and everyone was waiting to see the president leave. We hung around for about forty-five minutes, but didn't want to waste any more of our precious single day in London, so we walked around the corner away from the crowd and sat down on a nearby park wall to map out the rest of our day.

Just as we sat down, the president's motorcade pulled out of the palace. We groaned that we hadn't waited a few more minutes, but then the motorcade turned, heading directly toward us. Hundreds of people lined the palace gate, but we were all alone on the sidewalk well away from the crowd. The motorcade drove right past us, only about ten feet away, a procession of screaming police motorcycles followed by limousines with British and American flags waving from hood mounts and red lights flashing from behind their grilles. They were followed by the new presidential limousine with extra-large windows, which had just been built. We could easily see the president, and we all waved. He looked right at us standing alone on the sidewalk and waved back.

A few hours later we stopped at a stand near one of London's train stations to buy some film. The clerk told us that we should go into the station because she had just heard the Queen was on her way. The police had roped off part of the station, and we could see the royal train cars waiting to receive their royal passenger. Few people had gathered, so we walked up to the barricade and waited. Within a few minutes, a quiet procession of burgundy Rolls-Royces rolled into the station. The doors of each automobile were decorated with a small gold crown. The cars passed within four feet of us, the Queen seated in the back of one of them.

We were duly impressed, and agreed that the second procession was even more magnificent than the first. And who would have thought that on our one day in London we would see both the president of the United States and the Queen of England?

Back in port, it felt strange to climb down into the sub. Here I was in England for the first time, after having been submerged in the ocean for nearly a month. London was fun, and there was so much more to see and do, but we didn't have time. The sterile smell of the sub was depressing after being out in the fresh air. But I realized that this was part of my choice to serve in the Navy. I'd get to see a lot of the world, but maybe not have much time to spend there. As we cruised back out to sea, I felt grateful for the port call, and I would have been grateful even if we had been in port only a few minutes.

The remainder of the cruise seemed to go more slowly than the first half. My qualification was coming along well, and I had more free time than ever. I had bought a few more tapes while we were in London, but they all started to sound the same after a while. Sometimes I would just walk around the sub, going from one end to the other, through every level and compartment, just for something to do.

I had gotten to know some of the crew members, especially the guys in the missile control center, where the computer systems that control the missiles are located. The room was enclosed and soundproofed, so we could kick back and shoot the bull. All around us were banks of computer equipment, with rows of flashing lights. In these computers was all the information needed to deploy the missiles toward potential targets thousands of miles away.

The missile control panel itself was ominous, with dozens of lighted indicators and gauges to mark the status of the missile launch. In the middle of the panel was a small safe door, a black combination dial on its face. Behind this door was the trigger that launched the missiles. With the system enabled, this trigger was the final step in the launch sequence. Next to the safe door was the practice trigger, for use in drills. It was wired into the panel with a coiled black wire, like a heavy-duty telephone cord. It looked like the handle of a toy gun, as if the chamber and barrel had been sawed off. Molded of thick, black plastic, it was curved to fit the hand, with a small trigger protruding near the top of the handle where the index finger would rest. The practice trigger is exactly like the real trigger except that the real trigger, behind the safe door, is bright red.

Of the many drills practiced on the sub, the missile test was one of the most frequent. In the drill, every step in the launch process is followed, right down to pulling the trigger. Everything is the same; except the missiles don't launch.

I remember my first time in the control center during a missile drill. It was an eerie feeling watching the launch rehearsal and seeing the trigger pulled for the first time. To everyone else, it seemed mundane. It was just another drill they had repeated dozens, perhaps hundreds of times. But it was all new to me, and as I watched the panel lights clicking through the launch I couldn't help but think of what they represented: the immense power of destruction wrapped up in the simple click of that trigger.

Ever since plebe summer, I had known that the mission of a missile submarine is not to attack but to provide deterrence. In deploying missiles on submarines, virtually undetectable to the enemy, we count on the threat of mutually assured destruction to prevent a nuclear conflict. I had heard many times on my cruise that if our sub really had to launch its weapons, it would have failed its mission.

It made sense, and deterrence had been remarkably effective through the decades, at least in preventing nuclear war. But there was something uncomfortable about sitting at the launch panel and watching the launch sequence. It reminded me all too clearly of the teeth behind that logical explanation. These weapons were real, and they stood poised only yards away from where I was sitting.

There was a time in war when you had to look someone in the eye as you killed him. Today, we see charts, displays, and numbers; we push buttons and pull triggers, and I wonder if it hasn't become too easy. Like our computer simulations at the academy, the battle has become painless and abstract, and death is merely an afterthought.

As the ready light for the first missile lit, the officer in charge pulled the trigger, holding it down until the next indicator lit. "Missile away," an operator reported blandly. I sat next to the officer, half expecting the sub to lurch under the force of the missile ejecting from its tube. The cycle continued, missile by missile, the panel lights flashing, the trigger slowly clicking its way through the sequence.

Near the end of the sequence, the officer offered the trigger to me. "Do you want to give it a try?" he asked, as though bestowing a special honor.

I looked at it for a moment, and then answered, "No, thanks."

My response had come out a little more quickly than I expected, and I was concerned the officer might feel insulted. But he seemed more understanding than surprised by my response. I guess there had been a first time for him as well.

As the end of the cruise approached, I began to look forward to youngster year at Annapolis. I was anxious to see my friends again and even missed the routine of academy life itself.

I could only imagine how different life there would be now that plebe year was behind me.

Finally, we surfaced and headed back into port. I had to stand a few watches in the conning tower as a lookout, scanning the horizon with binoculars to keep an eye out for ships. After nearly seventy days underwater, even that bleak picture, with nothing but water spreading out in every direction, was a marvelous sight. The sunset on the open sea was like a display of silent fireworks, with brilliant hues of red, gold, and blue streaked across the sky.

The cruise had been long, but a great success. I had passed my final submarine qualification boards with flying colors. In fact, all the mids on board qualified, which was a first for any group of midshipmen on that sub. Before returning to Annapolis, all of us mids met in port with the submarine squadron commander and were presented our certificates of qualification and our dolphins.

It was amazing to think that I had already served on board a submarine, visited England, and earned my dolphins. I had done and seen things in a short few months that some people will never experience in their lifetimes, and there was so much more to come. The adventure I had hoped for, the challenge and excitement of a naval career, was everything I could have dreamed of, and I had never felt happier or more satisfied with my decision to enter the academy.

Back in Annapolis, it took me a while to get used to my new freedom as a youngster. During the first few days, I walked the hall cautiously, almost expecting to be yelled at for not chopping. I felt like Pavlov's dog. I had learned to associate these hallways with plebe year, and even after a summer away I couldn't quite shake that conditioning.

The most tangible sign of my freedom was seeing the new plebes chopping through the halls. Watching them reminded me not only of my own plebe year, but also of the fact that I had survived to become a youngster. I had made it through the toughest year, and now I could look forward to the easiest. Listening to chow calls almost made me feel nostalgic for the "good old days" when I was a plebe. Within a matter of hours, my classmates and I were commenting on how easy the plebes had it, and how ours had been the last *real* plebe year at Annapolis!

My class was the first to undergo what came to be known as "the scramble." The academy officials decided that it would be better for all the plebes to be scrambled after plebe year and assigned to new companies. The purpose was to give everyone a clean start, to let those plebes who had not done very well start the rest of their time at Annapolis with a clean slate.

Although many people were opposed to the scramble, I could understand the logic behind it. Even as a plebe, I had seen upperclassmen who were not respected by their classmates. They were often the subject of jokes and ridicule, even in front of us plebes. This open disdain was almost always the result of some incident or poor performance during their own plebe year that had transformed into a lingering curse. This kind of negativity affected everyone and helped no one. Those mids who had not fared well during plebe year often just gave up trying, realizing they would always get poor performance ratings because of their plebe-year image. I had done well during plebe year, ending the year ranked second of thirty-four plebes in my company. I realized that another purpose of the scramble was to keep the pressure on those of us who had earned top rankings—we couldn't just skate through youngster year on our good reputations.

I was moved to 35th Company, on the other side of Bancroft Hall. Living in a new part of this vast building took some getting used to. As plebes, we had avoided the hall at all costs, entering only at the point closest to our own company areas. Although I could now walk through the hall with impunity, it was a couple of weeks before I could easily find my way around its endless maze of halls and stairways.

To compound the difficulty, some of the stairways, or "ladders," as we called them, were designated for use by firsties only. These rules applied to other areas as well. Some doorways into Bancroft Hall could be used only by the second class or firsties. There were benches in the yard that only firsties could sit on. In the dining hall, certain aisles between tables were reserved for second class or firsties.

Although these distinctions might seem insignificant, they

were considered important and were strictly enforced. Privileges
at Annapolis are hard earned and vigorously defended. Taking
advantage of them—"usurping upperclass privileges"—is a punishable conduct offense.

None of my new company mates were from 11th Company, but I did know one guy from the choirs. We decided to
room together along with a friend of his named Greg Brooks.

Before coming to Annapolis, Greg had been enlisted in the
Navy and brought with him a more realistic, relaxed view of
military life than we who had lived at the Academy. Although
it's never easy to live with someone in such close daily proxim-
ity, Greg and I always managed to get along well, thanks to his
keen sense of humor and easygoing style. Although we had an
opportunity to change roommates every semester, Greg and I
continued to room together during our remaining years at Annapolis.

Youngster year was so dramatically different from plebe
year that my entire life at Annapolis seemed to take on a whole
new meaning. My moment-to-moment thoughts were no longer
focused on rates and surviving until the next day. Now I could
breathe easy, walk the halls without fear, and basically enjoy
life. Classes were still tough, but not having to deal with plebe
drudgery made them seem easy by comparison.

I continued to spend most of my free time singing with the
choirs and glee club. I had done well as a soloist at Sunday
church services, and early in the year our director, Dr. Barry
Talley, asked me to start doing some solo work with the glee
club as well.

The glee club took two major tours during the year, and
it was on the first tour youngster year that I broke my self-
imposed ban on drinking. This was the result of two forces.
First of all, I was feeling as independent as I ever had in my
life. I had grown a lot in just one year. My classmates were
from all parts of the country; there were some from other
countries attending as foreign nationals. Experiencing that diversity made me look at my own background from a new,
broader perspective.

The second force, and perhaps the more powerful, was
good old-fashioned peer pressure. Drinking and the military

have always gone together, and Annapolis is certainly no exception. Drinking is not allowed on campus, and because no one can leave campus during the week, mids have to catch up by partying extra hard on the weekends. Trips with the glee club followed the same principle, becoming a continuous cycle of singing and intoxication. And although plebes were not allowed to drink even if they were of age, youngsters were. Now that my classmates and I were youngsters, we were expected to join in or be chastised as wimps and faggots.

Drinking also gave me the perfect excuse for not chasing women. When we were hosted at dances on tour, I would force myself to dance for a while and then sit down with my buddies and get plastered. As time went on, I shed more and more of my puritanical shell. I started swearing more often and telling cruder jokes, working ever harder to fit in. Even my wild friend Rob Connor was impressed.

But there was something more invidious in my drinking as well. Going to dances reminded me all too much of my homosexuality, of the fact that I wasn't comfortable faking the heterosexual norm. Almost everyone around me seemed to be enjoying themselves, doing what was natural for them, but it wasn't natural for me and I hated it. By drinking myself into oblivion, I not only had an excuse to opt out, I had a means of forgetting. What I could no longer avoid consciously, I would escape through unconsciousness. In a way, I could feel that it was the first step toward self-destruction, but I didn't care. Now more than anything else, I simply wanted to forget.

Everything else in my life was going great. I was doing well academically, especially in my physics class where I had a 100-percent average. I had previously chosen systems engineering as my major, but about halfway through the semester I decided to switch to physics. That meant dropping an engineering class and staying for summer school to catch up. As in the previous summer, I would only have about two weeks off, but I figured it was worth it.

As a youngster, I was working with the plebes in my squad to help them learn their rates, to make sure they were ready for the second class. As youngsters, we didn't scream at the plebes— our job was to help them out and to make sure they were up to

speed. If a plebe was constantly screwing up, it was our responsibility to find out what was going on and help solve the problem. Working with the plebes was a powerful lesson in
leadership. One of the first things I learned is that everyone's
personality is unique, and that each individual is motivated in
different ways. A leader has to understand the needs, desires,
expectations, hopes, talents, and limitations of each person he is
leading. That meant being able to adapt. I learned quickly that
you can't choose one ironclad leadership strategy and expect it
to work with every person in every situation.

But perhaps the most important thing I learned about leadership is that in order to be truly effective, you have to care
about the people you're leading. I had experienced plenty of
negative leadership during my own plebe year, and it did nothing to motivate me. In fact, when confronted with negative
leadership I found myself exerting only the minimal amount of
effort necessary to get by. I knew that no matter how well I did,
it wouldn't make a difference, so I didn't do more than I needed
to. That didn't mean there weren't situations when I had to get
tough—sometimes it was necessary. But there was always a
sense that I was being tough for a reason, not just because I was
having a bad day.

Unfortunately, these weren't the kinds of things we were
taught in our naval leadership classes. They were helpful for
providing a conceptual framework and some basic rules, like
always praising a subordinate in public, and always reprimand-
ing in private. But developing our own day-to-day leadership
style was pretty much left up to us, and that meant everyone had
his or her own approach.

These approaches varied widely, especially when it came to
the plebes. Some mids treated plebe year like one big fraternity
initiation ritual, expecting the plebes to deal with at least as
much shit as they had had as plebes, with little or no reason
other than tradition to back it up. They didn't take the time to
think about what they had learned from plebe year, what had
helped and hurt them; they just wanted to pass it on. This was
one of the most frustrating things about trying to do a good
job—there was so little focus on consistency or the purpose
behind what we were trying to teach the plebes.

About halfway through the first semester, Dr. Talley surprised me with some remarkable news. The commandant had asked him to recommend a midshipman to sing the national anthem at the Army-Navy game in December, and he had volunteered me! I was going to sing the national anthem before a packed football stadium live on national television!

I was so worried about forgetting the words to the anthem that I practiced it endlessly. On the way to classes or formations I hummed it to myself, mentally singing the words, or repeating them as fast as I could without stopping—like a national anthem come-around. A few weeks before the game, I started practicing with the Naval Academy band, which is made up of enlisted musicians stationed at the academy. The band members actually serve in the military solely as musicians, playing for academy parades and other military events.

The rehearsals went well, but I knew conditions in the stadium would be difficult. Dr. Talley warned me to expect a long delay in the stadium's amplification system—which meant the loudspeakers would be blaring what I had sung a second or more earlier. I would have to stay exactly with the conductor, regardless of what I was hearing in the background.

My parents were apparently more nervous than I was. I received an index card from my mom with all the words to the anthem typed out in capital letters. She suggested I hold it in my hand during the anthem "just in case." On the week before the game, she found a penny and taped it to the side of the television for good luck. I wasn't sure whether to interpret these acts as well-intentioned precautions or an indication that my parents thought I was going to blow it.

In any case, by the time game day rolled around, I must have sung the anthem at least a thousand times. And as the brigade began its march into Veterans Stadium in Philadelphia, my nervousness turned into great excitement.

Back home in Warren, my parents were huddled with a dozen of their friends in front of the television. At the American Legion hall, the women's club stopped in the middle of their annual prayer breakfast and moved into the bar to watch on the big-screen television, while around town most everyone in Warren was waiting to see someone from their hometown sing on national television.

Immediately before the game, I walked onto the field with

an academy chaplain, who was giving the invocation. I had
brought a pitch pipe to get the starting note, but all during the
invocation a helicopter kept flying over the stadium and I kept
losing the pitch. Finally, the invocation was over. I gave myself
one last pitch and moved to the microphone. With television
cameras swarming, thirty thousand people in the stadium, and
millions more watching on television, I sang one of the best
anthems I've ever sung in my life. Hearing my voice echo
through that stadium, and the crowd's deafening applause, is
something I will never forget. Back home in Warren, everyone
agreed it was a job well done, and my parents breathed a huge
sigh of relief.

After Christmas leave, the second semester went by slowly.
I had switched into all the high-level physics courses, and they
were proving far more difficult than I had anticipated. They
were nothing like the normal courses, and the mathematics were
killing me. It seemed like I was spending twice as much time on
the material and only understanding it half as well. By midterms
I was struggling to get C's and starting to worry that I had made
a serious mistake.

Militarily, I was doing as well as ever. My performance
reviews had gone well, and I was earning a reputation as a
squared-away, competent leader. About halfway through the
semester, I was notified that I had been selected to interview
with our battalion striper board for a possible leadership position in the brigade. These boards are composed of officers from
each battalion, interviewing two midshipmen from each company. Of the twelve mids from each battalion, two were chosen
to go on to the brigade boards, which help select the second-
class chain of command for next year. Because the firsties ran
everything, these positions would be only administrative. But a
good showing at these boards meant a chance at being called
back for first-class boards the next year.

My interview with the battalion board went well, and I
ended up ranked first of the twelve candidates. A few weeks
later I interviewed with the brigade board, which also went well.
Now it was just a matter of waiting. The second-class leadership
positions wouldn't be announced until the end of the year.

The semester was the culmination of many different

stresses. Rehearsals for the spring musical were taking most of
my free time, just when I needed to spend more time studying.
Academics were wearing on me, and I began to question for the
first time if I should stay at Annapolis or consider transferring to
a civilian school while I still had the chance.

I was feeling very depressed, like nothing I had ever experienced in my life. At the heart of this depression were recurring
thoughts about my sexuality. I was working so hard to ignore
them, to shut them out, but I could not turn off a part of my
own mind. These thoughts were always there, always resurfac-
ing, reminding me that I was avoiding something. Our minds
are so powerful, so complex, yet I thought I could control my
mind and shut off a part of my being. It was a battle I was losing.
On the outside I was in control as always, but inside I was
self-destructing.

One night before midterm exams, I was trying in vain to
study in my room. My ability to concentrate was at an all-time
low, and I simply couldn't focus. There were so many pressures
to deal with, so many things going on in my head. Finally, I just
couldn't take it anymore. I slammed my books shut, threw on
a pair of sweats, and walked down the stairs and out of the hall.

The night was pitch-black, and it was raining lightly. A
heavy mist hung in the air, glowing around the dormitory, its
windows completely lit, with mids studying for exams. I walked
slowly across the grass practice field toward the seawall, immersed in my own churning thoughts. I finally sat down against
the chain fence surrounding the field and started to cry, the rain
slowly soaking through my sweats.

I was so completely frustrated. Since the first inkling of
doubt about my sexuality, the first spark of attraction to men, I
had resisted. I had fought, prayed, and hoped that it was just a
phase, that I would wake up one morning and the attraction
would be gone. But every day it was there, lingering in the
background waiting to pounce.

There were times when I would forget, when I was concentrating especially hard on difficult homework or practicing
with the choirs. But then something would happen to trigger my
memory and the sinking feeling in my stomach would return,
the feeling of dread and shame and most of all the loneliness that

came from having to hide a part of myself. My family and friends had always been there to help me when I needed it, but somehow this was different. I felt so alone.

From the beginning, I had avoided dealing with my sexuality, but it didn't feel like avoidance anymore. Now it felt like a lie—a lie whose perpetuation was beginning to sicken me, to eat away at my soul. I had crossed the line between doubt and certainty months before, but I kept lying to myself. In my mind, two incompatible thoughts were waging battle: The first was my own stereotypical prejudice toward homosexuals; the second was the realization that I was one of them. For a while, I had managed to suppress this conflict by assuring myself that I was not really gay. But I could no longer deny my sexuality, and I could not continue down the path toward self-hatred. That would be a living death.

And then there was Annapolis and the military. I knew the military didn't allow homosexuals, but I had invested so much here already—so many dreams were tied to this place. How could I give them up, quit for that I knew were all the wrong reasons? I knew now that keeping gay people out of the military was wrong. I knew because I was one of them, and I had done as well as any of my classmates. I only wondered how many others there were like me, how many more silent voices in the crowd.

Deep down inside, I knew I could never leave Annapolis. The problem wasn't the academy; it was me. I had to quit running away and finally accept the fact that I was gay. I wasn't going to be able to change, and even if that meant hiding a part of myself forever, I didn't care. This place had become the focal point of my life. It meant as much to me now as anything else. No matter what, I was going to stay here and continue working toward the goals I had held for so long.

After what seemed like an hour, I finally got up and started walking back to the hall. I still didn't completely understand what it meant to be gay, or even fully accept my homosexuality. A part of me still wanted to be straight, to be "normal"— because I felt it would make my life easier. But I had taken a first crucial step toward acceptance. That step was the beginning of a long process of "coming out." It would not be my last step, and it would certainly not be my most difficult. Unfortunately, it is a first step that many young gay people do not have the strength to take. They choose self-hatred over self-acceptance, and embark on an impossible path leading all too often to self-destruction through drug addiction or suicide.

For the first time in many months, I finally felt at peace with myself, and as the year went on I thought more and more about what it meant to be gay. I began examining and questioning the attitudes toward homosexuals that I had grown up with. The more I thought about them from my own perspective, the more I began to see the ignorance that lay behind these prejudices. Now, when I heard a negative comment about homosexuals, I no longer thought, Yes, they are like that. I thought, No, I'm not like that. Despite enduring the loneliness of living in the closet, I was finally breaking away from the feelings of guilt and shame that had tormented me for so long.

That rainy night on the practice field was a great turning point in my life. I had finally stopped fighting who I knew I was and began accepting myself. I have often heard people ask why anyone would choose to be a gay, but there is no question more flawed in its misunderstanding of human sexuality. None of us, gay or straight, choose our sexualities. They are defined within us, most experts believe, by a combination of genetic and environmental factors long before we ever become aware of our feelings. Few heterosexuals who believe people choose to be gay stop to think about when they chose to be straight. That just isn't the way it works.

No one wanted to be gay less than I did. Everything in my life, from my conservative upbringing to the path in life I had chosen, was opposed to accepting my sexuality. I had a vast storehouse of negative reinforcement to back up my own prejudices toward homosexuals, and I drew upon those forces to help me ignore and evade my own feelings.

But like many gay men and lesbians, I discovered that there is no hiding from yourself. Homosexuality is simply not a choice; it is an identity. The only real choice we have is whether to continue fighting, evading, and denying that identity or to finally accept it, heal, and get on with our lives.

As my youngster year drew to a close, I began to break out

of my long depression, slowly gaining strength as my understanding and self-acceptance grew. For the first time in many months, I felt complete and in control of my life. Everything was starting to make sense now, and I no longer denied my feelings or felt ashamed of them. They were simply a part of me. I knew that my choice to stay at the academy would not be easy—living in the closet never is. But for now I was willing to hide. It was enough to know that I was no longer hiding from myself.

6

—☆—

A Matter of Time

Second-class summer is one of the busiest a midshipman has, and having to take summer school meant another summer with only two weeks' leave. Instead of a cruise aboard a ship, this summer consists of several week-long tours of various naval service branches—surface ships, submarines, air and Marine Corps. It is designed to give us a taste of each before we make our service selection during first-class year, when we officially choose the branch in which we will serve after graduation.

One of our more exciting weeks was spent at the Navy flight training center in Pensacola, Florida. We each had the chance to fly with instructors in jet and prop aircraft and helicopters and take over the stick in the air. Another week was spent playing Marine at the Marine Corps training center in Quantico, Virginia. In addition to such treats as running the obstacle course, repeatedly cleaning our M-16 rifles, and rappelling down walls, we got to stage a mock assault against an opposing team for control of a group of concrete buildings called cinder-block city. The assault was complete with battle gear, a helicopter fly-in, smoke bombs, and plenty of M-16 blank ammunition rounds for us to shoot at each other. It was every kid's dream: getting to play army with really cool toys. Despite the high-tech approach, the day still ended in a series of classic disputes over who shot whom first.

Another week was spent aboard the Naval Academy's fleet of small training ships called yard-patrol craft, or YPs, which we navigated up a portion of the east coast. We eventually ended up at the submarine training center in Groton, Connecticut, where we all spent a few days aboard a submarine. Needless to say, there wasn't much new for me to learn that week.

Second-class summer ended with a training period at Annapolis where we completed a series of professional training programs. This time at Annapolis was actually rather enjoyable because we all had liberty every day after training. My friend from glee club, Rob Connor, and I were in most of the same training groups during the summer and spent most of our free time together, going out to bars or just hanging out in the hall. Rob was also a talented pianist, and we would often spent hours in Mitscher Hall, the auditorium where the glee club practiced, pounding on the piano, singing at the top of our lungs, and laughing until we were hoarse.

Rob was really a funny mixture. He was one of the most macho, irreverent, prototypically heterosexual mids I knew. He was constantly falling head over heels in love with one woman or another, and a bunch of us mids who hung out with Rob during the summer were always giving him shit about how "sensitive" and "caring" he was becoming. Of course, this drove him nuts and he would strike back with a stream of searing profanities or a quick punch to the shoulder.

Rob and I still clashed over our approaches to the academy, as we had since plebe year. I was extremely idealistic, always playing by the rules and sticking up for the academy, while Rob was constantly pushing the limits. But the better I got to know him, the more I realized what a truly caring and compassionate person he really was. There were times when we would sit and talk seriously, and he would open up to me about his frustrations and problems, and I would try to give him advice or cheer him up. And there were plenty of times when he did the same for me, making me laugh when I was down or overwhelmed by school.

Although there were a few classmates and friends that I felt attracted to, Rob wasn't one of them, and that made our friendship all the easier for me. But there was still a great distance between us, and I was constantly playing along with the heterosexual role, afraid to tell Rob about what was really going on in my head. There were a couple of times when I was tempted to come out to him, but I didn't have the courage. As much as I felt he might understand, I couldn't know for sure how he would react. He was a good friend, and for now I wasn't willing to risk that friendship.

When the summer training period finally ended, I started straight into summer school, taking a few classes to help lighten my physics load during the upcoming year. With only one more summer left after this one, I was beginning to wonder if I would ever have any real summer leave.

Shortly after the beginning of summer school, the new plebes arrived to start plebe summer. Watching them march around the yard and seeing their Induction Day transformation brought back my own memories of plebe summer. Everything had seemed so new then, so strangely exciting. I had come so far since taking my own oath of office on that hot July day, through experiences both good and bad. Seeing the new plebes reminded me of the idealism that had brought me here. It rekindled the deep pride that I felt in being a part of Annapolis, of its tradition and honor. The plebes were also a reminder of the most tangible fact of all: that I was one more year closer to graduation.

I was sharing a room with a company mate of mine, and we had combined our stereo components into a rather massive system, which I decided to put to good use. I thought the new plebes could use some inspirational music to pep them up for their first day, so I popped in a CD of Wagner's "Ride of the Valkyries," turned the speakers toward the windows, and cranked up the volume.

After about a minute of blaring music and a few amused glances from firsties on detail, I was startled by the sound of my door being kicked violently open. I turned around just in time to see it slam back in the face of an enraged officer known for his lack of humor. He pushed the door open again and stormed into my room as I turned down the music and snapped to attention. He was furious. Apparently, I had disturbed some important paper pushing in his office down the hall. He demanded an explanation, and I tried to tell him that the music was simply meant to inspire the new plebes on their first day. Still fuming, he ordered me to place myself on report and stomped back to his office.

What a wimp, I thought, walking toward the battalion of-

fice. If he's going to fry me, the least he could do is fill out the
form himself. In the office, I grabbed a conduct-violation form,
"Form 2," and wrote it up for violation of section 0707 of the
Midshipman Conduct Manual—excessive stereo volume.

When I turned in the form to the head midshipman on
watch, he couldn't believe the officer had ordered me to fry
myself for something so trivial, especially during the summer
when things are relatively relaxed. It was the only conduct violation of my career as a midshipman, and I served my punishment the following morning by sorting mail for an hour.

Because plebe summer is run by a selected group of first-
class mids, no one else was allowed to interact with or even talk
to the plebes. They ate their meals in a section of the mess hall
that was separated by partitions from the other mids at Annapolis for the summer. During meals, the mess hall was filled with
the clamor of the plebe section, as they screamed, cheered, and
shouted.

After the summer, the reassembling of the brigade signaled
the beginning of another academic year. Each class was required
to report before a designated time, starting with each of the
lower classes and ending with the firsties. It was exciting to see
everyone again, and catch up on their stories from cruises that
had taken them to all corners of the world.

The first academic day of second-class year is an especially
important one in the life of a midshipman. During the first two
years at Annapolis, a midshipman can choose to leave at any
time without incurring an obligation for military service. But
after attending the first academic class of second-class year, that
option expires, and my classmates and I were now obligated to
seven more years in the Navy: the remaining two years at Annapolis, plus a five-year obligation as an officer after graduation.

To mark this step beyond the point of no return, the entire
second class gathered on the evening of the first class day for a
party known traditionally as two-for-seven night, complete with
food and, of course, several thousand cans of beer. Most of the
high-ranking officers were there as well—the superintendent,
commandant, and a well-known partygoer among the mids, the
deputy commandant, Captain Al Konetzni. Captain Al, as he
was known within the brigade, was a brash, straight-talking,

no-nonsense kind of officer who wasn't above going for a drink
with mids. He was also a die-hard supporter of the football
team, and even showed up to lead a pep rally one night before
a big game wearing an ape suit.

Despite the partying that typifies two-for-seven night, as
second classmen we knew there was a risk involved in crossing
this threshold as well. After this point, if any of us were kicked
out of Annapolis for academic or military reasons, the obligation for service still stood and we would be required to fill our
commitment through service in the enlisted ranks of the Navy.
It was a risk that a few of our classmates weren't willing to take,
especially those hanging near the fatal 2.0 GPA mark, and they
had already tendered their resignations. For the rest of us, the
two-for-seven obligation was just one more spike poised be-
neath us if we failed to meet the challenge of Annapolis.

Any anxiety that we might have had about our new service
obligation was enhanced by the understanding that second-class
year is dreaded by midshipmen as the most difficult year academically, with notorious classes in electrical engineering, celestial navigation, and thermodynamics. The year also begins
increased professional responsibilities, which primarily involve
overseeing the professional development of the plebes. Traditionally, this means being tough and carrying forward some of
the stress of plebe summer into the academic year.

By this point, the first class have had their turn with the
plebes, they've survived second-class academics: they're on the
top of the heap and counting the days to graduation. They
basically don't want to be bothered with plebe development any
more than they have to. It's the second class's turn to take up the
reins, and most of them did it with a vengeance.

Because of this tradition, there was a lot of pressure to be
extremely tough on the plebes. Although I was definitely tough
as a second class, I was also determined to avoid being a mind-
less flamer. My own plebe year had taught me it just doesn't
work. If I had to be tough, it was going to be for a reason, and
if I didn't need to be an asshole to get the job done, I wasn't
going to be.

I was lucky enough to have squad leaders that year who
trusted my abilities and gave me free rein to do what I wanted.

My approach worked well, and I believe the plebes were better served by fairness and consistency than random, meaningless harassment. They learned quickly that if they came to me prepared and knowing their rates, they were going to avoid getting screamed at. Conversely, they knew if they weren't prepared, they were going to regret it. Because my reaction was always predictable, they learned that their treatment was directly and solely related to their own performance—in many ways, they controlled the come-around.

Academics that year were every bit as tough as I had anticipated. My physics classes were going especially badly, and I realized that if I didn't do something quick, I was going to end up between a rock and a hard place. Mathematics had never been my forte, and I found it increasingly difficult to get excited about calculating the effect of imaginary electrical fields on three-dimensional mathematical surfaces. At least in my earlier physics classes I could see the purpose behind studying the ballistic trajectory of cannonballs, but this stuff was downright boring. And why did I need to learn these things anyway? I was going to be a naval officer, not a physicist. I had never had trouble in school before, but now I was struggling with C's and even D's in some of my high-level physics classes.

It was becoming obvious that my switch to physics had been a serious mistake, and now I had to either give up everything else I was involved in and focus solely on academics for the next two years, or transfer to a new major. After four more weeks of frustration, I finally requested a change of major to economics. It was a less-demanding curriculum, and I figured that it would at least have some real-world applicability if I decided to get out of the Navy someday.

Convincing the academic dean to let me switch majors during second-class year wasn't an easy proposition. If my GPA had been below 2.0, I could have switched to the physical science major, an easy catchall major used to salvage failing mids (most of whom turned out to be football players). But finally, after considerable effort, I was allowed to transfer into economics. It meant switching into some classes already under way and spending my final summer in summer school again, but it was more than worth it. I hadn't come to Annapolis to spend all my time on academics—that just wasn't what this place was about. It was about being involved in lots of things, being well-rounded, or as the academy would say, growing as a "whole man."

Even with the extra work of having to catch up in my new classes, my change of major took a big load off my mind. Within a few weeks, things were back to normal, classes were going fine, and I wasn't losing sleep over whether or not I was going to flunk out. My roommate, Greg Brooks, was also having trouble with his major, electrical engineering, and was so impressed by the results of my transition that he decided to transfer to economics as well. This was especially helpful because we ended up with most of the same classes, which made studying for tests a lot easier.

Shortly before Christmas leave, the stripers for the second semester were announced, and I was assigned as a regimental commander. It was the second-highest command position in my class, next only to our class brigade commander, which meant I was responsible for half of my entire class. Although I felt I had done well at the striper boards, the ranking was far beyond what I had expected and a bit of a shock.

This position was simply administrative—the firsties still ran everything—but it meant that if I played my cards right, I would almost certainly be in line for a striper position during senior year. I had worked hard to develop my skill as a leader during my previous years, and it was especially encouraging to have my progress recognized in such a tangible way.

Among other duties, I was placed in charge of the brigade's professional-knowledge program, which created and administered weekly quizzes to the plebes. I had a staff of other second classmen working for me, so I spent a lot of time delegating and tracking the assignments that were passed our way. That meant a lot of meetings and rushing around, but for the first time I felt like I had a hand in the inner workings of the brigade.

Later in the semester, I was given the unique chance to serve on a committee of high-ranking second-class stripers to rewrite the *Plebe Indoctrination Manual* and the plebe-summer *Squad Leader's Manual*. These were the books that defined plebe summer and how it was to be run, and I recognized that this was an opportunity to change plebe summer for the better.

I had always felt that too much of the summer was simply
a meaningless ritual that undermined the professional goals of
the academy. When the committee started discussing the future
of plebe summer, I made my feelings known and, to my surprise, the majority of my classmates agreed. Much of the information we had been forced to memorize during plebe summer
was useless gibberish, created simply for the sake of memorization. If the plebes were going to be forced to memorize information, why not at least make them memorize information on
ships and weapons that they would eventually have to learn
anyway? We agreed that plebe summer was being run too much
like a fraternity initiation and that unprofessionalism led to
events like the sweatbox, which I learned was only one of many
similar incidents that had occurred during my own summer.

Over the course of the next few weeks, we revised much of
the format for the summer. Reaching agreement on what to
change wasn't easy, especially with a few of the committee members fighting tooth and nail to keep the summer as anachronistic
as before. "This is tradition," they would whine. "It's always
been done this way." But most of the changes survived, and by
the time we were done, I felt satisfied that plebe summer had
evolved into something better. It was still going to be as tough
as ever, but it would accomplish the goal of indoctrinating the
plebes in a more professional, mature, and effective manner.

With my new responsibilities as a second-class regimental
commander, the year seemed to scream by. Every year at Annapolis is different, and each year seems to get better, probably
because each year brings new privileges and responsibilities.
Second-class year is a major transition toward responsibility,
and during this year at Annapolis, it was remarkably satisfying
to be so busy and involved.

I had also come a long way since the beginning of my own
coming-out process the year before. I had read and learned what
I could about homosexuality in books and magazines, slowly
piecing together a broader intellectual understanding of the issue. I wanted to start meeting other gay people, to start dating
and having sex like everyone else I knew, but I was far too afraid
to risk any openness about my sexuality. I had no contact with
or even sense of the gay community, and although I knew there

were gay bars in nearby Baltimore and Washington, D.C., I was too paranoid to go to them.

It was a frustrating dichotomy to feel so sexually isolated and constrained while my friends and classmates were free to pursue their heterosexual lives without any fear whatsoever. I was especially frustrated by the double standard that I felt inherent in the military's policies toward gay men and lesbians. Although the military was vicious in discharging homosexuals, regardless of any evidence of sexual misconduct, heterosexual sex was accepted as a common, everyday aspect of life at Annapolis. Sometimes even the most egregious cases of heterosexual misconduct were overlooked or excused.

One incident that demonstrated this hypocrisy occurred during the second half of the year. Late one night, a classmate in my company was awakened by a bumping sound coming from the room next door. He brushed it off at first, but when the noise continued, he decided to investigate. The room was shared by two male youngsters. When he walked into the room and turned on the lights, he found one of the youngsters in flagrante delicto with a black female youngster who was also from our company.

It was quite a scandal, and both of them were fried for having sex on academy grounds, a separation-level conduct offense. After the smoke cleared, the woman was kicked out of the academy, but the man was retained. He was punished by being forced to spend a year in the enlisted ranks of the Navy before being allowed to return to the academy and pick up where he left off. It was a perfect example of the "boys will be boys" mentality that often dictated the administration's reaction to such offenses.

Although these cases of sexual misconduct were usually punished severely, they were not at all uncommon. It was only uncommon for people to get caught. I knew several guys who had sex in Bancroft Hall or on the academy grounds with female midshipmen or civilian women they managed to smuggle in. Despite the risk, it was encouraged by the macho environment of the academy. It was even a tradition for a mid who had sex with a woman in his room to proudly display a Chiquita banana sticker on his door nameplate.

In addition to strict rules regarding sexual misconduct, mid-shipmen were also banned from getting married or having children. These restrictions were designed to keep midshipmen focused on their duties and responsibilities at the academy. The "offenses" of marriage and paternity/maternity were the first two conduct offenses listed in the *Conduct Manual* under Section 0709, Standards of Behavior. Violation of either was a separation-level offense.

Although it wasn't common for midshipmen to risk separation by marrying, I know one classmate who had been married since his youngster year. He was a good mid, and plenty of people knew that he was married. It had actually become something of a running joke in our class, until the administration found out, and he was separated. It seemed a shame to lose a classmate over something so inane. He had obviously managed to handle being married without any problems, and his military performance and conduct record hadn't suffered as a result. Nonetheless, rules were rules, and according to the academy, he had to go.

The paternity/maternity rule posed even more difficult questions. Despite weekday restrictions, the vast majority of midshipmen, like any other normal group of college students, are sexually active. Even with everyone trying to avoid pregnancy, there are going to be accidents. This point was especially highlighted for me when one of my best friends told me late in the year that he had gotten his girlfriend pregnant.

He wanted to marry her and have the child, but he was terrified of getting kicked out of the academy. Now that he was bound to a military commitment, that meant not only separation, but spending the next few years of his life trying to raise a family on an enlisted man's pay. It was a serious matter, with repercussions that could follow them for years to come. In the end, they decided that their only real option was an abortion. It would have been a difficult decision for anyone, but it enraged me that their choice was dictated, in part, by the academy's outdated regulations.

Near the end of the year, I was called to striper boards again, this time directly to the brigade board. The deputy commandant, Captain Konetzni, was in charge of the board, as he had been the previous year. The striper board was made up of officers and a few high-ranking firsties, and the panel members took turns asking questions about how I would improve the brigade and what steps I would take to boost morale. After a while I got the feeling that many of these questions were designed not so much to test my creativity, but to see how much I might challenge the academy's existing policies. There is usually some tension between the first-class stripers and the academy's officer staff because the firsties usually want to change more things than the officers do. And because the officers, particularly the commandant and deputy commandant, have final say over what policy changes are implemented, they wanted to make sure the stripers weren't going to push for too much.

A few days after the striper board, I met with the academy's commandant, Captain Steve Chadwick, to follow up on the striper board and give him a chance to ask his own questions. Captain Chadwick was an academy classmate of my sponsor, John Morrow. Captain Chadwick's only question was to ask what position I was hoping to get in the brigade. I explained that what I really wanted was a command. "If it's a choice between having five stripes as a staff member, or four stripes as a commander, I would rather have the command," I told him bluntly. I thought my statement might have seemed almost demanding, but he smiled and I knew he understood where I was coming from. I asked John about it later, and he said I had said the right thing. Chadwick was the kind of guy who respected a direct, honest answer, and he knew the difference between a command and a staff position.

Later, I met with the superintendent, Rear Admiral Charles Larson. Admiral Larson knew me from my singing with the choirs, and we had talked several times during receptions and other events at the academy. During my four years at Annapolis, there was probably no officer who was more respected by the brigade than Admiral Larson. His career had been every naval officer's ideal. He had been chosen as brigade commander during his time at Annapolis, and after his graduation, he was the first naval officer ever granted a White House fellowship. He entered the submarine service, was promoted rapidly throughout his career, and eventually returned to Annapolis to serve as superintendent. It was a great honor, and everyone agreed he was on a fast track to becoming chief of naval operations.

After a short discussion, Admiral Larson congratulated me on becoming "one of the top midshipmen in my class" and shook my hand. Coming from him, it was a compliment I would never forget. After the striper boards and meetings were over, it was once again a matter of waiting until the striper positions were announced. None of us would hear anything until at least the end of the year.

Near the end of second-class year, my classmates and I received the most coveted of midshipmanly possessions—our class rings. They were the ultimate symbol of pride and accomplishment, and we had waited over a year since ordering them as youngsters. I had ordered my ring without a stone so that I could handpick the perfect one. On the weekend after my ring arrived, I spent hours searching through jewelry stores in town looking for the ideal stone.

Finally, in a store in the historic district across from the city dock, I found a brilliant blue topaz that was nearly blinding in the sunlight. I left the ring to have the stone set and picked it up the following weekend. It was beautiful, but beyond mere aesthetic appeal, it was a tangible reminder of how far I had come. I hadn't even dared to think about it until now, but the ring was proof that graduation was close at hand. Three years down—only one to go.

Officially, we were not allowed to wear our rings until the ring dance—a formal dance held during graduation week for the second class. But in reality, we wore them whenever we could get away with it. Although it was technically a serious conduct offense (usurping upperclass privileges), according to tradition, if a firsty caught a second class wearing his class ring, the firsty was due a free soda. That could get expensive, so we generally just wore them in our rooms. We would walk into the room, pull the ring out of the desk and put it on. Then, if we had to leave, we would return the ring and put it on again when we came back. Although this might seem a little obsessive to the casual observer, to us the ring meant everything. It was power, satisfaction, accomplishment, and pride all rolled together into one chunk of gold. Annapolis is an institution with many traditions, and the ring dance stands out as one of the most important. It was an occasion not to be missed, and arriving at the ring dance without a date was considered a major disgrace. Of course, this put me in somewhat of a jam. I obviously wasn't dating any girls, and I was at a loss as to whom I could ask.

I had met the sister of a glee club friend of mine on a recent tour, and we had hit it off pretty well. When I asked him about inviting her, he thought she would certainly want to go. I felt guilty calling and asking her to the dance, like I was using her— and I was. But using people was just another part of what living in the closet was all about.

When she accepted, I felt an uncomfortable mixture of relief and anger. I was relieved and grateful that I had a date, and angry because I knew that asking her was a lie. It was a lie to her and to everyone who would be there. I was so sick of the hiding, the pretense, the charade of heterosexual conformity that came from being completely closeted. It made me angry that I had so many good friends at Annapolis, people I had known for years through the happiest and most trying of times, but none of them knew the first thing about who Joe Steffan really was. This dance was supposed to be a highlight of my time at Annapolis, but I knew it would only be a reminder of everything I had come to hate.

On the night of the ring dance, I arrived with my date, Laura, at the pre-dance reception at the Michelson-Chauvanet Courtyard. It was quite a spectacle—a myriad of gold-buttoned dress-white uniforms and formal ball gowns. We met up with my roommate, Greg, and his girlfriend, Sarah, and the four of us walked over to Dahlgren Hall to go through the ring ceremony. Greg and I had planned on arriving early so we could get to the ring ceremony and officially wear our rings.

Outside the dance floor in Dahlgren Hall, a huge representation of the class ring was positioned next to a binnacle, or compass stand. In place of the compass was a container filled with water from each of the seven seas, sent to the academy by Navy ships from around the world especially for this ceremony. As each couple took its turn, the midshipman's date took the ring, which she was wearing on a ribbon around her neck, and dipped it in the water. The legend is that once the ring is dipped, it will always return to its owner if lost. Then the couple enters the opening of the large ring, she places the ring on his finger, and they kiss.

For Greg and Sarah this was a doubly significant night because it was also the night of their engagement. In keeping with another academy tradition, Greg had bought a miniature class ring as an engagement ring and presented it to Sarah before they kissed inside the ring. After congratulating Greg and Sarah, Laura and I took our turn, and then we all returned to the reception.

After a formal dinner later in the evening, the dance began in Dahlgren Hall. Most of us stuck around for only a short time before leaving to party off campus. A bunch of second class in our company had rented a block of rooms in a hotel just outside Annapolis, so we drove out to spend a few hours partying with them. I was scheduled to leave early the next morning for my summer cruise, which was a convenient reason to cut the night short. After the party, I dropped Laura off at her parents' hotel. (They had come up to see the graduation week ceremonies.) I kissed her good night and drove back to the academy. Although the evening had been fun, I couldn't help thinking that it was just another heterosexual hoop I had dutifully jumped through. By the time I got back to the academy, I was just grateful it was over.

Early the following morning, I left for my first-class summer cruise aboard the USS *Kinkaid*, a destroyer out of San Diego. A friend of mine from glee club, Jack McCauley, was on the same cruise, so we met up before the flight out to California. It was an early cruise, so we would be missing graduation, which was still two days away. As I had done before on my youngster cruise two years earlier, Jack and I switched to our first-class shoulder boards before leaving the academy. A famous admiral once said that the two best ranks in the Navy were admiral and midshipman first class. Although I didn't know about being an admiral, if it felt half as good as finally putting on those first-class shoulder boards, he was definitely right.

In addition to my cruise and summer school, I had also been chosen to serve on plebe-summer detail during the second half of the summer. Luckily, this cruise would be a short one.

We were scheduled to be at sea for about twenty days, which would leave me just enough time to return to Annapolis to start summer school.

First-class cruise is similar to youngster cruise, except that the first class don't serve in the enlisted ranks, they serve as junior officers. It's a chance to get accustomed to life as a young officer aboard ship. Serving on the *Kinkaid* was considerably less stressful than my sub cruise. We weren't working for a qualification, so we didn't have to spend all our free time studying. We stood watches, primarily as junior officers of the deck, assisting the officer of the deck in overseeing the navigation and operation of the ship.

The cruise went by quickly, and as we neared the end, the ship docked in Portland, Oregon. It was the first time I had ever been to Portland or anyplace in the Pacific Northwest. The city was beautiful, and we had arrived just in time for an annual festival. Jack and I and the other mids on board spent the last days of the cruise partying our way through the Portland bars and eating at seafood restaurants.

I remember one afternoon when four of us were in town watching a parade that was part of the celebration. I noticed a woman working her way down our side of the sidewalk, asking people to sign something she was holding on a clipboard. As she drew closer, I overheard her mention that she was seeking volunteers as part of an environmental group working to protect endangered sea life. One of the mids wanted to get going, so we started walking down the street toward her. Just then, she finished speaking with someone and turned toward us, starting in on her spiel. She realized immediately from our short hair that we were in the Navy. Before even finishing her first sentence, she stopped and said, "Oh, you're just a bunch of fucking squids. You don't care about anything." And with that, she turned away and continued down the street.

I stood there shocked, my mouth practically hanging open. Although I knew that some people didn't like the military, it was the first time I had ever been judged and dismissed by someone in less than ten seconds simply because my hair was short. None of us had even said one word, and yet the woman had immediately made up her mind about us. Although that incident lasted only a few seconds, it has always stuck with me as a reminder that prejudice is a two-way street. Whenever we judge people by categories, no matter what those categories are, we judge them unfairly.

After our final days in Portland, I flew back to the academy with Jack and checked in at the summer battalion office. All mids at Annapolis for the summer, other than the plebe-summer detail, are organized into a single battalion called the NASP, an acronym for Naval Academy Summer Programs. The midshipman on watch saw my name on the list.

"Steffan, here you are," he said. "Looks like you're the NASP battalion subcommander."

"Are you sure?" I asked, having heard nothing about this before leaving.

"Yeah," he said, pointing to a line on his computer printout. "It says so right here, next to your room number."

After signing in, I caught up with the NASP commander, a firsty from last year's class who was graduating late after missing part of the year due to an automobile accident. He explained that the positions had come down after I had left Annapolis.

Because it was a first-class striper position, albeit a summer one, I had the rank of midshipman lieutenant and wore rank insignia with three stripes. My duties actually turned out to be minimal. I helped the battalion commander, filling in for him at formations if he was unable to make it and taking care of administrative details. This left me with plenty of time to keep up with my summer-school classes and catch up with friends who dropped in on their way to and from summer cruises.

Early in July, the new plebes reported for Induction Day and the start of plebe summer. I was scheduled to serve in the second set, which wouldn't be taking over for another three weeks. Within a few days the plebes were marching in their platoons around the academy grounds. The speed of their transformation amazed me, and it was hard to believe they were the same bunch of kids that had just wandered through the front gate. I wondered if I had looked the same to my firsties on that summer day three years before. Then, I had seen the firsties around me as gods; now, it was all reversed—and I still felt as mortal as ever.

On my own Induction Day I had revered the academy, with it the iron gates and stone buildings, its tradition and prestige, and the rare opportunity to be forever linked to it. Now, like all midshipmen, I hated the academy and I loved it. The two were never quite removed from one another. I hated it for the freedoms it took away from me; I hated marching, practicing for parades, not being able to come and go like a normal human being, being constantly watched, governed by bells, and by rules too numerous and inane to count or comprehend.

I hated being subject to the whim of some officers who were at the academy simply for the power trip, back for their chance to gain by default of rank the respect, or should I say deference, they were incapable of earning. I hated standing watch, wondering if my room was going to be inspected while I was at class, filling out log books, folding my towel in three, and the thousand other trivialities that I was bound by fear of punishment to obey.

But at the end of the day, after bells and marching and standing watch and having my room inspected twice; after three formations and a night of studying thermodynamics and electric engineering and differential equations; after knowing I would miss half my weekend liberty because of a home football game that we all had to march to and attend; after all this, there was one crucial fact, one ultimate, telling point that I could not avoid: I was still here.

Each of us could have left anytime during the first two years; we could have resigned and packed our bags and walked out the gates, free of military or financial obligation. But we had chosen to stay, and the mere fact of our continued presence at Annapolis exposed an underlying truth that no self-respecting midshipman would ever utter in the presence of other midshipmen. For all its limitations and imposed sacrifices, there was something undeniably incredible about life at Annapolis. Deep down inside I felt a bond with this place, with my classmates, and, in a way, with everyone who had ever lived the life of a midshipman.

Like the new plebes, I had come here with an idealistic vision—a vision that reality had inevitably tarnished over time. But a part of that idealism had survived, as I believe it did with most mids. The idealism was sometimes obscured, but always there at the core of my motivation. Seeing the plebes was a chance to experience that vision anew. The plebes would learn that Annapolis and the military are not perfect. But in that knowledge, in recognizing the military's imperfection, lay the real hope for change.

For me, that hope was to someday be able to serve in the military without having to hide my true identity. Since that rainy night as a youngster, I had grown each day in the acceptance of my sexuality. And the more I understood and accepted it as a part of my identity as an individual, the more it hurt me to hear the common antigay remarks that permeated the homophobic brigade, spawned as much by sexual insecurity as anything else. But for now, I could simply continue to hope, and to hide in a closet that was shrinking each day.

Working on plebe-summer detail was one of the high points in my academy career. The detail is divided into two battalions, port and starboard, and I served as the starboard battalion subcommander. I once again held the rank of midshipman lieutenant, with three gold stripes to indicate my rank.

My battalion commander was Tom Olton, a classmate I had known from our work together as second-class stripers. Tom and I had a very similar vision as to how plebe summer should be run, with a focus more on professional development and evaluation as opposed to basic abuse. This vision was in stark contrast to that of the port battalion, whose leadership had chosen a focus much the opposite to our own. Needless to say, we didn't spend much time conferring about indoctrination strategy.

Tom and I would often leave a meal only to find the port battalion subcommander and his henchmen frothing at the mouth while berating any number of plebes they had managed to capture returning to their company areas. I had heard the saying that power corrupts, and absolute power corrupts absolutely. And if anyone has absolute power, it is a first-class midshipman during plebe summer.

Before each meal, any number of plebes would arrive outside our door to report for battalion come-around—a punishment worse than death. It usually takes a major screwup before a plebe makes it to battalion come-around, with numerous trials at the platoon and company levels before finally being ordered to report outside our door. These visits were not ordered lightly by the firsties, but were often arranged in advance with some discussion with us about the problems the plebe was experiencing. Our goal was to evaluate the plebe and attempt to resolve the problem.

In order to succeed, a plebe needed ability as well as desire. There were a few plebes who had the ability to survive the academy but lacked the desire. Some of them had come here only to please their families or uphold a family naval tradition. This was a common situation, as many Navy officers hope that their daughters and sons will follow in their footsteps by entering the academy. Sometimes the kids grow up with this goal, never stopping to think about whether it's what they really want. Plebe summer is unfortunately often the first time they question their motivation.

The most difficult plebes to deal with were those who were at the academy for the wrong reasons but had just enough internal motivation to sneak by. Sometimes they made it through the summer unscathed, but a few found their way to our door. Our job then was to force them to look inside themselves and decide whether the academy was for them.

It wasn't enough to simply want to stay at the academy. It was a sad thing to find a plebe who had vastly underestimated the difficulty of academy life. Some of them arrived with little or no understanding of what the academy is about, or what life at a service academy is like. I found this quite surprising, considering the long and difficult process of obtaining entry. I remember one time during the previous summer when I was standing watch in the summer battalion office. The plebes who had chosen to resign during plebe summer were switched over to our side before being processed out. One of the plebes had submitted his resignation on the day after Induction Day. His only explanation for resigning was that he didn't want to go to a college that didn't have fraternities and sororities. You'd think he might have stopped to look at the school catalog sometime during the two-year application process.

Plebe summer was also the time when plebes auditioned for

entry into the glee club and choirs, and I would often stop by Dr. Talley's office to sit in on auditions or discuss the prospects for the choirs. Because tenors were always hard to find and several of our strongest had graduated that year, I kept an eye on those plebes who were selected for tenor positions in the choirs. I wanted to make sure they didn't freak out during plebe summer and decide to quit the choirs in the hope that it would give them more free time during the year. They didn't yet realize how important that escape would be to their survival.

One plebe who had auditioned for the glee club was a fellow named Pete Corcoran. Dr. Talley said he had a good voice and would be a needed addition to the choir, so I took the time to keep an eye on his progress through the summer. He seemed to be having a pretty difficult time of it, so when the choir selections were posted and he was on the list, I decided to pay an unexpected visit to his room. Now, the last thing any plebe wants to see during plebe summer is three stripes walking into his room. A one- or two-striper is bad enough.

When I walked through the door, he and his roommate jumped to attention, reciting the standard name, rank, and alpha code as fast as they could. They were clearly wondering what the hell they could have done to attract a three-striper to their room. After they had finished, I walked around the room slowly, examining a few details just to let the tension build.

"Mr. Corcoran," I said finally.

"Yes, sir," he answered in a quick but obviously nervous tone. I paused a moment longer, while beads of sweat glistened on his forehead. He was preparing for the worst, the most dreaded of plebe-summer nightmares. A three-striper had tracked him down and was obviously going to eviscerate him right here in his own room, and he wasn't even sure why.

"I hear you made it into the glee club," I said, relishing the shock of surprise that crossed his face.

"Yes, sir," he responded, not quite certain if this was good or bad.

"Congratulations," I said. "You're going to enjoy it."

A huge grin broke out across his face. "Thank you, sir," he said. And with that I walked out of the room, leaving them both in a state of mild shock and relief. I figured it wasn't much, but it was probably the least critical thing he'd heard that summer, and I hoped it might provide a little bit of needed encouragement.

Another plebe I had noticed on the list was Alan Kinney, who was in the platoon that would enter my company after the summer. About halfway through the second set, Alan had screwed up on something and had been ordered to report one evening for battalion come-around. Surprisingly, he never showed up. Obviously these things did not go unnoticed (or unpunished), so I stopped by his company area later that evening to track him down.

The summer company was in the middle of a group comearound, so I pulled Alan away and into the doorway of our company officer's office. I was livid that he had missed comearound, and he knew it. After only a few seconds he was literally shaking and dripping with sweat. I expected him at least to have some excuse, but he finally admitted that he had simply forgotten the come-around. It was a monumental screwup in what had obviously been a tough few days.

I was pissed off, but I was also concerned about him. He was clearly on the verge of snapping, of being overcome by the pressure that surrounded him, and I decided to back off for a minute by changing the subject. Remembering his involvement in the choir, I asked him how things were going so far. To my surprise, he said he had decided to drop out of choir because it was taking up too much time.

I knew his decision was a big mistake, especially this early in the year. Although I couldn't order him to change his mind, I was in an ideal position, considering his missing come-around, to propose a "bargain." I told him that he could choose between showing up for battalion come-around every day for the rest of the week, or sticking with the choirs into academic year. He was obviously surprised by the offer and happy to choose the latter option. It was a decision he would thank me for many times later.

As plebe summer ended and the brigade returned, we transferred back to our academic-year companies. During first semester, I held the rank of squad leader, heading up my own squad of twelve midshipmen. Being a squad leader was sort of like having a family. I worked closely with my squad every day, and the squad looked to me for guidance and support. We ate our meals together, kept track of each other for formations, marched together, and helped each other with homework. Although there was something uniquely challenging and exciting about working as a high-level striper, my experience as a squad leader helped to put everything into perspective. It reminded me that the military, like any organization, is nothing more than the people in it. The key to successful leadership lies in understanding and respecting the people who work for you.

In addition to being a squad leader first semester, I was also elected president of the Catholic choir. I took on the responsibility of managing that group and organizing its various trips, performances, and rehearsals throughout the year. One of the choir's annual trips was to New York to sing at St. Patrick's Cathedral. Part of the reason behind this trip is that Cardinal O'Connor, whom I would later come to recognize as one of the nation's leading homophobes, was formerly chief of chaplains for the Navy, holding the rank of rear admiral. Before that, he had served as the chief of chaplains at the Naval Academy.

I had been to New York City several times singing with the choirs but had never really had a chance to see much while we were there. Nothing was ever organized for us to do in our free time, so we spent most of it just wandering around the streets with no comprehension of where to go or what to do. Because this would be my last choir trip to new York, I wanted to do something memorable and decided to arrange tickets for the choir to see *A Chorus Line* on Broadway.

I had never seen a show in New York before and knew nothing about *A Chorus Line* beyond its reputation. Nearly the entire choir was there—about sixty mids looking pretty obviously military, even in our civilian clothes. Toward the end of the show I was taken by surprise when one of the characters, a young dancer named Paul, poignantly described coming to terms with his own homosexuality. Through the entire scene, I was transfixed. Everything he related I had felt myself—the same uncertainty and fear, the same denial and self-hatred. I had also experienced the self-acceptance that made all the suffering worthwhile—the great reward of finally discovering the beauty of the person he had fought so hard to extinguish.

It was the first time I had ever experienced a realistic, positive, and compassionate depiction of a gay person, the first image that didn't make me feel ashamed. And when Paul described his parents' accepting him after discovering he was gay, I longed more than anything to feel that same reassurance. I wanted to know that my parents would still love me, that my sisters and all my friends would still accept me even if they knew I was gay.

I had half expected a few moans when the gay theme came up, but there were none. It wasn't until afterward that I realized how deeply the show had affected the other members of the choir. Several of them, both men and women, had been moved to the point of tears. They were grateful and appreciative that I had made the effort to arrange the tickets. For me, it was an unexpected and moving personal experience, a small, crucial moment of reassurance that I would never forget. As I left the theater, I wondered how many of my fellow choir members were having the same thoughts.

That evening, Dr. Talley and his wife, Marcia, asked if I wanted to join them for dinner with friends of theirs who lived in town. They added a sort of disclaimer to the offer, explaining that their friends were a gay couple—a former Navy officer named "Copy" Berg and his friend Paul Nash. Copy had sung in the glee club back in the 1970s when he was a midshipman. While serving in the Navy after graduation, he had been given a dishonorable discharge for homosexuality. He gained national attention when, together with Air Force Sergeant Leonard Matlovich, he filed a lawsuit, which was eventually settled out of court but changed the military's policy of giving automatic dishonorable discharges to all gay service members regardless of the character of their service.

Needless to say, I was thrilled by the chance to meet Copy and Paul, but I didn't want the Talleys to think I was overly eager.

"It doesn't bother me," I said. "I'd still like to go."

"Don't feel like you have to if you really don't feel comfortable," Marcia responded, making sure I had an out.

"No, really," I said, "I don't mind." If only they knew, I thought.

If I thought seeing the show had been moving, it was noth-

ing compared to meeting Copy and Paul. Here were two perfectly normal-looking guys, nothing like the horrid stereotypes
I had grown up assuming all gay people were like. They were
charming, witty, and unpretentious. There were a million things
I wanted to know, but I was too afraid to ask. It was enough, at
least, to simply spend time with two men who were completely
comfortable and open about their sexuality, neither flaunting
nor(hiding it, but simply being themselves. And it was so encouraging that they were friends of the Talleys', a couple to
whom I had grown so close over the past four years. At least I
knew that when I decided to come out to them, they would
accept me as they accepted Copy and Paul.

Although I was still completely closeted, I knew I would
eventually have to come out in some way, to someone. Meeting
Copy and Paul in New York, seeing *A Chorus Line,* my own
growing understanding—these all helped me feel better about
being gay, and to shed the final remnants of guilt that had surrounded every thought about my sexuality. I had come to accept
myself in the vacuum of Annapolis and with essentially no outside support. And although I had been successful through that
long journey, it had been an isolated and lonely one. From the
beginning I had sought only self-acceptance. But now I needed
more than that. I needed to know if my friends would accept me
as well.

Since the beginning of the semester, I had spent a good deal
of time with Alan Kinney and Pete Corcoran. Because of my
early contact with them, we usually talked and hung out together during choir rehearsals and trips. They both seemed constantly to be in some kind of academic or other trouble, and I
was always trying to cheer them up and keep them motivated.

After a while, a friendship and trust had developed between
us that I didn't feel even with some of my own classmates. I
think the difference in our ages and the fact that I was a senior
made our relationship more like that of an older brother with his
younger brothers, which was something I had never had growing up.

When I finally made the decision to come out to a friend at
the academy, it was Alan Kinney who I decided would be the
first. Later that semester, on a glee club trip out of town, I told

him that I was gay. Although I was extremely nervous about
confiding in another midshipman, even Alan, his reaction was
positive and understanding, and our friendship continued unal-
tered. We continued to discuss my homosexuality on other occasions and even to joke about it privately. I was so encouraged
by Alan's reaction that I decided to tell Pete Corcoran shortly
thereafter. Although his reaction was similarly accepting, it was
clear that the whole concept bothered him a little. He was from
a highly conservative background, not unlike that of many midshipmen, and although our friendship continued, we didn't
spend much time discussing my being gay.

Neither of them was gay, so it was reassuring to me to
know they valued my friendship more than the homophobia
they were exposed to daily at Annapolis. And despite the risk I
knew my confidence involved, I trusted their promises to keep
it between us. It was a powerfully liberating feeling to know that
at least two of my friends realized I was gay and still accepted
me. It was as though the burden I had been carrying for so long
was finally starting to lift off my shoulders.

Later that fall, I was saddened by the news that my sponsors, John and Anne, had decided to sell their home and move
to Florida. We had become very close over the years, and I had
spent many of my free weekends at their home. They were
determined not to abandon me, though, and arranged for another couple in Annapolis to "adopt" me for my remaining
year.

As I was overcoming the depression of losing John and
Anne, Dr. Talley informed me that I had again been chosen by
the commandant to sing the national anthem for the Army-
Navy game in December. I would be the only person ever to
sing it twice at the game. After gratefully accepting, I set to
work practicing once again for the event. When the day of the
game finally arrived, I gave what I felt was a considerably better
performance than my sophomore rendition. Of course, this time
I had the benefit of experience—and my mom's lucky penny
taped inside my wallet.

Before Christmas leave, the second-semester striper positions were announced and I was assigned to be the 6th Battalion
commander. This position was one of the ten highest command

ranks at Annapolis, with direct command of one sixth of the brigade, or about eight hundred midshipmen.

I returned from Christmas leave wearing the four gold stripes of a battalion commander on my sleeves, and overseeing a staff of five first-class midshipmen. Along with the rest of my staff, I moved into a set of three staff rooms next to the battalion office. My new roommate was Brad Schmidt, my battalion adjutant, who was also from 35th Company.

As part of the brigade's command structure, I was directly responsible for all aspects of the battalion's operation, from leading formations to creating and implementing new policies. I also met every week as part of the "brigade staff" with our brigade commander and his staff, as well as the two regimental commanders and five other battalion commanders. During these weekly meetings of the academy's highest-ranking midshipmen, we discussed and debated new ideas and policies affecting the brigade. Although the brigade commander reserved the power to make each decision, our input and advice were a crucial part of the decision-making process.

In addition, I met daily with our regimental commander and the two other battalion commanders in our half of the brigade. These were followed by meeting with the six company commanders in my battalion. In this way we passed along information regarding formations, events, and new policies, assigned tasks, and gathered input and suggestions. These daily meetings made up the lines of communication between each of the many command levels at Annapolis.

With my new responsibilities as battalion commander, it was all I could do to keep up with academics and my involvement in the choirs. But I was doing exactly what I had always hoped to do.

Pete Corcoran had not been doing well militarily or academically, and he told me shortly into the semester that he had decided to quit Annapolis. He had already made it through most of the year, and I tried to convince him to stay, at least until youngster year. After considerable effort, however, I finally accepted that there was no keeping him.

During the spring, I interviewed for admission into the Navy's nuclear power program for submarines. Submarine service is one of the most selective specialties in the Navy, and candidates had to qualify just for the opportunity to interview in Washington, D.C. Those of us who were selected went through a day of interviews with submarine officers and civilian specialists to evaluate our academic and professional qualifications. After these interviews were completed, we each met individually with the admiral in charge of the entire submarine service.

Altogether, it was a nerve-racking day. The fact that I had earned my submarine pin gave me some advantage, but my mathematics scores weren't particularly outstanding. One nightmare interview focused almost exclusively on a discussion of differential equations, my worst subject. The other interviews went much better, and my submarine experience proved especially helpful. My roommate, Greg, also interviewed, so we spent the weeks after the interviews trying to keep each other from worrying about the results.

The letters eventually started trickling in from Washington. When mine showed up in my mailbox I brought it to my room, breathed a deep breath, and ripped it open. I immediately spotted the magic introduction, "Congratulations!" and knew I had been accepted. After years of anticipation, I was finally certain that I would enter the submarine service following graduation. Greg's acceptance arrived a few days later, and we celebrated with a dinner in Annapolis with Sarah. It seemed almost too good to be true, but our futures were set.

That semester had been the culmination of everything I had hoped to achieve at Annapolis, more than I dared dream possible. With only a few short months to graduation, we would soon be throwing our hats in the air. The finish line was in sight and the senior countdown had begun. Now it was simply a matter of time.

7

⟶☆

"Are You
a Homosexual?"

One day early in March, I stopped by glee club practice. We were beginning to prepare for our annual spring oratorio and this year we would be performing Handel's *Ode for St. Cecelia's Day*. It was a piece I had first heard during my youngster year and it had so impressed me that I recorded it for Dr. Talley.

He was equally impressed and agreed that we should perform it. Although he had already made plans for the next spring oratorio, he offered to use it during the spring before my graduation. The tenor solos would be mine, he promised, as a graduation present.

Dr. Talley had arranged private voice lessons for a few soloists during the year, and I was on my way to a lesson out of town. I had just stopped by practice to catch up with people and kill a few minutes before I had to leave. As practice got under way, I grabbed my things and started for the door.

Just then, Alan Kinney came up and said he needed to talk to me. He looked upset, and I assumed he was in some kind of trouble. We walked out to the hallway, and I asked him what was going on. "This afternoon," he said, pausing for a moment, "I was called in for questioning by the Naval Investigative Service. They're investigating allegations that you're a homosexual."

I looked blankly at him, feeling my heart drop deeper in my chest. I was stunned, as though my whole body had suddenly become numb, drained of feeling. Everything was silent, except for the sound of blood rushing through my head, driven by the deep, hard pounding of my heart.

"And what did you say?" I asked quietly, speaking as if from mere reflex.

"I denied everything," he said. "I told them you never said anything about it."

"Did you ever tell anyone?" I asked.

"Only my girlfriend," he said, "and I know she would never tell anyone. I'm sure she wouldn't. She wasn't upset about it or anything; it was no big deal to her."

I didn't know what to think, whether to believe him, what to believe. I asked him to call his girlfriend and find out for sure if she had told anyone. The only other person it could have been was Pete Corcoran, but I couldn't believe he would tell anyone. After all, he was back home. He wasn't even part of the military anymore.

As I drove out of town, I was still in a daze. This day had started like any other, with the sound of bells ringing through empty hallways. I had put on my uniform as I had a thousand times before.

But this day had become like no other. In a only few short moments everything had changed. For the first time, I felt fear— deep, biting, overwhelming fear. I was only two months from graduation. After all that I had endured, I couldn't believe this was happening. I had been so stupid, I thought, so completely insane to trust anyone with something this important.

The following day, Alan told me that he had contacted his girlfriend. She said she hadn't told anyone. I wasn't sure whether to believe her or not. Even if she was lying, as long as Pete hadn't said anything I might be all right. They couldn't kick me out for a simple rumor. At least I hoped they couldn't.

During the next few days, I tried to simply forget about the whole thing, to forget that Alan had even mentioned the investigation. If they really wanted to kick me out, I thought, there was little I could do to stop them. Even without any real evidence, they could probably do anything they wanted. If there was one thing I had learned in four years, it's that mids really have no power at all. We are completely at the mercy of the officers who run the academy. If they want to destroy any one of us, right or wrong, they'll find a way.

As the week went on, I found it increasingly difficult to avoid thinking about the investigation. I wondered who else the NIS would call in for interviews, how many of my friends would be questioned, and how long it would take until the rumor started circulating through the brigade. Once that happened, I knew there was no stopping it, regardless of whether the rumor was true or not. My parents were going to be coming out for graduation in only a few weeks. What if the administration dropped a bombshell on me at the last minute? What if they had already decided not to let me graduate?

I had to find out what else was happening, who else they had contacted. I finally decided to call Pete. He was the only other person who knew anything at all.

That night I called Pete from the battalion conference room next to my room. When we started talking I didn't really mention anything specific at first—just asked him how things were going back home. He seemed uncomfortable, and after our initial small talk, he asked if anything was wrong. I told him about the investigation and asked him if he had been contacted by anyone. He explained that about two weeks earlier, an NIS agent had visited him at home and questioned him about me.

"And what did you say?" I asked.

There was a pause for a moment. Finally Pete said, "I told him what happened."

"What do you mean, you told him what happened?"

"I told him you said you were a homosexual," Pete answered.

I couldn't believe it. He had betrayed me. My grip on the phone tightened, and I felt my face growing hot with rage.

"I can't believe you value your loyalty to them more than to me," I said bitterly. "You've ruined my entire fucking life!" I slammed the phone down so hard I thought it would break. The phone's bell reverberated from the impact.

My hands were shaking, and I could feel my heart pounding so hard in my chest that I could barely catch my breath. After a few minutes, I got up and walked back to my room in a daze. I sensed everything slipping through my fingers. It was as if waves were washing over me, each one pounding in reality deeper and deeper: my career, the submarine corps, my battalion—my parents. My mind was racing through scenarios like a high-speed chess game.

Why would Pete have even spoken with the NIS? Alan had lied, committed an honor offense to protect me. Pete wasn't even a midshipman anymore; he had no duty to the military. Why would he want to hurt me? He could have told the NIS agent to go screw himself without fear of any retribution, but instead he had chosen to seal my fate. Whatever Pete's reasons, whether his disclosure was intentional, whether he had told his parents and they had forced him, it just didn't matter anymore. The damage was done.

I had to find a way to fix this. I hadn't come this far to simply roll over and play dead; but I didn't know who to turn to or who I could trust.

I decided that talking to one of the chaplains would be the best route. I had gotten to know Captain Byron Holderby, the academy's chief of chaplains, from singing in church. I also knew his wife, who sang in one of the church choirs. They were two of the kindest people I had ever met, and I trusted that Captain Holderby would be understanding. Maybe he could suggest something I hadn't thought of.

The next afternoon, I went to see Captain Holderby at his home on Captains' Row, the nickname for a road on the academy grounds lined with old brick houses assigned to the academy's highest-ranking officers. Just across the street was the commandant's house, and around the corner, next to the chapel, was the superintendent's residence.

I was very nervous and feeling overwhelmed by the whole situation. Should I be taking the risk of telling someone, even a chaplain, about what was going on? What if I was wrong about telling him, and it just made everything worse? All the NIS had now was the statement of one person, but once I told the chaplain, they would have irrefutable proof of my admission. All of these thoughts were streaming through my head as I rang the doorbell.

To my surprise, a female classmate of mine answered the door, but I remembered that the Holderbys were her sponsor family. I asked if Captain Holderby was in.

"He's taking a nap in the living room," she said.

I didn't want to wake him, but I knew if I didn't do this now I might not be able to build up the courage to come back. And things were moving so fast that I had to take care of it immediately.

"I'm sorry to ask this," I answered, "but it's very important. Could you possibly wake him? I really need to speak with him."

"OK," she said, seeing how concerned I was.

After a moment, she and Captain Holderby returned. He greeted me warmly, and we moved into the living room. I apologized for waking him, but he said it was no problem, closing the door behind us as I sat down on the couch. He pulled up a chair and sat down.

"So, how can I help you, Joe?" he asked.

"Well, sir," I said, "I've got a serious problem that I need to discuss with you."

"Go ahead," he said softly. I paused for a moment, not quite sure where to begin.

"I guess I should start by telling you that I'm a homosexual," I said, "but that's not really the problem—I mean, I'm pretty comfortable with it. It doesn't bother me or anything." I glanced up at him.

"Go on," he said, speaking in the same soft voice and nodding.

"Well, the real problem is that I told a few friends about it, and now there's an investigation. The NIS questioned the people I told and one of them told them everything. Now I don't think they're going to let me graduate."

The captain looked concerned. "I'm so sorry, Joe," he said. "This is serious."

"Do you think there's anything you might be able to do?" I asked. "Do you think they'll let me graduate?"

"I don't know," he answered, "but I would be willing to speak with the commandant about it. You've come this far and you have an outstanding record. Maybe they would be willing to let you graduate and just withhold your commission."

I was uneasy about having him contact the commandant. Although I was sure he and the superintendent knew about the investigation, I didn't know how much they knew or how badly they wanted to kick me out. Once Captain Holderby made his plea, there would be no turning back.

But I didn't feel like I had much choice; the wheels were already turning. Now it seemed certain that they would at least withhold my commission, but would they also deny me my diploma? After all, I was a top midshipman, finals were only two weeks away, and I really hadn't done anything wrong. I had simply told the truth about who I was.

It seemed like a better plan to take action rather than just wait. I knew that would drive me crazy, wondering when or if I would get a message to report to the commandant's office. At least this way I had some control over my own fate. Maybe if I came forward now and agreed to forfeit my commission, they would allow me to finish classes. I finally agreed with Captain Holderby that he should speak with the commandant.

It was difficult to go through the motions of the next day, not knowing when I would hear from Captain Holderby or what the commandant would have to say. It was all I could do to pay attention in classes, to do my work, wondering if I would even be back for classes the next day. I felt good about talking to the chaplain; I only hoped his news would be positive.

When I returned to my room after classes, there was a message on my desk to call Captain Holderby. I phoned him immediately and his secretary put me through.

"Good afternoon, sir," I said.

"Joe," Captain Holderby answered, "I'm afraid I don't have good news for you."

"What did the commandant say?" I asked.

"All he suggested is that you seek legal counsel. He said you should talk with the midshipman legal adviser in Mahan Hall."

"And what about graduation?"

"He didn't think that was possible. I'm sorry, Joe. Let me call the legal adviser and set up a meeting for you. I'll let him know what's going on."

I thanked him for his help and hung up the phone.

It appeared as though things had gone from bad to worse. I had truly believed in the chaplain's plan. After all, why would they not let me graduate? I had come this far. It was a question I would ask myself many times.

The following afternoon, I met with the midshipman legal adviser, Commander Reidel, in his office in Mahan Hall. The legal adviser is a military lawyer assigned to help midshipmen with legal problems. Mahan Hall also housed the academy's auditorium. I had spent many hours there rehearsing and performing in the annual spring musicals put on by the men's and women's glee clubs. Only a few weeks earlier I had performed a role in Gilbert and Sullivan's *Ruddigore,* and my parents had flown out for one of the performances. I couldn't even think of how much my parents would be devastated by the news, or how I would even begin to break it to them.

Although Commander Reidel seemed like a nice guy, I wasn't sure at first how much I could trust him. After all, he was a naval officer bound to follow his commanders like everyone else. Captain Holderby had filled him in on the details, and he wasn't very hopeful about the outcome.

"Legally," he started, "when you entered the military, you didn't forfeit any of your constitutional rights as an American citizen. But no matter what anyone tries to tell you, the bottom line is that at Annapolis, midshipmen really have no rights. The academy and the military can pretty much do whatever they want to you."

"What do you mean?" I asked.

"Do you remember the Bellistri cocaine case?" he responded.

"Yes, sir, I do." It was a case that had been covered a lot in the local papers. Early in 1986, the academy had attempted to discharge a firsty named Jeff Bellistri after a urinalysis, given randomly to test midshipmen for drug use, had come back positive for cocaine. Bellistri rigorously denied the allegation, insisting that he had not used the drug and that there must have been some error. Nonetheless, the academy's conduct and academic boards had suspended him and recommended his discharge. With the help of lawyers, he fought the discharge and won, and he was reinstated in time to graduate with his class.

Commander Reidel continued, "I worked with Jeff's civilian lawyer to help him win that case. My job is to help represent midshipmen in legal trouble, and I did it well. In fact, I did it too well. My reward from the academy was notification that I'm being transferred to another duty station. You see, the academy doesn't want midshipmen to be adequately represented; they don't want you to be able to fight back. They want the absolute power to do anything, and if they can't have it one way, they'll figure out another."

Mission accomplishment, I thought, that's what it's all about. Those two words describe basically everything the academy had taught me about working in the military. Excuses are irrelevant—the bottom line is simply getting the job done, no matter what. If the administration wanted to kick me out, they were going to do it regardless of whether or not they had adequate proof. What difference did it make to them? Even if I tried to fight back, it would take years of costly litigation, something they knew I probably wasn't financially or emotionally prepared to undertake.

"So what can I do?" I asked. "Captain Holderby has already talked to the commandant, and he said I'm not going to graduate. Do you think I should try a direct appeal to the superintendent? Maybe I could convince him to let me graduate."

"Well, it's certainly worth a shot, but I should probably put you in touch with a good civilian lawyer in the meantime. I'd be glad to put you in touch with Jeff's former lawyer. He knows as much about military law as any lawyer in the area, and he might be able to put you in touch with a civil rights group that would be willing to help you fight the discharge."

"That would be great," I said.

"I'll give him a call this afternoon and set up an appointment for you."

"Thank you, sir."

"No problem, Mr. Steffan," he said. "And be sure to let me know if any of the other mids start giving you a hard time about this. Just give me a call and I'll take care of it."

"Thanks," I said, and walked out of his office. I felt sorry for him, getting screwed by the academy for doing his job. At least I felt I could trust him. In any case, I was hopeful that a civilian lawyer might be able to help me out of this mess.

That afternoon, I wrote up a special request form asking for

a meeting with the superintendent concerning a "personal matter," and started routing it by hand up the chain of command.
That chain of command started with my new company officer,
Major Herdering, a tough, no-nonsense Marine Corps officer
who had taken over the job at the beginning of the year.

My request was certainly not a common one, especially
coming from a battalion commander. In fact, I had never heard
of anyone submitting a request of this type. Major Herdering, in
keeping with Marine Corps tradition, was determined to take
care of the problem right then and there. He was particularly
upset when I declined to discuss it with him and pressed me to
disclose the problem. He continued to question me but I continued to respectfully decline. I was tempted to just tell him;
after all, I expected him to guess it any moment. Finally, he
asked me, "Did you get a girl pregnant? Is that it? Don't worry
about that, Joe. We can take care of it."

"Not quite, sir," I responded, realizing now that he would
never guess it. "I really can't discuss it right now, but I appreciate your concern." And with that, he finally signed the form
and sent me on my way. I was greeted with similar responses
from my battalion officer, and the deputy commandant, Captain Konetzni. Neither of them appeared to have any idea what
was going on, but they put up less of a fight than Major Herdering had in approving the request.

Now I was only one step away from the superintendent.
Unfortunately, that step meant getting approval from the commandant, and he would know the reason for the request. I
turned in the request to his secretary. The commandant was
busy, so I returned to my room.

A short while later, I received a message to report to the
commandant's office. As I walked through the hallways toward
his office, I felt a sense of calm determination. Whatever was
going to happen was going to happen. I just needed to trust
myself and to not forget who I was or what I had learned.

The commandant's office is located in a hallway just off the
main entrance to Bancroft Hall. The same hallway also houses a
number of other administrative offices including the deputy
commandant's office, the conduct office, and the commandant's
conference room among others. The hallway is strangely quiet

amid the flurry of Bancroft Hall, thanks in part to a layer of carpeting over the tile floor and the fact that the area is off-limits to midshipmen not on official business.

I walked into the commandant's outer office and reported to his executive assistant, a junior officer assigned to serve as his aide. He said the commandant would be right with me, and asked me to take a seat. The strange quietness of the hallway seemed to permeate everything, and although the EA's greeting had been cordial, there was an obvious tension in the air. He undoubtedly knew the purpose of this meeting as well, and I began to wonder how long it would take before it leaked to the rest of the brigade.

I tried to keep calm, but it was difficult to ignore the obvious importance of this meeting. What would happen in the next few moments would likely determine, to a very large extent, the rest of my life. My feelings were a strange mixture of fear, anger, and pride, and I was determined that, no matter what, I was going to maintain my sense of dignity.

Finally, the EA signaled that the commandant was ready and led me into his office. The commandant of midshipmen, Captain Howard Habermeyer, was waiting just inside the door as we entered. He greeted me, shaking my hand, and motioned for me to sit as he returned to his desk. The office was relatively opulent by military standards, with dark wood paneling and blue carpeting. Behind the commandant's large wooden desk stood the United States flag and the blue-and-gold flag of the Brigade of Midshipmen. The walls were covered with pictures and plaques, memorabilia from his service as an officer in the submarine service.

Captain Habermeyer was tall, bespectacled, and quite thin, almost to the point of frailty. He and the superintendent had taken over during the previous summer, replacing Captain Chadwick and Admiral Larson, both of whom I had come to know quite well during my previous years. I regretted that they were not here now, and that my fate rested in the hands of two officers who barely knew me. I sometimes wonder if they had been there instead whether it would have changed the outcome at all. Perhaps it would at least have been more difficult for them.

I had first met Captain Habermeyer at a small leadership retreat held for the top incoming stripers of my class. The retreat was relatively informal and was held at an Annapolis hotel. At the time, he impressed me as an intelligent and articulate officer, and we had shared a conversation about his admiration of Japanese culture. It was an interest that had grown through several tours of duty he had in Japan.

I had heard since then that Captain Habermeyer was a stickler for regulations. He played everything exactly by the book. My suspicion was confirmed when the EA remained standing in the doorway as the commandant began to question me about my request. He had apparently been ordered to remain as a witness to the conversation. Despite an outward sense of cordiality, I was beginning to feel like a criminal under interrogation.

As with the previous officers, I refused to discuss the purpose of my request with the commandant, but he continued to question me. He finally stated that no one in the military has an inherent right to meet with anyone above his own commanding officer, which for midshipmen is technically the commandant. If I refused to disclose the purpose of the meeting, he would deny my request. When he again questioned me, I finally answered, "The meeting concerns a situation of which you are already aware."

"You're referring to the NIS investigation presently under way?" he asked.

"Yes, sir."

He responded; "Are you willing to state at this time that you are a homosexual?"

The moment of truth had arrived. In a way, I was surprised that he was even asking the question. Captain Holderby had already basically told him the answer. Was he offering me an out, a chance to deny it, to say that it was all a big misunderstanding? Was he offering me a chance to lie?

I looked him straight in the eye and answered, "Yes sir, I am."

It was a moment I will never forget, one of agony and intense pride. In that one statement, I had given up my dreams, the goals I had spent the last four years of my life laboring to attain. But in exchange, I retained something far more valuable—my honor and my self-esteem.

In many ways, the commandant's words were more than a simple question—they were a challenge to everything I believed in, and to the identity I had struggled to accept. In giving me the opportunity to deny my sexuality, the commandant was challenging that identity. He could just as well have asked, "Are you ashamed enough to deny your true identity in order to graduate?" More than anything I have ever wanted in my entire life, I wanted to be an outstanding midshipman and to graduate from the Naval Academy. And I firmly believe that if I had been willing to lie about my sexuality, to deny my true identity, I would have been allowed to graduate.

I had come to the academy to achieve my potential as an individual. These four years had been filled with trials and lessons from which I learned a great deal about life and about myself. But none of these lessons was more difficult, important, or meaningful than coming to understand and accept my sexuality—in essence, to accept my true identity. By coming out to myself, I gained the strength that can come only from self-acceptance, and it was with that added strength that I had been able to persevere through the many trials and difficulties of life at Annapolis.

The commandant's question was also a challenge to my honor as a midshipman. The Honor Concept at Annapolis is based on the tenet that personal honor is an absolute—you either have honor or you do not. No one can take it from you; it can only be surrendered willingly. And once it is surrendered, once it is compromised, it can never again be fully regained.

I knew that my graduation would mean absolutely nothing if I had to lie to achieve it, especially if that lie was designed to hide the very fact of my own identity. I would have given up my honor, destroying everything it means to be a midshipman. And I would have given up my identity and pride—everything it means to be a person.

The only way to retain my honor and identity, both as a midshipman and a person, was to tell the truth. I was honor bound not simply by the Honor Concept, but by its foundation: the respect for fundamental human dignity. The academy had the power to take away everything tangible that I had attained, but only I had the power to destroy my honor. Even if the academy discharged me for being gay, I could live with the knowledge that I had passed the ultimate test. I was willing to give up everything tangible to retain something intangible but far more meaningful: my honor and my identity. Even the military could not take them away from me now.

Captain Habermeyer said that he could not grant my request to speak with the superintendent because he would eventually sit in judgment over me. A performance board would be scheduled the next day, the first step toward discharge from Annapolis. Although I explained that I still desired to graduate, the commandant assured me that he did not believe the superintendent would allow it.

Before leaving, I looked at the commandant and said, "I'm sorry it had to end this way." He answered, "So am I." I truly believed him, which didn't make the imminent destruction of my life much easier to deal with. It would have been so much easier to have someone to hate, a person to blame for everything that was happening. But there was no one to blame. I couldn't blame myself because I had done what I believed right. There was only a military policy, a rule like countless others that define life in the military, rules that we learn to instinctively enforce and obey.

My perception of what was happening seemed almost detached at times, and I wondered how long it would be before I woke up to realize this was all a horrible dream. In retrospect, I don't doubt that I was suffering from shock, so completely overcome by emotion that I couldn't feel anything at all. I wanted to scream or cry or something, but there was too much to deal with, and I wondered if I would be able to stop once I started.

Not only was the nature of my life changing rapidly, but I was also anticipating how each of my relationships with other people would change. Would my parents and friends reject me as I had feared for so long, or was I not giving them enough credit? In any case, I knew it would be only a short time until the news of my disclosure would leak to the brigade, and I had to be prepared before then. I had heard a story about two male mids who were caught in bed together a year or two before I was inducted. That evening, they were both dragged from their rooms, wrapped in blankets and beaten by other mids in what was called a "blanket party." In a way, I doubted whether anyone would dare do that to me, but I wasn't too excited about the possibility.

There was no doubt in my mind that the story would leak, probably within twenty-four hours. After that, it would spread like wildfire. Annapolis is such a rumor mill that I could expect to hear about five hundred colorful variations of the story within a few hours. I decided that the best way to combat this inevitability was through a controlled release of information, and that release had to start with my closest friends at the academy.

I spent the rest of the afternoon telling six of my friends what was going on. Each of them was shocked and surprised, but they were universally supportive, even more so than I had hoped. I told them I wanted them to hear it from me first, but that they should keep it under wraps for now. I also took the time to go to each of the teachers I had in classes that semester to inform them personally. I felt a need to do this first out of respect for them, and second, to make sure that they knew I was not ashamed to face them. If I was going to leave the academy, I wanted it to be with the same level of pride I had felt as a battalion commander. I didn't want anyone to think I was running away, departing under a cloak of deserved shame. I wanted to show them I was the same person as before—exactly the same.

My professors were also universally supportive. I particularly remember the reaction of my military-law teacher, a Navy lieutenant commander. During our classes on the Uniform Code of Military Justice, he had often jokingly used "homosexual bed wetters" as the subject of military discharge proceedings, to the general amusement of my classmates. I had sat quietly in my seat, trying to chuckle along but feeling anger instead. Perhaps more than anyone, I questioned how he would react to my disclosure. He had probably been involved in a few such cases during his service as a military lawyer.

Much to my shock, when I told him he almost started to

cry. His eyes teared up as he explained that he had seen many discharges for homosexuality. And without exception, he said, they were all of individuals who were outstanding performers. He said he was truly sorry about what was happening to me, and it was obvious that he was profoundly touched. I wonder if he has ever used the "homosexual bed wetter" example since.

Another reaction that took me by surprise was when I told the Navy commander who was the officer representative for the glee club. I had gotten to know him and his family quite well during our many glee club functions. He was a serious, professional, and highly idealistic officer. Although I had great respect for him, I seriously wondered how he would react when I told him.

To say that he was stunned would be an understatement, but his reaction was one of complete personal support. He even offered to speak at the performance board on my behalf. It was not a hollow offer—he knew as well as I that it could easily have ruined his career. In that moment, the respect I felt for him grew ten times. Of all the officers I told, all of whom had been personally supportive, he was the only one willing to take a personal risk on my behalf. He never gave me any sense that my sexuality was a problem at all; in fact, before I left he gave me a hug! It was the last thing I expected from someone as straightlaced as he was, but it proved what a caring person he was, in addition to being a fine naval officer. It never ceased to amaze me how completely clueless everyone was about the possibility that someone they knew might actually be gay. I guess it comes from a complete lack of education on the subject. People come to the academy with their own ideas and prejudices about homosexuality, few with any frame of reference beyond the standard stereotypes. The primary reaction of my friends was one of disbelief. They simply could not reconcile their stereotyped understanding of homosexuals with someone they had grown to know and like over a period of years.

When I returned to my room later that afternoon, I knew my toughest task was still ahead—breaking the news to my parents. Graduation was only weeks away, and they were already making plans for their trip out, not to mention their four-year-old hotel reservations. But I knew the longer I waited, the more difficult it would be. I walked straight to the phone room and into one of the phone booths and called home.

My mom answered the phone; Dad was still at work. The conversation started with the standard small talk—the weather, things back home, schoolwork—like so many other phone calls I had made over the years. How can I break the news gently? I thought. Is there any way to take the pain out of what I have to say? I was tempted to just end the conversation and hang up as if nothing was wrong, but that would only make things worse.

But my mom had already sensed that something was wrong, whether by intuition or a tone of depression in my distracted conversation. "What's wrong, Joe?" she asked. In the quiet moments that followed, I explained to her that I was gay and being separated from the Naval Academy. I spoke softly, choking back the tears I hated to feel, knowing that I was breaking her heart, but at the same time not wanting to feel ashamed.

Her first response was simply, "Oh, Joe," in a soft voice, like a sigh overcome with sorrow and compassion. We talked a while longer, and I asked if she would tell Dad, but she didn't think she had the strength. I would have to call that night and tell him myself. I understood and told her I would call back that evening. As I said good-bye, she said, "We still love you, Joe." As tears welled up in my eyes I answered, "I love you too."

Despite everything that was going on around me, I felt an overwhelming sense of relief. I knew my mom well enough to expect that she would be as loving and accepting as ever. I had no idea how my dad would react. I suspected it would not be nearly as well.

There was plenty to do before I had to make that phone call, however. I had asked a couple of friends to stop by later that afternoon to help me start moving some things out of my room. The last thing I wanted to worry about was moving my belongings out of the hall after the story broke. Although my friends had reacted positively, I was a little concerned over whether they would show up. I thought they might be afraid of being seen with me so soon before the brigade would find out that I was being discharged. After all, they had their own reputations to worry about.

My concerns were alleviated when everyone showed up,

including a few friends I hadn't even spoken to. To my surprise, they had secured a pickup truck as well as another car to help with the move, and we immediately began packing up my things. A few minutes later, my staff roommate, Brad Schmidt, showed up and was obviously surprised to find us moving all my things out of the room. I didn't want to tell Brad anything before our staff meeting, which I had scheduled for eleven o'clock that evening. But he continued to press. Finally, I just looked at him and said, "Brad, I'm being separated for homosexuality."

At first, he didn't believe me. "Come on, Joe," he said. "You can tell me the real reason." It wasn't until Rob Connor looked at him and said, "He's not kidding, Brad," that he finally believed it.

I asked him not to tell any of the other staff members before the meeting that evening—I had to keep a lid on it for now. I thought he might be upset to find out his roommate of several months was gay, but his reaction was as kind and positive as everyone else's. He told me how sorry he was that this was happening and he helped us finish moving my things out. I was beginning to wonder if everyone was going to be so supportive. Where was all the ignorance and prejudice I had seen displayed so often at Annapolis? Was it all just a facade?

Thanks to the organization of my friends, we completely cleared out my half of the room in less than twenty minutes— the accumulation of four years: books, clothing, uniforms, my computer, and stereo system. A few minutes later we were on our way out the main gate to Dr. Talley's house.

When we arrived, Marcia was waiting for us at the door. She had tears in her eyes, and as I walked in and hugged her, the whole force of what was happening hit me like a brick wall. I started to cry as well. I didn't want my friends to see me like this, so I walked back out the door and down the street, tears streaming down my face. It was dark and cool out, and I took in deep breaths of the damp air to help calm down. It was only the second time I had cried since coming to Annapolis. Not since that night over two years earlier, the night I had sat drenched against the football field fence. If I could have seen then what was happening now, I wondered if I would have had the strength to stay at Annapolis.

More than anything, I hated feeling like I had done something wrong, like I had committed a crime. I answer "yes" to
one question and my life disintegrates—there's got to be something wrong with that. I'm the same person I was last week—
isn't that all they need to know? It seemed so obvious and
simple to me; if only they could see it from my perspective they
would understand.

When we got back to the academy, it was time to complete
the most difficult task so far—calling home to tell my father. His
was the reaction I feared most, perhaps because since childhood
it was him I had tried most to please. There was a time when I
felt like a great disappointment to him, as the skinny, uncoor-
dinated son he had so hoped would grow up to be a star football
player. But now that had all changed. I had turned out to be a
good athlete, albeit not in the sport of his choosing, and I had
achieved things at the academy far beyond his hopes or my own.
I had done things that no one from my hometown had ever done
before, things that I knew made him incredibly proud. My father had his dream son, someone he could brag about to his
friends at morning coffee. Like all fathers, he saw in me an
opportunity to relive his own youth, and perhaps a chance to
improve upon it. It hurt me terribly to think how devastated he
was going to be, perhaps not so much by my homosexuality as
by the shattering of the dreams and goals he had come to share.

When he answered the phone, the first words out of his
mouth were "I know everything—Mom told me." The fact that
he was talking in a normal tone of voice sent a wave of relief
through my body. I had called with no idea of how to even
begin telling him, but Mom had fortunately spared me that
terrible burden.

Our discussion was short, but he seemed to be taking it all
very well, almost too well. What I had thought would be far
more difficult than telling my mother turned out to be easy. His
simple message was "Do what you have to do, hang in there,
and let us know what's happening." I hung up the phone feeling
surprised and relieved. Since coming out to myself, I had often
thought about when and how I would tell my parents, and now
it was done.

At eleven that night, my staff of five was assembled in the

battalion conference room. I had also asked another battalion commander friend of mine and the brigade commander to join us. The brigade commander and I had discussed everything earlier that afternoon. My staff members had seen us moving my things out and were anxious to find out what was happening, but I had told them I would explain it all that evening.

I started by saying that, as they had probably guessed, I was being separated from the academy. I told them the separation was for homosexuality, that I was gay, and that no one else was involved. A few rumors had already started circulating through the brigade, and I wanted enough people to have the truth firsthand to keep the rumors down. I explained that the brigade commander would inform the other battalion commanders the following morning, and they in turn would inform their company commanders. That way, everyone in a position of authority would have the correct story.

They were obviously shocked, perhaps as much by the honesty and directness of my explanation as its content. My subcommander said, "You've really got balls, Joe." I dismissed the group, and as they filed out of the office, each of them shook my hand, explaining how sorry they were that this was happening. One of them had tears in his eyes. They were all good people, and we had become friends in the three months we were together as a staff.

After the meeting, I drove out to stay with the Talleys. I didn't want to be at the academy the next morning as the story was spreading. That night I barely slept. I just lay there on the edge of consciousness, amid a daze of swarming thoughts and emotions. It all seemed so unreal.

I arrived at the academy at about noon the following day, checking in with the officer of the watch, as I had been ordered by the commandant. The performance board was scheduled to begin at one o'clock, and I reported about ten minutes early to meet with the deputy commandant, Captain Konetzni. From the beginning of our meeting, I had a feeling I wasn't going to like what he had to say.

He explained that he would be in charge of the board and would ask me several questions during the proceedings. If I wanted things to go easy, he explained, I shouldn't give any answers that would make the proceedings adversarial. He warned me in a threatening tone that the academy could make things much tougher for me if it wanted to. His statements angered me, but I believed him. I was sure the academy could do just about anything it wanted to me, and there was little doubt in my mind that I would be discharged.

He then tried to mellow his tone by saying that his only concern was to make this as easy for me as possible. But there was little doubt in my mind that his true goal was to make this as painless for the academy as possible. Right now, I was a problem that the administration wanted solved. Graduation was only a few weeks away, and the last thing they needed was a scandal breaking just while the eyes of the nation were focused on the service academies.

Captain Konetzni left his office, and a few minutes later I was called into the commandant's conference room for the performance board. Seated around the large wooden conference table were the seven board members—Captain Konetzni at the head, five of the six battalion officers (excluding my own), and the brigade commander, the only midshipman on the board. They were seated three on each side of the table, with an empty chair for me at the end opposite Konetzni. Major Funk, the performance officer, was seated in the corner to observe and tape record the proceedings. I entered the room and approached my chair, standing at attention. "Midshipman Steffan reporting as ordered," I said. "Take a seat, Mr. Steffan," Konetzni responded.

Konetzni began by reading an explanation of the purpose of the performance board, which is to formally evaluate midshipmen who have demonstrated consistently unsatisfactory military performance. He listed and described the five basic requirements of military performance—performance of duty, attitude, leadership, bearing and dress, and finally, growth potential. But everyone in the room knew I wasn't here because of any deficiency in those areas. To the contrary, it was because of my excellence in military performance that I had been chosen for battalion commander. Konetzni admitted this obvious contradiction of purpose by stating, "I would normally ask your company officer to present a résumé, but since this has all occurred within a day, there is really no sense for me to do that. Your performance here as a midshipman and the issues that we look at have been outstanding."

I was here because of a special section of the Naval Academy *Performance Manual* that lists "certain traits which are undesirable in commissioned officers." More specifically, section 2.15.3e—homosexuality. It reads: "The basis for separation may include previous, prior service or current service conduct or statements. Homosexuality includes the member engaging in, attempting to engage in, or soliciting another to engage in a homosexual act or acts. It also includes statements by the member that he or she is homosexual or bisexual, or the member marrying or attempting to marry a person known to be of the same biological sex." The basis for the Naval Academy's policy is a military-wide policy banning homosexuals from military service which has been in effect since the 1940s.

After reading the explanation of the military-performance system, Konetzni asked me a series of yes-or-no questions to make sure I understood the process. I answered quickly, not wanting to appear "adversarial," as he had warned. But the final question took me by surprise. He asked, "Do you desire to be commissioned as an officer of the naval service by continuing as a midshipman at the Naval Academy?" Obviously, I wanted to graduate and everyone knew that, but that wasn't really the question. I knew that being commissioned was completely out of the question. He and the commandant had already made that clear. The answer he was expecting was "No," and I was afraid that answering otherwise would be adversarial to the proceedings. I paused for several seconds before answering, "No, sir."

After reading the commandant's account of our conversation of the previous day, Konetzni asked me for the record, "I'd like your word, are you a homosexual?" I answered, "Yes, sir." That one question would serve as the entire basis of my discharge. I had not been accused of any homosexual conduct, and the academy didn't have to prove conduct in order to discharge me. The military's policy not only allows but requires the discharge of service members who simply state that they are homosexual.

After Konetzni's obligatory questions, I was dismissed

from the room for the vote. About one minute later, I was called back into the room and Captain Konetzni read the results: "Mr. Steffan, the brigade performance board has voted secretly, and it is the vote of the brigade performance board to forward your case to the commandant of midshipmen with the recommendation of an F in military performance by reason of homosexuality and subsequent discharge from the Naval Academy."

It was a moment that I had felt was inevitable, but hearing the words made my heart sink. It had all gone so smoothly, so quickly. No one other than Captain Konetzni and I had even spoken, no additional questions were asked. The entire proceeding was simply a ten-minute formality, free of any pretense of justice. From the moment I had walked through the door, everyone had known the result that was required.

I had instantly dropped from an A in military performance to an F, as if they could simply ignore reality and rewrite history to their liking. No homosexual could be a good performer, so they would simply change my performance grade to an F. Then they would recommend my discharge for performance deficiency.

Captain Konetzni explained that the recommendation of the board would be forwarded to the commandant for his approval. After that, the commandant's recommendation would go to the academic board, the highest board at Annapolis. Only the academic board has the authority to recommend the separation of a midshipman to the secretary of the Navy. He also informed me that I was no longer a battalion commander and ordered me to vacate my room in Bancroft Hall. I would be assigned a room in Ricketts Hall, a building used to house visiting sports teams. "I think it's important that we do that," he said, "for you as well as for the Brigade of Midshipmen." I was dismissed from the room, and Major Funk brought me into his office to go over some papers.

Of all the people directly involved in these proceedings, Major Funk was the only person I felt I could trust. He had a calm, relaxed attitude, and he always treated me with great courtesy. He made me feel at ease, speaking casually about the papers I had to sign and what was going to happen next. It was his job as performance officer to coordinate the brigade performance system, including all performance boards, and he had seen a lot of board proceedings. But my case was unusual, and I knew it disturbed him. Every time he explained something, there was a tone of apology in his voice, as if to say, "I know this is bullshit, but it's my job to explain it to you."

When I sat down with Major Funk, I told him I was concerned about answering no to Captain Konetzni's last question, and that after thinking about it, I felt it didn't represent my true desire. I asked him if I could submit a letter with the board's recommendation to the commandant to explain that even if the academy wasn't going to allow me to be commissioned that I still wanted to graduate. He said I would have to wait until the hearing of the academic board to make that statement. He was expecting that a special board would be convened within the next few days.

Before the performance board, I had been willing to cooperate with the academy in the hope that they might allow me to graduate. But listening to Konetzni read the description of the purpose of the performance system drove home the hypocrisy of everything that was happening. I had been an outstanding midshipman and I deserved at the very least to graduate. But if the academy wasn't going to let me graduate, I needed to start thinking about other options.

After my meeting with Major Funk, I talked with a few friends about what was going on in the brigade. They said that after morning formation and during early classes the story had spread like wildfire. By ten o'clock, everyone at the academy knew that the 6th Battalion commander was being discharged for homosexuality. A plethora of rumors had also inevitably popped up, and throughout the day my friends kept me abreast of the most humorous ones. They began with stories of how I was caught in bed with my roommate, which later evolved into my being interrupted during a shower with a janitor. But by later that afternoon, nearly all the rumors had been squelched by people who knew the real story, primarily as a result of the information release I had set up the previous night.

The rumors were also denied by friends who were willing to stick up for me in my absence. I learned that Rob Connor had nearly punched out one mid who was spreading an obviously false rumor in one of his classes. A number of my other friends, including choir members and other stripers I had worked with, had also publicly stuck up for me against the rumors that were spreading through the brigade.

I was pleased and actually surprised at how much my friends had pulled together for me. I had expected that most of them, through either ignorance or peer pressure, would simply not want to associate with me. But it was becoming clear that I had vastly underestimated them, as well as the strength of our friendships. These were friendships that had developed over years, through often trying and difficult times. I had worked, partied, sweated, and studied with these people. It was exactly what the military wanted. Everything we were taught at Annapolis was geared toward group cohesion, toward developing a lasting bond of trust and loyalty between classmates that would extend into the fleet after graduation.

It was also an incredible test of the character of my friends. People have been discharged from the military for merely associating with known homosexuals, and although none of us expected that to happen, it was clear that my friends' continuing association with me posed at least some level of formal or informal risk. They had their own reputations to worry about, but without exception they chose to stick by me—in spite of the academy—because they knew it was right to.

The core of direct support during this week came from a group of about six friends, most of whom I had come to know through glee club and the choirs. They had been there to help me move out of my room, but even now that the brigade knew what was going on, they were in constant contact with me. They kept me up to date on what was happening, relayed messages of support from other people, brought people by to visit me, and generally made sure I was all right. They understood the tremendous stress I was under, and in the days following the performance board they actually organized a rotation among themselves so at least one person would be with me as often as possible. They tried to keep my spirits up, making me laugh despite the pressure that was tormenting me.

Over the next few days, my friends were constantly relaying messages and notes from other midshipmen, some of whom

I barely knew, who wanted to lend their support. They wanted me to know how much they admired my integrity and honesty, and how terrible they felt it was for the academy to be losing someone as dedicated and capable as I had been. Even when I was walking around the academy grounds, people would come up to me and shake my hand, ask me how I was doing, and give me a word of encouragement. At first I had completely avoided everyone, walking around outside only in-between classes, afraid that someone would scream "fag" or "queer" as I walked by. But within a day I was walking the academy grounds freely, and I never received a single derogatory comment from anyone.

Perhaps the biggest surprise of the week was when two friends I had known for years at the academy came out about their own homosexuality to me. Neither of them knew about the other, and they had each waited until no one else was around before finally sitting me down and telling me. Although they were terrified by what was happening, they each felt compelled to let me know how clearly they understood what I was going through.

In a way, I felt sorry for them. At least for me the truth was out. No matter how painful that might turn out to be, I knew it couldn't be as tough as living a life of secrecy and constant fear. Although one of them was fairly comfortable with his sexuality, the other was still trying to come to terms with it. I tried to be encouraging, but I couldn't ignore the harsh reality of my own situation. Life in the Navy was going to involve a constant risk, and the best advice I could give either of them was simply to be careful. As it happened, they both eventually graduated from Annapolis, one of them near the top of his class, and they both continue to serve today.

One of the lessons of my first few days after the disclosure was that there is a big difference between understanding and acceptance. Although most of my friends had no way of truly understanding or appreciating what it was like to be gay, they were nonetheless capable of accepting me. I remember Rob Connor asking, "Can't you just wake up one morning and decide that you're going to be straight—decide that you're going to like girls from now on?" I answered, "That would be just as easy as your waking up tomorrow and deciding that from now on you were only going to be attracted to men."

He got the point, but I found it remarkable that he had never viewed my sexuality in the same way that he viewed his own. He had only envisioned it as a deviation from some universal norm. Like many people, Rob initially saw homosexuality as a behavior, without any regard to the underlying basis of sexuality. It is not the physical act of sex that defines us as gay or straight, it is the innate physical and emotional attraction that we feel toward members of the same or opposite sex. The physical act of sex is simply one of many ways we may choose to express that attraction.

That evening, I called my parents from the Talleys' to see how they were doing. My father answered the phone. When I said hello, he tried to speak, but started sobbing so uncontrollably that he could only get out a few words. He was completely out of control, crying and muttering "Why?" over and over and saying that he could not understand how I could be gay. His reaction took me completely by surprise, and my face went hot with anger.

Finally, my mom took the phone away from him. She explained that he had had a delayed reaction and wasn't taking my coming out very well, which was obvious. But I didn't care—it was my life that was falling apart. What gave him the right to make it harder on me? I was the one who had survived four years of hell for nothing. I was the one studying every fucking night and working my ass off to make it this far. I said, "You tell him that I can come home as who I am, or I can come home in a coffin," and I hung up.

A few minutes later my father called back to apologize. "It's a difficult time for all of us," I said, "but I need all the support you can give me." He said he understood, but remained unstable through that week. Mom said he spent most of his time in a daze, sometimes crying to himself. I guess it's sort of like a death. You wake up one morning and find out your son is gay—someone you never really knew. And the dream son—the straight one—is gone forever, along with his wife and children and all the dreams you had for them.

As the days dragged on following the performance board, I

HONOR BOUND

became more and more upset about the absurdity of my discharge. I had talked to Dave Simison, the civilian lawyer that Commander Reidel had suggested, but he didn't think there was anything we could do before the academic board met to make their final decision. In the meantime, I decided to call Copy Berg about any ideas he might have. At least he could understand what I was going through.

Speaking to Copy was remarkably helpful. He could empathize with what was happening to me, having dealt with the reaction of his friends and family to the disclosure of his own sexuality. He was extremely encouraging but warned me that if I chose to make a public issue out of my discharge I should be fully aware of the possible consequences. He related some of his own experiences: being followed by NIS agents, having his car broken into and documents stolen. It could be a harsh experience trying to fight against an organization with essentially unlimited resources. He suggested that I give it some thought before making a decision.

It was clear that the academy was extremely concerned about the possibility of my fighting the discharge. I had learned that the academy's public affairs officer had called Dr. Talley in for a meeting to see if he could find out what I was up to. Although Dr. Talley wouldn't disclose any specifics, he made it clear that I wasn't the type of person who would just sit around and wait for the end without taking some kind of action.

Within a day of his comments, Dr. Talley had been subtly informed by someone in the commandant's office, presumably Captain Konetzni, that the academy was considering the possibility of court-martialing me if I tried to resist being discharged. "Court-martial me for what?" I asked him. "I haven't even done anything." I discussed it with both Copy and Dave Simison. Although they both agreed there were no grounds for a court-martial, they also knew that while I was still a midshipman, the military was in a clear position of power to do just about anything it wanted, legal or not.

Several days had passed since the performance board with no word on scheduling the academic board, but I could already feel the screws tightening. I began to wonder whether the information being channeled to me was real, or simply a bluff to make me back down without a fight. In any case, I needed to be prepared. I figured there was a fine line to be walked, and I had to make sure the academy knew that I wasn't going to be a pushover without pissing them off so much that they wouldn't consider giving me my diploma to avoid a public battle.

So far, I had been cooperative and well behaved, and I expected that would weigh in my favor. But they also needed to know that they had something to lose as well. I hoped that message had come across. In the meantime, Copy had been in touch with friends of his at the American Civil Liberties Union in New York, and they were very interested in taking on the case. I spoke with Nan Hunter, one of their attorneys, about a possible lawsuit, and agreed to contact her following the academic board hearing.

Marcia and I had been invited to stop by that evening at the home of one of the choir reps, a senior officer on the academic staff. He and his wife had accompanied us on most of our choir trips during the year, and I had grown to know and like them both. I was especially glad that they were concerned enough me ask me over.

When we arrived everything seemed perfectly normal—I talked with the commander and his wife and they expressed their concern about what was happening. Then the commander asked to speak with me privately and led me to a small living room in the back of the house. I started to wonder if this invitation had an ulterior motive—it was starting to look a little more orchestrated than I had anticipated.

The commander sat me down and started asking me about how I was feeling, how everything was going, how I was dealing with the reaction of my parents. It was obvious that he was leading up to something. Finally, he said there was something he felt certain could prevent my discharge from the academy. I was a little confused about what he could mean, but anxious to hear his idea. Before I knew it, he had pulled out a Christian tract and was reading to me about how my soul could be saved by Jesus.

My heart sank as I politely listened, trying to quell my disappointment and frustration. These were the same things I had learned through years of involvement in the church, things that had only added to the torment and guilt that I had endured

162   HONOR BOUND

in coming out. I had finally freed myself from those thoughts, and now someone I knew and trusted was trying to shove that self-denial and self-hatred down my throat again. I thought I should feel anger, but I knew he was only trying to help. All I felt was a kind of pity that he was unable to comprehend the magnitude of his ignorance. And then came the most incredible statement of the evening. He said that if I was willing that evening to accept Jesus as my personal savior and renounce my homosexuality, he would personally call the commandant and inform him that I had been converted and recommend that the proceedings against me be dropped.

I could hardly believe what he was saying; rather, I couldn't believe that someone I knew and respected, an otherwise intelligent, thoughtful, and compassionate person, could be so ignorant, and so capable of the cruelty that flows from it. I politely declined, thanked him for his concern, and left. When I explained to Marcia what had happened, she apologized for having brought me over. She had had no idea what he was going to do. Of everything I experienced at Annapolis, there was nothing more depressing or disturbing than realizing how many good, intelligent people simply have no concept of what homosexuality really is.

Finally, on Monday, Major Funk informed me that the academic board had been scheduled for that Wednesday, April 1. April Fool's Day, I thought, how appropriate. Maybe I'll get in there and they'll tell me this has all been a big joke.

Although a lawyer was not allowed to represent me or speak on my behalf at the academic board, I was allowed to bring an official observer. Dave Simison and I felt it would be best if he didn't attend the hearing—the academy was upset enough with him after the Bellistri case, and I didn't want to make them overreact. I knew that bringing any lawyer would be enough to let them know I meant business, so Dave's assistant, Christene, agreed to join me.

On the night before the hearing, I prepared a short statement that I wanted to read during the board proceedings:

Throughout the past four years, I have attempted to be a model midshipman. I have worked to the limit of my abilities, not only professionally, but through my involvement in many extracurricular activities which directly support the Naval Academy. I believe that my performance and conduct records speak for themselves in support of my statements. Although the past week has been a very difficult time for me, I am proud that I have weathered the storm with my honor, integrity, and self-esteem intact. If the board votes to separate me today, I will be faced not only with dismissal from the academy, but also with a considerable setback in the completion of my degree. Because a civilian school requires a minimum number of resident hours, I would be required to complete at least one year of school elsewhere. This comes at a time in my life when I need most the chance to be given a clean start. Considering my past record at the academy and the fact that dismissal would essentially be a punishment beyond simple dismissal, I do not believe that it is beyond the scope of reason for me to be permitted to complete the academic requirements to earn my diploma.

Early the next morning, Dave, Christene, and I met with Commander Reidel in his office to prepare for the hearing. When I showed them my statement, Dave suggested I change "I have attempted to be a model midshipman" to "I have been a model midshipman." "I guess you're right," I said, but I was already beginning to question whether anything I had to say would make a difference to the board.

Christene and I arrived outside the commandant's conference room about ten minutes early for the hearing, which was scheduled for nine that morning. Captain Konetzni was talking with some other officers outside the conference room, and it was obvious that he was not pleased at the sight of a civilian attorney accompanying me. He called over Major Funk, and they spoke for a few moments before Major Funk approached us. He was wearing his classic I-know-this-is-bullshit-but expression. "Captain Konetzni wants you to go have the stripes taken off your uniform," he said. "You mean right now?" I asked. "The academic board is supposed to start in five minutes." "Yes. He said you lost your battalion commander rank at the performance board, and you don't rate wearing four stripes anymore. Head down to the tailor shop now—we'll wait for you to get back." I was incredulous. There was clearly no way

I was expected to have my uniforms restriped before this hearing, especially when I had no idea of when it would be held. But arguing was senseless; this was simply a little taste of Konetzni's warning from before the performance board—you fuck with us, we're going to fuck with you, only worse.

I quickly walked through the rotunda to the other side of Bancroft Hall toward the basement tailor shop. Some mids were coming to and from classes, and although a few clearly recognized who I was, none of them said anything. Just as I reached the stairs to the basement, I ran into a friend of mine I hadn't spoken to since the story broke.

"Joe," he said, "what's going on? I heard—"

"Sorry," I interrupted, "I've got two minutes to get my stripes removed. We'll have to talk later."

"Good luck," he said, as I disappeared down the stairway.

"Thanks," I answered. "I'll definitely need it."

By the time I got to the tailor shop, Captain Konetzni had already called to tell them what was happening. I took off my uniform jacket, and two women hurriedly worked, opening up the black wool sleeves and snipping away the gold star and three of the four gold stripes above the cuff of each arm. They could just as well have been cutting out my heart as I watched them pluck the stray gold threads from where the stripes had been. And then, with the precision of dueling surgeons, they stitched the seams shut again, leaving the solitary stripe of a midshipman in ranks, a first-class midshipman with no command authority. As I walked quickly back through the hall to the academic board, I could feel the heat of my reddened face and the sickening grind of humiliation in my stomach. I wondered if this gave Konetzni pleasure, or if it simply made me easier to face, easier to reconcile with his image of who I was now.

When I was called into the boardroom, eight of the academy's highest-ranking officers were seated at the table, including the superintendent, Admiral Marryott. I reported as before, and was seated. Admiral Marryott began by reading the commandant's letter reviewing the performance board's findings and concurring with the recommendation for my discharge. The letter said that as a homosexual I had "insufficient aptitude for military service," by definition.

When the superintendent finished, I was granted permission to speak. I read the statement I had prepared the night before, making the change Dave had suggested. When I finished, Admiral Marryott simply said that he didn't feel there was anything they could do—the military's regulations were clear. I pointed out that the academic board had complete control over my situation. If they felt it was appropriate to let me graduate, it was well within their power to allow it. But Admiral Marryott just stared blankly back at me. I glanced around the table; no one else was even looking at me. They were just staring down at their papers. For them, the decision was already made. It had been made when I first met with the commandant. They were never going to take a chance on this case—it might mean the end of their careers.

I finally realized the futility of my hopes. Despite everything that had happened, I had still believed there was a chance. But for all the academy's idealistic teachings, its glorification of truth and personal honor, when push came to shove the bottom line was covering your own ass. Every single one of them knew I was right. They knew I was as completely capable of serving my country as they were, but it didn't matter. I was dismissed for the vote.

Moments later, I was called back to learn that the board had voted unanimously for dismissal. I walked out of the room and into the hallway. As the officers filed out, several of them came up to shake my hand and speak with me. My battalion officer said I shouldn't be disappointed. "You were a great midshipman, Joe," he said. "You could easily have been the brigade commander. You can do anything you want in life." I want to serve my country, I thought bitterly, shaking his hand. He even offered to write letters of recommendation on my behalf, but the truth was that the last letter he had written was to the performance board recommending my discharge. It was all so cordial, so professional. It was sickening.

Major Funk called me into his office to explain the next steps. He said that, technically, I had two choices: I could submit my resignation in light of the board's decision or I could write a letter to the Secretary of the Navy explaining why I should be retained. He said that the latter option was futile because I had admitted my homosexuality, and to his knowledge, no one had ever been retained who admitted being gay. He added that if I appealed and was discharged, my discharge certificate would have a code that meant "homosexual," and that could turn up to haunt me in the future. But if I resigned, my certificate would just say "voluntary resignation." The bottom line was that I was getting kicked out of the Navy and my only real choice was how long I wanted it to take.

Christene and I drove to Dave Simison's office outside town to discuss our next move. I told her and Dave that before we did anything, I had to call my parents and let them know what was going on. I hadn't told either of them about a lawsuit. When I discussed the possibility with my mom, she was completely opposed. This was all difficult enough, she explained, without turning it into a national case. I tried to reason with her, but it was useless.

I was incensed, but she pleaded with me not to do it, to just get it behind me and get on with the rest of my life. In the end, I agreed that she was probably right. What was the use of fighting against the government? What I really needed was to get my life back on track.

I walked into the next room and told my lawyers that I had decided not to fight the discharge. I explained that it was simply more than my family or I could take right now. They were understanding, and we called Nan Hunter at ACLU to explain my decision. She also understood, and assured me that it was a decision only I could make. I thanked them all for their help before Christene drove me back to the academy. That afternoon, I handed in my resignation.

During the next two days, I completed the tasks of separation. There were forms to fill out, papers to sign, boxes to pack. As the final insult, I was even ordered to turn in my class ring. On the day before I was to leave the academy, I walked into town wearing my ring. I went into a jewelry store and handed it to the jeweler. He didn't believe me when I told him to pry the stone out of it, but he soon realized I was serious. It was my stone and I was going to keep it, the single memento of a former life. That afternoon, I turned in my class ring exactly as I had received it—without a stone.

On the way out of Bancroft Hall, I stopped in the academy's main office to complete the final task: checking out on leave for the last time. "Leave pending separation," the academy calls it, graciously allowing me leave before the paperwork for my discharge was completed by the Secretary of the Navy's office.

The following day, I packed everything I owned into my car and drove away from Annapolis, leaving behind four years I never wanted to think about again.

8

※

The Simple Truth

My long trip from Annapolis ended in Syracuse, New York, the home of my aunt and uncle, Jane and Harvey Lillestol. They were two of our closest relatives, and when my parents had called to explain my discharge from Annapolis, they had offered to take me under their wing. Jane was a dean at Syracuse University and had also offered to help me transfer to Syracuse to finish my degree.

When I arrived they were very comforting, and they made an effort not to overreact to my discharge. They wanted me to know that they cared while trying to keep me positive and motivated toward the future.

I moved my things into a small bedroom on the third floor. It was pretty cramped, but at least it was my space—no roommates, no inspections, no bells in the morning. The first thing I moved in was my stereo, and I spent much of my newfound free time listening to music.

It wasn't long, though, before I found that most of the recordings I owned reminded me too much of Annapolis. This was music I had studied and fallen asleep to over the years. It had been such a part of my life there, a quiet respite from the drudgery and pressure. I found myself playing the few new discs I had bought recently over and over again. They were new, different—like my new life. I didn't want to look back. I just wanted to pick up the pieces and move on, to cut those lost years out of my life, my memory—to move on and never think of them again.

As my battalion officer had pointed out, I now had the chance to do (almost) anything I wanted. That meant earning a business degree and starting work on a career outside the military. If I was going to overcome this devastation, I would simply have to discard my old dreams and create new ones. This would only be a brief stumble, for if Annapolis had taught me anything, it was how to survive.

Jane was wonderful. She helped me speed my application through the administrative red tape, and even worked out a special two-year curriculum to finish my last year of undergraduate school and complete an MBA at the same time. We also spent time talking about my parents and their reaction to what was going on. She was very supportive and understanding, and her years in college environments and living in more metropolitan areas had given her a broader perspective on the issue than my parents had.

My classes weren't scheduled to begin until the summer, so I spent a good deal of time watching television coverage of the Iran-contra hearings, which had captivated the attention of the country. I was particularly interested because Oliver North, John Poindexter, and Robert McFarlane had all graduated from the Naval Academy. McFarlane's son, Scott, was a classmate of mine at Annapolis, and we had sung together in a church choir and glee club. Although Scott and I weren't close, I had met his father at an Army-Navy-game party during senior year that the McFarlanes had hosted. McFarlane seemed like a good, well-meaning person, and I was sorry to see him and his family hurt by the incident.

Iran-contra had been a hot topic during much of my senior year at the academy, and Oliver North had practically been elevated to sainthood in the eyes of most midshipmen. After all, he was only circumventing the wishes of Congress, who were just a bunch of liberals. At the time, I considered myself pretty conservative, but I had had serious concerns about the whole incident.

I remember an interesting letter that I read in a magazine one morning while I was waiting for a haircut at the academy. It was written by a classmate of Oliver North's who had served as brigade commander during then Midshipman North's senior year. The former brigade commander explained in the letter that

North had been involved in a serious car accident while he was a midshipman. He was left with injuries that were not debilitating, but might have precluded his commissioning as an officer in the Marine Corps, which had always been his goal.

Late one evening, well after taps, when all midshipmen were required to be in their rooms, the brigade commander found Midshipman North in an administrative area of Bancroft Hall. When asked why he was up past taps, North told the brigade commander that he was looking for his medical file. He explained that he wanted to remove the records related to his car accident so they wouldn't jeopardize his entrance into the Marine Corps.

Although North's actions would clearly have been a conduct offense as well as an honor offense, the brigade commander was so moved by his apparent dedication to service that he decided not to intercede or report the incident. He never found out if North had achieved his goal, but North was allowed to enter the Marine Corps following his graduation from the academy.

Only years later, the former brigade commander explained, had he come to see the full effect of his failure to uphold the Honor Concept. On that evening years before, Oliver North had proven that he was willing to do whatever was necessary, to lie and cheat, to destroy documents, in order to advance his own goals. And although the reason seemed good, almost honorable, back then, the brigade commander discovered too late that the reason is not all that matters. In that moment, Oliver North had shown his true character. He had crossed the line beyond which the ends justify the means, and beyond which honor is irrelevant.

As I watched Oliver North proudly testify that he had lied to Congress, that he had willingly and gallantly deceived the American people to advance his own agenda, I wondered what had been the worth of my sacrifice. What was the value of honor when so many people, including President Reagan, lined up to pay North homage for his dishonesty? I began to wonder whether honor really exists at all, or if it's just an old principle stored away in old institutions, kept like a jewel in a dusty box to be taken out on occasion and admired.

Within a few weeks of my arrival in Syracuse, I began

feeling restless to return to Annapolis. My departure had been too quick, and it had felt too much like I was running away. Also, my classmates were going to be graduating soon, and I wanted to see them one last time before they shot off to all corners of the globe. Showing up for graduation would have been too painful, so I decided to return for one of the last weekends before graduation week. It would be healthy, I thought, like getting back on a horse right after a fall. A part of me also wanted people to know that I wasn't ashamed or afraid to show my face there.

My weekend back at Annapolis was spent with friends from the brigade, and on Sunday I attended services at the academy chapel. At church, I saw many of the people I had come to know from my weekends spent singing there. Although the story of my discharge had never really become public, nearly everyone associated with the academy knew what had happened. The only local publicity had been a small article in the Annapolis paper, *The Capital*, reporting that an unnamed midshipman had been forced to resign from the academy after admitting his homosexuality.

Both before and after the service, I was surprised by the number of people who came up to greet me and to see how I was doing. Many of the people who went to church at the academy were retired officers and their families whom I had gotten to know over the years, and they went overboard to let me know how happy they were to see me again. I hadn't really had a chance to say good-bye to many of them before, and it was clear that they had been concerned and worried about me. I got a lot of hugs and pats on the back, and it felt good to know that I hadn't been forgotten.

I even spoke with the commandant and superintendent and their wives following the service. The "supe" complimented me on how good I looked in a suit. "You look just like a regular businessman," he said. I tried to smile politely, knowing that he meant well, but I hated the image. Despite my efforts to avoid blaming them for what had happened, I couldn't ignore the anger I felt inside as we spoke. They may have simply been doing their jobs, but that didn't mean that what they had done was right.

I felt strange talking with everyone about my acceptance to
Syracuse, the classes I would be starting soon, and my plans for
a new life. Although I tried to appear upbeat, I felt a tug in my
gut every time I thought about that life. It was a life I had never
wanted, a choice I had never made. As my friends shared their
own postgraduation plans, I simply couldn't stop thinking about
the plans and hopes that had once been my own.

All around me, the academy was exactly as I had left it,
every nuance, every detail. The people I knew were still here,
and we talked and laughed as on each of a hundred Sundays
before. In many ways, it was like I had never left at all. If not for
my new clothing, I could have rejoined it all so smoothly, without even missing a beat.

But there was a barrier to those dreams, a barrier that was
both invisible and impenetrable. It was not a barrier of ability,
enthusiasm, or dedication—it was purely a barrier of perception. I saw that barrier in the eyes of the commandant and the
superintendent, and even in the looks of some of my own
friends. I had returned, in part, to prove that I was the same
person as before, the same person that they had all known,
respected, and even admired. But in their eyes, I could see that
that person no longer existed. To them, I had become someone
else.

That feeling of transformation reminded me of a book entitled *Black Like Me,* which I had read back in high school. It
was written by a white man who used drugs and dye to change
the color of his skin while traveling through the Deep South
during the 1950s. He wrote about how it felt to be treated as a
black man one day and a white man the next, sometimes by the
same people. He had seen the barrier of race, sometimes subtle,
sometimes blatant. Although his book had deeply moved me, it
wasn't until that Sunday morning at Annapolis that I truly came
to appreciate what he had experienced. In the eyes of so many
people, I was no longer Joe Steffan, the battalion commander,
outstanding midshipman and leader—I was simply Joe Steffan,
the homosexual. That one aspect of my identity, only one part
of who I am, had suddenly expanded to eclipse everything else.

Part of the reason I had returned to Annapolis was to experience the sense of belonging I had known as a midshipman,

the feeling of being a part of that place and its uniqueness, its history. It was clear to me now that I had missed the chance to savor that feeling during my final days. There was no real closure to my life there, simply a quiet void, a nothingness that echoed my own feelings of emptiness. I no longer belonged there. I was just a visitor, like any other tourist walking the yard and wondering what it would be like to live there as a midshipman, to be a part of Annapolis. Unlike a visitor, I had once known that feeling; I knew how it felt to belong there. As I said my good-byes and drove out the main gate on my way back to Syracuse, I wondered whether those memories were a gift, or simply a source of bitter regret that I would carry with me for the rest of my life.

Shortly after returning to Syracuse, I began preparing for my first trip back home. Most of my family was planning to meet for Easter at the home of relatives in Fargo, North Dakota. I was particularly anxious about seeing my parents again for the first time since my discharge. Even though I knew this meeting would be uncomfortable, I wanted my parents to see that I was all right, and that I was still the same son they had always known.

When I arrived in Fargo, everyone avoided the topic of my discharge from Annapolis. Only a few relatives knew why I had really left, and everyone else had been told that I simply chose to resign before graduation. Either way, they knew it was a sensitive topic and avoided it.

Even my parents and I evaded our inevitable discussion until practically the last moment before I left, when they finally asked to speak with me alone. We went upstairs to an empty bedroom away from everyone else. I could tell by their faces that it was time to have a serious discussion about what was going on.

They began by asking what I wanted to do about my homosexuality. When I seemed confused by the question, they explained that they would be happy to spend whatever it would take to treat me, that they would find the best psychologist in Syracuse to help cure me.

At first, I was surprised. They had seemed relatively accepting during our conversations over the past weeks, despite my dad's initial reaction. If anything, I had actually felt encouraged. Now it was obvious that their acceptance had not been at all complete.

I tried to explain that my sexuality was not an illness, mental or otherwise, and it was not a "problem" as far as I was concerned. The categorization of homosexuality as a mental disorder was abandoned over twenty years ago, and not even the military considers it an illness. The so-called cures for homosexuality are nothing more than attempts at brainwashing in its most classic and obscene form.

In one variation, the patient is administered a drug to induce nausea and then shown a series of homoerotic images. Sometimes, a painful electric shock substitutes as the conditioning stimulus. After a long series of these "treatments," the patient's mind eventually learns to associate homosexuality with pain. The result is not heterosexuality, but a partial and temporary suppression of homosexual thoughts. The same method could just as easily be used to suppress heterosexuality, but it changes nothing in reality. It is simply an invidious means of hiding what lies within, another chance at denial.

I tried to explain to my parents that homosexuality is a normal orientation for about 10 percent of any population, and I was one of those 10 percent. What I really needed was not to be treated like an outcast—I had already had my fill of that. I just needed them to accept me for who I am, not who they would like me to be.

But the more we talked, the more they resisted accepting the reality of my homosexuality. This was their last chance to deny that I was really gay. They were pressing for me to tell them that I wanted to change, trying every parental trick in the book, from bribery to good old Catholic guilt, but none of them worked. I had endured plenty of guilt in my own acceptance of my sexuality, and I was much harder on myself than my parents were. The more they pushed, the more angry I became, until I finally refused to discuss it any longer. I had dealt with enough ignorance, stupidity, and intolerance at Annapolis to last me a lifetime; I didn't need it now from my parents.

Since leaving the academy, I had experienced my first real taste of freedom from outside control. I had more freedom than

I had ever known, but now I felt like I was suffocating. My parents were trying to cram me back into the old image they had of their son. In my anger over their reaction, I became determined to become truly independent, to take complete control of my life. I couldn't live under my parents' thumb or stand having them watching over me.

I was determined to find a job, leave Syracuse, and work my way through school. I didn't want anything from my parents, and I wasn't going to let them pay my way. I was going to do it myself, free of obligation to anyone else.

I extended my stay in Fargo through the week and interviewed for a job at a computer software company. The following day, I was offered a position. I flew back to Syracuse, packed up my car again, and drove for two days back to North Dakota.

Within a few weeks I started work and completed my transfer to begin night classes at North Dakota State University in Fargo. A good portion of my credits from Annapolis were transferable, and even after all the military credits were stripped out I still had more than were required to graduate with a Bachelor of Science degree. But like most schools, NDSU required at least one full year of credits at their school as a minimum requirement for graduation.

After starting my job, I began taking night classes, working until five, and then attending classes until nine or ten. It was a frustrating situation. At Annapolis, I had been only weeks from graduation. Now, with more than enough credits to graduate, I would have to spend at least a year and a half taking part-time classes. With little time to study, I was tired, depressed, and completely devoid of motivation.

My depression was only worsened by nagging thoughts about the academy. I had tried to keep from thinking about Annapolis, concentrating on moving ahead. But as weeks turned into months, I couldn't shake the memories of my discharge. Every night as I fell asleep, images of the board hearings kept flashing through my head. My mind was constantly replaying them, trying to figure out what had happened or to find the missing piece that might have salvaged everything.

Since first questioning my sexuality, I had practically made an art out of suppressing my emotions. I was still trying to carry on that tradition by ignoring the trauma of my discharge. But as hard as I tried, I could not avoid thinking about what was clearly the most difficult experience of my life. Every day was filled with thoughts and emotions spilling over from that week at Annapolis.

Despite the obvious difficulty of my discharge, I also thought about what it had taught me about life. Up to that point, I had been too career- and goal-focused, all but ignoring the true value of my relationships with other people.

But, as with any great trial, I learned important lessons that will forever shape my outlook on life. If there is one thing I brought away with me from Annapolis, it was the realization that people are truly the most important part of our lives. In a matter of moments, I had lost what I had perceived to be everything of value in my life—my hopes, my career, years of hard work and dedication to a goal that I had placed above all else. I was left with nothing, as if the previous four years of my life had simply been erased.

If it had not been for the support and compassion of my friends at Annapolis, I wonder if I could have endured the trauma. When everything else was gone, I looked into the bare core of my life, the most basic part of what makes life worth living. I discovered just how transitory and uncertain life is, and that we truly possess nothing. Never has this reality been more clear to me than in those nights I spent alone in Ricketts Hall, with only a metal cot and desk, and my uniform hanging from a hook on the wall. I will never forget how it felt to face a circumstance I had never dared to conceive turned into stark reality.

Certainly I had survived that onslaught, choosing my identity over self-destruction, but the mental effects of that negative reinforcement were only slowly starting to wear off. By coming out, I was using my energy to fully accept and understand who I was instead of destroying myself a little bit each day. My frame of reference was changing, and as it did, the events of my discharge came into clearer and clearer focus.

At Annapolis, I had accepted my discharge as appropriate punishment for simply being gay. When I lived in that environment, with virtually no support or understanding, my entire world, my value system had been linked to the beliefs of the military and shared by practically everyone I had known.

Now I was struggling to build a new value system, struggling to make a transition back to civilian life. With every day away from the academy, I realized more and more how much I had been changed by my indoctrination into the military. Surviving in such a stifling environment had changed my personality and my self-image. I had become completely invested in my goals of graduating and serving as a submarine officer. Now that these were gone, I was trying to discover what was left. I looked back on who I had been in high school—energetic and hopeful, the perpetual optimist and planner, the person voted most likely to succeed by his classmates. Somewhere during the last four years I had lost touch with that young man, and I needed to find him again.

In many ways, it was like starting from scratch. Most of my friends were gone—off to new places and careers. Although we still kept in touch through letters and phone calls, I could already sense them slipping away. After all, what did we have in common anymore? For the first time in my life, I felt I'd fallen behind my peers, and I couldn't build the motivation to try and catch up. My own career and goals were gone, and I was unable to create new ones or build up my hopes for the future. I was filled with too much regret to even be angry; I felt unable to commit to anything, try too hard or invest too much. Deep down inside, I was afraid that I would lose it all again.

I started taking voice lessons from a professor at school, hoping that singing again would make things seem more normal. I even auditioned to be a cantor at the local Catholic cathedral and was hired to sing at weekend services. Music and singing had always been such an important, consistent part of my life. If I wanted to begin building that life over, it seemed like the right place to start.

Eventually, I made new friends through work and school, and I became more accustomed to civilian life. I also began meeting other gay people in the area, people who I was happy to discover were as "normal" as I was. After several months, I even built up the courage to go with some friends to the gay bar in

Fargo, My Place, which happened to be the only gay bar in the entire state of North Dakota.

I had never been in a gay bar before in my life. It too was surprisingly "normal," and although not as nice as the other bars in town (it was essentially a Quonset hut), everyone seemed to know everyone else and they actually talked to each other. It was as much a meeting place or a community hall as it was a bar.

The concept of the gay community is one that took some time for me to appreciate. In many ways, it was a group of people I was very wary of. After all, I was still dealing with my own prejudices and homophobia. I felt like a pretty regular guy, but who was to know if most other gays were just like the stereotypes I had known? After all, I didn't know that many gay people so far.

At that time, I especially disliked people who I felt perpetuated the gay stereotypes—the effeminates, the queens, the guys in leather, those who visibly flaunted their sexuality. To me, they were a problem and a threat. They were why the rest of society wouldn't accept us, because this was society's image of who we were. I felt that if everyone would just try to act and dress more mainstream, life would be a lot easier for all of us.

By getting to know other gay people in Fargo, visiting the bar and going to parties where everyone was gay, I began to get a sense of the gay community. I began to understand that, like any community, we were bound together by shared experiences. It seemed that no matter where we were from or how diverse our backgrounds, we all had something important and intensely personal in common. It wasn't simply the fact that we were gay; it was that we had all, in our own unique ways, come to terms with our sexuality in an often unaccepting society.

In our own isolated corners of life we had struggled with thoughts and feelings we couldn't understand, emotions that didn't seem right. We had shared a difficult experience, often isolated and alone, not knowing if anyone else like us existed in the world. Now we were finding each other, people who had shared these experiences, and it was as though we were all old friends reunited. The stories and experiences of our coming out,

whether discussed or not, created a common ground of understanding and friendship.

Something I discovered quickly among my gay friends was
their ability to accept people without judging them against a
preconceived set of standards. They had all known, in one sense
or another, what it felt like to be judged by other people, to have
someone else impose standards on their lives. I had also known
this feeling, but it still took time for me to overcome the elitist
attitudes that had been ingrained in me at Annapolis.

I began, slowly, to appreciate the value of people even if
they didn't conform to my own standards of normalcy, to shed
some of my own prejudices. Uniformity had been such an integral part of my military experience that I had lost much of my
ability to appreciate and value diversity.

One of the important lessons of my coming out was the
appreciation of my own vulnerability. For the first time in my
life, I had learned what it feels like to feel vulnerable in this
society, to recognize how skewed it is toward certain classes of
people. Our social standards and mores are the product of historical development, designed by and for white, heterosexual,
Christian men.

When I fit this identity, it was difficult for me to believe
that our society had faults. I had come from that protected
mold, and during high school and my early days at the academy
I could never understand why people in our country were dis-
satisfied. I knew society was fair and good because I had never
known hunger, bigotry, or discrimination. I had never been
called "nigger," "fag," or "kike." To me, America was ideal, a
place of limitless opportunity, a place where no one had a right
to complain. If anyone was badly off, I thought, it was simply
his own fault.

My experience at Annapolis changed my perspective forever. Once outside the golden mold, important choices and decisions about my life were made without my consent—decisions
based on ignorance and hatred. Now other people were choosing what I could and could not do, and I learned what it felt like
to be powerless and vulnerable. In that moment, my image of
the American dream crumbled before my eyes. America was no
longer a land of opportunity, and I was no longer the favored

child. Now I was simply another minority, to whom some doors were open and others tightly closed.

During my last few days at Annapolis, a professor had given me his recording of *Peter Grimes*, an opera by the English composer Benjamin Britten. He was already my favorite composer, and I was especially captivated by the opera. Since leaving Annapolis, I had listened to parts of it nearly every night as I fell to sleep.

In the beginning of the story, a fisherman named Peter Grimes is accused of negligence in the death at sea of his young apprentice. Although the charges are dropped during a hearing, he is warned by the judge that people will remember the incident, and whether he is guilty or not, the aura of guilt would follow him for life. Unwilling to accept his fate, he sings:

> *Then let me speak—*
> *Let me stand trial!*
> *Bring the accusers into the hall—*
> *Let me thrust into their mouths*
> *The truth itself,*
> *The simple truth.*

As I listened to these words, I couldn't help but think of my own hearings at Annapolis. My demeanor in those hearings had been polite and restrained; I had exercised the calm composure I had learned so well during plebe year. I had called no witnesses in my defense. What would they have said—that I was a good midshipman? The deputy commandant had already admitted that during the performance board.

I had spent so much time poring over my memories of that turbulent week, trying to discover a reason for what had happened. Somehow, I could not escape the feeling that I was somehow to blame for my discharge. If I had only kept my mouth shut, if I had not dared to trust anyone, I might have survived.

Now I was beginning to see it all so much more clearly, and much differently. What had happened to me was wrong; it was a pitiful abomination of justice. I had done nothing more than tell the truth. I had been true to everything I valued: the Honor Concept, my self-esteem, and my basic dignity as a human being. It was the academy, by its own policies and the actions of its officers, that had ignored the truth. And without truth, it is so clearly said, there can be no justice.

Although I had paid dearly for the truth, I had also chosen to ignore it by accepting my discharge without a fight. Bullied by the academy, and under pressure from my family, I had walked away from a discharge that I knew was wrong and unjust. I had been trying very hard to move on, but I could not run away any longer. Allowing this unfairness to stand was contrary to everything I believed in, and it had tormented me from the beginning. I knew that I would never be able to live with myself or accept what had happened without making some effort to fight back.

By not fighting back, I was passively supporting the military's actions. I wondered who would be next, and who they would have to turn to. If everyone who was discharged simply walked away, what hope would there be for the future? How many more lives would be destroyed? It was time to stop running and to meet this injustice face to face.

Although nearly six months had passed since my discharge, I decided to contact Copy Berg about the possibility of filing a lawsuit against the academy. He was encouraging, and put me in touch with Lambda Legal Defense and Education Fund, a non-profit gay-rights litigation group in New York City. Although the ACLU had initially expressed interest in the case, Copy felt Lambda would probably be best for a suit of this type.

Most of my initial contact was with Abby Rubinfeld, Lambda's legal director, and Paula Ettelbrick, a staff attorney. Abby explained that Lambda had the resources to take only a small number of cases each year. Before making a decision, they would have to carefully review the facts of my case and determine whether there was a real possibility for victory.

Over the course of the next few weeks, I worked closely with Paula, sending her copies of all the documents related to my discharge and preparing a detailed account of the events leading up to it. After all the documents were in, I waited for a decision from Lambda.

Several weeks later, when I still had heard nothing, I was beginning to worry that they might not take the case. When I finally called Abby to find out what was going on, she could tell me only that a decision had not yet been reached. She also mentioned that they were concerned about the legal ramifications of my "resignation" from the academy. Despite the pressured circumstances, they worried that a court might regard a resignation as a forfeiture of my right to sue. Although I had no legal training, it seemed like a circuitous argument. If it hadn't been for the existence of the policy, I would never have been put in the position of having to resign in the first place.

But the decision-making process dragged on, and I was becoming increasingly impatient and frustrated. When I shared my concerns with Copy, he suggested that I fly to New York and meet directly with Lambda's executive director, Tom Stoddard. Copy knew Tom well and had talked extensively with him about my case. Copy arranged the meeting and agreed to join me. A few weeks later, I flew to New York City.

In our meeting, Tom seemed excited about the case, but he shared Abby's concerns about the resignation issue. He was also worried about whether Lambda could wage a worthy fight against the military and its practically unlimited resources.

Copy stressed the need to make cases against the military a higher priority, if for no other reason than to educate the public about the issue. Thousands of good people were being discharged from the military every year, and yet few people knew about the military policy or the cruelty with which it was being administered. Even if the courts rejected our claim, it could only help to focus attention on the policy.

Tom acknowledged that the facts of my case were almost too good to pass up—a high-ranking midshipman whose entire discharge was based solely on a statement. If any case was going to have a chance, not only legally, but in appealing to the public's sense of justice, it was this one. By the time our meeting was over, I was convinced that we had made our point as best we could. All I could do now was wait.

Finally, several months later, Paula called to inform me that Lambda had decided to take my case. I felt a deep sense of relief and was grateful that our lobbying efforts had paid off. If it hadn't been for Copy helping me, though, I question whether we would have been successful.

Four-wheeling on a frozen lake during one of my much appreciated visits home on Christmas leave.

Moving in with my roommates at the start of second-class year. We're obviously not looking forward to making this mess shipshape and ready for inspection.

Two company mates and me after our last intramural soccer game of youngster year. Our company didn't fare very well, and we're displaying our season record—0 and 8.

Performing in Gilbert & Sullivan's musical Ruddigore *during the spring of my senior year at Annapolis.*

Standing in Times Square with some friends from Catholic choir during our trip to New York senior year. This was the weekend when I saw A Chorus Line *for the first time.*

One of the hundreds of public glee-club performances I sang in during my Academy career. This one was at Sea World in Orlando, Florida, during my youngster year.

My parents, Connie, and their friends, who had packed into our family room to watch the anthem that morning on television.

PHIL HOFFMAN

Singing the National Anthem at the Army-Navy game for the second time. This performance was during my senior year.

Receiving a special commendation for outstanding leadership from the commandant, Captain Habermeyer, only a month before my discharge.

Posing with then Vice President Bush and former chief of naval operations Admiral Crowe after a choir performance in Washington, D.C.

Copy Berg and me at the press conference following the filing of my lawsuit on December 29, 1988.

Former ROTC cadet Jim Holobaugh and me wa iting to be introduced at American University in Washington, D.C.— A.U. was one of the many schools across the country where we spoke during the early stages of the ROTC protests.

With my family at our lake cabin in Minnesota. Left to right, Cheryl, me, Connie, Cindy, Dad, and Mom.

Paula Ettelbrick, Lambda's legal director, and me at the press conference following the filing of our lawsuit.

This was taken in Fargo, North Dakota, only a few months after my discharge. No one in my family had a recent picture of me, and because I didn't have a graduation picture, I asked a friend to take this one instead.

Over the course of the next few months we continued to prepare for the filing of the lawsuit, and the process dragged on. I was becoming stressed out, trying to prepare mentally for the filing, but never knowing for sure when it would happen. It was my first exposure to the slow pace of the wheels of justice. More than a year had passed since I had originally contacted Lambda, but every time we decided on a filing date, something else came up to delay it. I only hoped things would move faster once the lawsuit was filed.

As various filing dates approached, I debated about whether or not to tell my parents what was happening. When I was at Annapolis, I used to call them regularly, at least once a week. But since that Easter in Fargo, I rarely called them—I guess as a kind of punishment, a warning that they were going to have to accept me, all of me, if they wanted to continue our relationship. To me, that meant more than just accepting the fact that I was gay, but also that I was not willing to hide it or treat it like some kind of silent, undiscussed shame. They would call every few weeks to check on me, but our conversations were superficial—we discussed only work and school. They were careful to avoid the dreaded topic, and I lacked the determination to push it.

I could sense their concern about the distance growing between us. As a family, we had never really talked about personal things. I don't recall the word "sex" ever being mentioned in any context in our home. In the great Scandinavian tradition, we learned not to complain, to eat all the food on our plates, and to deal with our own problems. Too much communication made us uncomfortable. We avoided it at all costs, substituting a kind of mental guessing game in its place. Now I was playing that game to my advantage. By not calling my parents, I had sent a message that they clearly understood.

I was sure they would react negatively to the possibility of a lawsuit and the public exposure it would bring, and the last thing I needed was a big load of discouragement. It was enough to worry about how my life might be affected by undertaking a public challenge to the policy. Despite these concerns and our chilled relationship, I felt obligated to give them at least some warning. My chance came during one of my infrequent trips home since moving to Fargo.

On my last night home, I was sitting with my parents watching television in the family room. I sat there, silently, while my insides were churning, waiting for an opportune moment to tell them about the lawsuit. I wanted to put it off until I knew when we would file, but I knew I had to tell them. After avoiding the subject of the lawsuit all weekend, I finally built up the courage. Turning to them, I said in a calm voice, "Oh, by the way, I'm going to sue the military."

They both looked at me in quiet bewilderment, their faces reflecting the hazy white glare of the television.

"You're going to what?" my mom asked in a rhetorical tone.

I paused for a moment. "I'm going to sue the military to get back in," I answered, even though I knew they had caught it the first time.

Needless to say, they were less than pleased. My mom asked what I hoped to gain, and my father said in a disgusted tone that he couldn't understand why I would want to do something so stupid. Their reactions were exactly as I had predicted, but I was still angered by them. Our discussion was short and tense. I told them I was determined to do this, with or without their support. My father finally said, "Do what you want. I don't want to hear about it."

"Fine," I answered hotly as I got up and left the room. I packed my things and left for Fargo without a word. I had done my duty, and it was the last they would hear about it from me.

Back at Lambda, the process was again delayed when Abby Rubinfeld left Lambda and Paula Ettelbrick was named to replace her as legal director. Because of her new duties, Paula could not continue with the case, and another staff attorney would have to be found to replace her.

Just before December 1988, a new attorney named Sandra Lowe was hired by Lambda and assigned to my case. She had recently graduated from law school, and had spent the last year working as a public defender in Philadelphia. She was also concerned about the resignation issue, but she came up with a brilliant idea to weaken the Navy's argument.

What we needed, she said, was proof that the military would not have retained me, some evidence to show the futility of an appeal to the Secretary of the Navy. After poring over the military regulations related to resignations, Sandy came across a section that said I had the right to send a letter to the Secretary requesting that my resignation be withdrawn.

She suggested that I write such a letter outlining the facts of my situation at Annapolis and my forced resignation. I would request in the letter permission to withdraw my resignation from Annapolis and ask that I be reinstated. At first I couldn't understand what purpose this letter would serve. The Secretary would certainly deny the requests, and our efforts would be wasted. But as we discussed it, I realized how ingenious the idea really was.

In denying the request, the Navy would be giving us exactly what we needed to overcome the resignation argument. The government would argue that by resigning from Annapolis, I did not utilize the last avenue of appeal open to me—a direct appeal to the Secretary of the Navy. They would argue that he might have kept me in, but I would never know because I resigned. Of course they knew he would never have kept me in, just as I knew he would deny my request. But now, if my request was denied, we would have proof of Major Funk's assurance that no homosexual had ever been allowed to remain in the military. The Secretary's denial of my request would deflate the military's argument that I had not availed myself of all the avenues of appeal before me.

I mailed the letter December 9, stating that if I did not receive a reply by December 27, I would consider my request denied and would take "other appropriate action." That meant, of course, filing a lawsuit. If no response was received, we would file the lawsuit on December 29.

I half expected some kind of response, however negative, but by the week of Christmas, I was preparing to leave for Washington, D.C. Before leaving, I did an extensive interview with Cathy Mauk, a reporter with the local Fargo newspaper, *The Forum*. Assuming everything went according to schedule, she would break the story on the morning of the filing.

It felt strange talking about my experiences at Annapolis, especially to a reporter. But Cathy was very kind, listening carefully as she took notes. Her questions were thoughtful and intelligent, and I was encouraged by how she seemed to be moved by my experiences and what I had to say. She asked me about things I hadn't really discussed much—about my friends and what it was like to go through Annapolis, about my background and family.

Talking about Annapolis didn't hurt as much as thinking about it. It seemed to bring back as many happy thoughts as sad, and I actually felt comfortable talking about my sexuality. During the week of my discharge, I could never even bring myself to use the word "gay"—it seemed so foreign to me. I could only say "homosexual." It was a sterile, scientific term—as if I were talking about someone else. I guess, at the time, that made it a little easier.

Perhaps part of the reason I didn't feel embarrassed or ashamed talking about that time in my life was because I no longer felt like a victim. I was finally beginning to fight back, to stick up for myself and what I knew to be right. I had wanted to fight from the beginning, but I had given in—to pressure from Annapolis and my parents, as well as my own lack of confidence. I had allowed myself to become a victim—powerless and helpless. Now, win or lose, I would at least know that I had tried, and I knew that I could live with that.

We have so few real choices in life—much of what happens to us is simply beyond our control. But there is one choice that we always have, and that is the choice of how we choose to respond to the situations that confront us. It is in those responses, I believe, that our strength and freedom as individuals lie. Life is not always fair—it has the same randomness as any other natural process. We can choose either to be victims of that process or to work for change.

The next day I was on a plane to Washington, D.C. I had told my parents that I was spending Christmas with some friends in the area, which I was, but they had no idea of my real reason for being there. The only member of my family I had told about the filing was my oldest sister, Cheryl. She said I should tell Mom and Dad what was going on, but my father had made it clear that he didn't want to know. I said if she wanted to tell them she could, but I wasn't going to do it.

Back in Washington, I was becoming anxious and excited

about the filing. It was hard to believe after so much waiting and wondering that it was finally going to happen.

I had decided that I would attend the Christmas Eve service at the Naval Academy. I had heard the service was a beautiful one, but had never seen it because I'd spent all of my Christmas leaves back home in Minnesota. It seemed a fitting thing to do before filing the lawsuit, before I would be perceived as a public opponent of the academy and the Navy.

As I walked into the chapel that evening, I was filled with a deep sense of calm. I had always felt warmth and acceptance here, but on this night I felt it more than ever before. All of my anxiety seemed to melt away in that environment, that place in which I had spent countless hours rehearsing, singing, and contemplating my future as a midshipman. Now I was contemplating my future again, but in such a remarkably different context than before.

As part of every religious service at Annapolis, a special prayer is repeated by all midshipmen. The second stanza of the prayer had always carried special meaning for me, and as I heard the words again they struck me with all the significance of the trying days to come:

> Keep me true to my best self,
> Guarding me against dishonesty in purpose and in deed,
> And helping me so to live that I can stand unashamed and
>   unafraid
> Before my shipmates, my loved ones, and Thee.

A year and a half after my discharge, I had finally rediscovered my true, best self. For the first time since those horrible days, I truly stood without fear or shame, and most importantly, without regret as I faced both the past and the future.

On this night I looked at myself, at what I was about to do, and I felt good. I had tried to escape my memories of the academy, to erase that history, to simply forget. But I could not escape the fact that the academy was a part of my life, a part of who I had become. By deciding to fight, I was proving to myself exactly who I was and what I believed in.

As I stood singing in the chapel, I finally felt again the sense of belonging I had known as a midshipman, the belonging I had so longed to feel on my previous trips back to Annapolis. I had come to realize that my memories and accomplishments, the friendships and happiness I had shared here, were mine, and would be mine forever. No matter what the future would hold, no one could ever take them away.

9

Litigation

On the day before the filing I had another interview, this time with Frank Browning, a reporter from National Public Radio in Washington, D.C. His story would air nationally the following morning, and so he recorded the interview on tape, which felt a little uncomfortable at first. Frank's questions were intelligent and insightful, and he clearly understood the issue. The more we talked, the more comfortable I felt answering questions about my experiences at Annapolis.

I had prepared myself to deal with ignorance, with people saying, "But you're gay, of course they should kick you out"— the kind of mentality that I experienced in the military. But so far no one had taken that stance. There was only understanding and compassion—much more than I had expected. I was beginning to realize that the reactions I had anticipated from people were still skewed by my military experience. Either these interviews were anomalies, or things were going to go better than I had expected.

Later that day, I called Marcia Talley to let her know that the filing was still on, and that there was going to be a press conference held afterward. She worked in Washington, and wanted to be there to see it. But she knew Barry would end up taking some heat at Annapolis when the filing hit, and she didn't want her picture ending up in the paper. That would only make things worse. She told me she would hang out in the back of the room, and joked that it might be best for her to arrive in dis-

guise. We both laughed, and I felt a little more at ease knowing
that Marcia would be there.

On the morning of the filing, January 29, 1988, I arrived
early at the office of our Washington, D.C., cooperating attorney, Calvin Steinmetz. He and Sandy Lowe, my Lambda attorney, were to meet me there, and I was looking forward to finally
seeing them in person. I was especially anxious to meet Sandy.
We had worked closely during that month, and I had spoken to
her nearly every day as she worked to complete our papers for
the filing. We had gotten along well, and she had helped put me
at ease about the filing and upcoming publicity. Even though we
had never met, by now I felt close to her.

When I walked into the office, Cal stood up and introduced
himself and then introduced me to Sandy. She was a black
woman, a little shorter than me, with dreadlocks and a warm
smile that matched her personality. We sat down to discuss the
plan for the day. First, we would head to the Federal District
Courthouse to file the papers for our lawsuit. After the filing,
we would go directly to a press conference, which was being
held at the National Press Club building. Lambda had arranged
the press conference, and both Paula Ettelbrick and Copy Berg
would be meeting us there.

The actual filing was much less involved than I had anticipated. We simply handed our complaint to a clerk in one of the
court offices. In our complaint, the formal statement of our
allegations, we requested that the court grant three remedies.
First and foremost, we asked that the military's policy of homosexual exclusion be declared unconstitutional. Second, we
requested that I be granted my diploma from the Naval Academy, and finally, that I be reinstated into the Navy to continue
my career. The clerk then went behind a screen to pick a judge
for the case. The judge for each case is chosen by lot, and when
she returned, she informed us that the case was assigned to
Judge Oliver J. Gasch. Although Cal had heard of Judge Gasch,
he didn't really know much about him. After only a few moments of quick paperwork, the filing was complete and we
walked out of the courthouse.

I looked at Cal and Sandy in astonishment. "You mean
that's it—we're done?" It seemed a pretty anticlimactic two
minutes after over a year of waiting, work, and preparation.

They both smiled knowingly as Sandy assured me that waiting is 99 percent of what this and most lawsuits are all about.

On the way to the press conference, I worried about whether anyone was going to show up. After all, this wasn't the first time a gay person had sued the military to get back in. There had been several, starting with Leonard Matlovich and Copy Berg back in the 1970s, and later Perry Watkins and Miriam Ben-Shalom. I wasn't sure if the first suit against a military academy would bring much attention.

My doubts were answered when we arrived at the press conference, about ten minutes late. The room was packed with reporters and television cameras. Paula and Copy were starting to get nervous that something might have gone wrong. My heart started to race as we all sat down behind a long table at the front of the room amid the harsh camera lights and intermittent photo flashes.

Sandy began by explaining a little about our lawsuit, and what we hoped to gain. I was looking for Marcia at the back of the room, but couldn't see her anywhere. Then I noticed a strange-looking woman standing next to the door. When she waved at me and smiled I suddenly realized it was Marcia—she was wearing a grotesque black wig and huge sunglasses! She looked hilarious. Copy recognized her at the same time, and we both started to laugh. It was just like Marcia to pull a stunt like this.

After Sandy finished her introduction, I spoke in detail about my discharge and the events leading up to the filing. I was grateful for having done a few interviews before this—it all seemed to flow much easier after that practice. Marcia's surprise appearance also helped to lighten things up.

The reporters were great. They were interested in the story and asked many questions about Annapolis, my discharge, and why I wanted to get back into the Navy. They, too, surprised me with their level of understanding and appreciation of the issue. It was quickly becoming clear to me that many people questioned the military's policy. From their reactions, I could tell that they saw me and my successes at Annapolis as a contradiction to the military's claim that gay people are incapable of military service.

After Paula and Copy finished speaking, we split up and

spent about another half hour answering questions individually
for reporters. Most of it was simply answering the same questions
over and over again for different people, something I would get
used to after dozens of interviews turned into hundreds.

At last we were able to get away and spend some time
relaxing at lunch at a nearby restaurant. We all agreed we had
underestimated the level of interest in the lawsuit. We had expected some coverage, but within a few days it was clear that
people wanted to know more about this policy and why the
military was discharging qualified gay people.

After lunch, I taped an interview for CBS's *Night Watch*,
their late-night interview show. It was my first network television interview. Later on that day, I called my answering machine to check for messages. Besides the messages from dozens
of reporters across the country there were excited messages of
support from friends and a message from my parents asking me
to call them.

I spent much of the day returning phone calls, answering
questions, and arranging interviews. That evening after things
had calmed down, I called my parents. I felt guilty for not
having let them know what was happening, despite the anger I
had been feeling toward them since my trip home. Although I
expected that they would be quite upset, they were both remarkably calm, almost relieved that the filing had occurred.
They explained that Cheryl had told them about the filing two
days earlier, so they were at least prepared for it.

My parents said the filing had been the lead story on all the
local television news shows. They had been concerned about
reaction from their friends and other people in town, but they
were surprised that they had received many supportive and encouraging calls. I could sense that they were deeply relieved by
that reaction, which was far more positive than they had ever
expected.

The filing would be the turning point in my relationship
with my parents. Although much of the last year and a half had
been difficult for me, I began to realize just how much my
parents had to deal with at the same time. They had to deal not
only with my discharge from Annapolis, but also with my coming out. I had had years to deal with my sexuality and come to

terms with it, but my parents were hit with everything at once, and I had been unwilling to be patient with their acceptance. I just needed it too much to wait.

I admired their reaction to the filing and began to under-stand just how far they had come. In a way, they seemed almost excited that the story was out, that the whole truth was finally being told. As difficult as it had been for them to deal with my discharge, I think it had also been a great burden on them to keep it all a secret, because as a secret it somehow felt shameful. Now that everything was out in the open and I was fighting to get back into the academy, that feeling of shame was de-stroyed. In the light of day, it was so much easier to see that the only shame in my discharge was how I had been treated by the academy.

A few days later, I flew back to Fargo. Before leaving for Washington, I had told my bosses about everything, and they had been completely encouraging and supportive. I was grateful to be working for such a forward-looking company, and when I returned absolutely everyone at work was great. Many of them took the time to congratulate me and say they were proud of what I was doing. I had expected to be treated differently, but after things calmed down a little, life was pretty much back to normal. I was expecting to be fired as cantor at the cathedral, but nothing ever happened. I continued to sing as before, and even the choir members asked how things were going and en-couraged me to keep up the fight.

Before the filing, I had mentally prepared myself for the worst. I knew I wouldn't lose my job, but I wondered how people would treat me. But everything seemed so normal now, it was as though nothing had happened at all. I think part of the reason was something I had learned at Annapolis. I believe that people are very sensitive to your own sense of self-worth, to your own self-image. If you feel ashamed or afraid, regardless of whether you overtly show it, they can sense those feelings. People will inevitably treat you as you feel you should be treated. If you don't respect yourself, if you don't trust your-self, you will never be able to inspire that trust and respect in those around you. People reacted to me the same as always because I felt the same, and I wasn't ashamed or afraid of my identity—I was proud of it. They could respect that, even if they didn't accept or even understand my sexuality.

One thing I had not expected was the number of letters and phone calls I received from people I had never met offering their support and often telling of their own experiences of discrimination in the military. Within only a few weeks, hundreds of letters had been forwarded from television stations and newspapers that had interviewed me. And so many people were calling me that I eventually had to put in a second, unlisted phone line just to get some peace and privacy.

I felt overwhelmed. There were so many people with so many heartrending stories of discrimination, especially as a result of the military's policy. I was only beginning to understand how deeply it had scarred the lives of thousands—tens of thousands of people through the decades. Although my decision to fight had been a personal one, undertaken primarily to reconcile my own life, I realized now that my efforts had much broader implications. As much as I was fighting for myself, I was also fighting for these people—for their rights and, just as important, for their dignity.

Many of the letters were from gay and lesbian active-duty service members, including many who were graduates of the academy. I even received a number of letters and phone calls from midshipmen I had known at Annapolis in which they came out to me for the first time and related some of their own experiences at the academy.

These people began to wake me up to the reality that, even with the military's exclusionary policy and the academy's strict regulations against sex on campus, a good deal of homosexual conduct took place at the academy. The gay and lesbian academy grads and midshipmen who were still at the academy eventually related a number of stories to me about their sexual experiences at Annapolis.

One guy who had been at the academy only a few years before I arrived told me that he had not only carried on a sexual relationship with his plebe-year roommate but had also been having sex with his roommate's brother, who was also a midshipman at the academy. According to the former mid, neither of the brothers knew about the other.

Still other midshipmen told me about having sex with fellow mids during study hour or on weekends, either off campus or in empty rooms in buildings on campus. Apparently, one particularly common location for these encounters was the clock tower in Mahan Hall, which contained a maze of dusty, unused rooms and passageways. Those of us who had been in the musicals had rooted through this maze a couple of times during the free time of our rehearsals, and I imagine that it would have been as ideal a spot as any.

Other midshipmen's experiences had been a bit riskier. One fellow told me about a time when he had had sex with another midshipman in the varsity wrestling sauna room in LeJeune Hall, the academy's indoor swimming complex.

Although Annapolis was obviously not an ideal environment, a few mids told me that they had managed to carry on stable sexual relationships with classmates at the academy. Sometimes they would all but ignore each other during the week, only to spend all their weekends and free time away from the academy together. Other relationships were surprisingly open, at least by academy standards. A gay friend of mine who was at the academy after I left told me about a classmate of his who had a boyfriend from another company. They spent a good deal of time together during the week, and were even out to a few close friends in the brigade. A number of them, gay and straight, even joined them on their free weekends together, going out to dance at gay bars in Washington, D.C.

For many of the mids I spoke to, however, the negative reinforcement of the academy only added to the difficulty of dealing with their sexuality. I never gained any sense of a "gay underground" at Annapolis, either during my time at the academy or through contact with other gay mids and graduates—it was just too stifling a place.

As remarkable as some of these stories sounded to me, given the climate at the academy, they made me realize that, restrictions or no, there are always going to be people involved in sexual misconduct. The academy's rules prohibit all sexual relationships, gay or straight.

There are good reasons for these restrictions, and I firmly believe that there are clearly inappropriate situations for people to have sex, such as on a ship or on duty at a military base. The purpose of these regulations is to keep people focused on their work and to maintain the readiness of the military. The difference comes when duty is over or when people are off the ship. Whereas straight service members are free to have sex and pursue their relationships, gay men and lesbians are not.

As far as the military is concerned, *all* homosexual conduct is inappropriate and punishable, whether it takes place off duty, off base, or in the privacy of one's home. This negative atmosphere not only makes it more difficult for people to come to terms with their sexuality, it also makes it nearly impossible to explore and develop stable, lasting relationships. It is this lack of equality and freedom to be open about one's sexuality and develop healthy relationships that makes serving in the military as a gay person so difficult.

Although each of the people who contacted me with their stories was unique, they all shared one, overriding hope—that they would one day be able to serve their country openly. I sensed in their words much of the frustration I had felt myself living in the closet during my time at the academy.

One of the few anonymous letters I received struck me as particularly poignant, and indicative of the struggle of many gay men and lesbians, both in and out of the military:

Dear Mr. Steffan,
   You have my strongest, though anonymous, support. I served in the Navy as a career officer—a very successful career, which included combat and excellent assignments including command.
   You are absolutely right to say that one's sexual orientation does not come into the equation when doing one's job supporting his or her country. My efforts, first and foremost, were to serve well, do the best I could, and make a difference. For those efforts I have been decorated, received early selection and promotion, and had an enviable career. . . .
   Early in my career I wanted a family—I married and have children—a wonderful family. Today, perhaps, I might have done something differently—but years ago I made choices and now live with them—happily, but with some areas of my life unfulfilled.

On the other hand, I have an abundance of blessings and must be thankful for the gifts of health, education, family, and excellent careers.

I sincerely appreciate everything you do in behalf of better human understanding. . . . On behalf of any number of people whose voices are silent, I thank you. Many others in the future will benefit from your efforts.

Thank you. God bless you.

An unnamed supporter

Among the letters were many from people who were not gay, but who were simply outraged by the unfairness of the military's discrimination. They came from all walks of life—professional and working class, old and young. I was particularly moved by a letter from a physician whose entire family had watched a documentary television piece about my case. He and his wife had discussed it with their children and explained how wrong it was to discriminate against people for any reason. As he passed on the encouragement of his entire family, I felt a deep sense of hope that I had never dared to feel before. With the help of people like these, I thought, we really can change this policy.

Within a few months of the filing, I was still receiving many requests for interviews, and each interview seemed to lead to more and more. Essentially every minute of my free time was devoted to the lawsuit in one way or another, and I was beginning to fear that we might have created a monster.

The lawsuit itself was also growing out of Sandy's control, consuming more of her increasingly precious time at Lambda. As is usually the case with nonprofit groups, Lambda was overwhelmed with work and constantly trying to keep up with the needs of their many cases. With only three staff attorneys, they were carrying dozens of cases across the country challenging discrimination in everything from housing to employment to child custody.

With the increasing publicity surrounding our case, Sandy had received numerous requests for help from gay service members who were either being discharged or investigated for homosexuality. Each case was deeply disturbing, reminding me of my own experiences at Annapolis, but there was often little that we could do. The military has so much control in these cases, especially if they involve homosexual conduct, that we often felt helpless to assist these people. The whole issue of gays in the military was exploding in our faces, and we needed help, not only with growing media attention, but also with our increasing legal burdens.

At this point, Sandy and I were essentially the only people involved in the day-to-day aspects of the case. Ric Wanetik, a marketing consultant and a member of Lambda's board of directors, had been helping us with media relations, and had coordinated several print and television interviews. Ric also recognized that we were becoming overwhelmed, and contacted his friend Howard Bragman, a successful media consultant who had recently left Burson-Marsteller, a major public relations firm, as a vice president to start his own firm in Los Angeles. Howard agreed to help us, and I met with him on a trip to Los Angeles to speak before MECLA, the Municipal Elections Committee for Los Angeles, a gay rights political-action committee.

Howard Bragman is a tall, dark-haired man whose totally irreverent sense of humor kept me laughing through most of our conversation. We sat in his living room, talking about the case and eating blue corn chips and salsa, something previously unknown to me. Despite Howard's relaxed personality, it was clear that he was incredibly talented at his profession. We spoke for several hours about message points, sound bites, and the strategy of bringing our issues more effectively into the public view. "What we're really fighting here are two separate battles," he explained. "The first is a battle in the courts, and the second, perhaps more importantly, is a battle in the court of public opinion. Even if we lose in the courts, we still have a chance to show the American people that the military's policy is wrong. This is all really a question of fairness, and even if the public doesn't understand homosexuality, they can understand the unfairness of this policy."

With Howard on our growing "team," at least a part of our problems were solved. Now all we needed was more legal help. It was on a trip shortly thereafter to New York for a Lambda benefit that those needs were answered.

At the benefit I met a lawyer named Marc Wolinsky, a

partner at Wachtell Lipton Rosen & Katz, one of the most powerful and well-respected law firms in the country. He and his lover, Barry Skovgaard, who was also a lawyer, had been long-time supporters of Lambda. Marc and I discussed the case at some length, and he later mentioned to Tom Stoddard that Wachtell Lipton might be interested in joining Lambda as a cooperating firm on the case. Tom was more than enthusiastic, and Marc agreed to present the case for approval by the other partners at his firm.

A few days after I returned to Fargo, Sandy called to tell me that Wachtell Lipton had agreed to take on the case without charge, and that Marc would be assuming the bulk of the legal work. Sandy would still remain involved, but from now on, it was basically Marc's case.

I felt sad that Sandy and I wouldn't be working as closely as we had been. We had been through a lot already, and had developed a trust and friendship. I would soon learn, however, that with the considerable resources of Wachtell Lipton at our disposal, the military was facing a far more capable adversary.

At about the same time, I received a call one evening from a friend of mine at Annapolis. He explained that an officer at the Naval Academy was being discharged for homosexuality. The officer, Lieutenant Fred Steckler, had arrived at the academy after my discharge and had been serving as the executive assistant to the commandant, still Captain Howard Habermeyer. Although I had never met Lieutenant Steckler, my friend suggested that I call him to see if there was anything I could do to help him fight the discharge.

I got Fred Steckler's number from directory assistance and called him at home. He was obviously surprised when I introduced myself, but grateful for my calling to help him out. We spoke for nearly an hour, and he told me the details of what had happened at the academy.

Since being stationed at Annapolis, Fred had been fairly open in Washington's gay community, where he had several friends. Eventually, he was introduced to a close-knit group of gay retired naval officers living in Annapolis. For the most part, the retired officers were extremely closeted, and several of them still worked for the government in various capacities.

One of the officers, a former captain, took an immediate liking to Fred and began calling him and asking him out. Although Fred said he was flattered, he explained that he was already seeing someone in Washington. The captain, however, refused to take no for an answer and continued calling Fred incessantly to ask him out. Finally, Fred became upset and said bluntly that he wasn't interested in a date and that he didn't want to be bothered anymore.

The captain was incensed, but the calls finally stopped. Shortly thereafter, Fred heard through his friends that the captain had vowed to get even with him. Chalking it up to bruised feelings, Fred decided not to worry about it.

One day a few weeks later, while working in the commandant's office, Fred was called in for questioning by a group of officers. It seemed that the Naval Investigative Service at the academy had received a letter from an "anonymous midshipman."

The letter said that Fred was a homosexual, and it went on to make a series of false statements, starting with accusations that he had made unwelcome sexual advances to midshipmen at the academy. Although none of the midshipmen's names were mentioned, the letter stated that Fred "also had an affair with Joe Steffan." Apparently, the "midshipman" had forgotten to check the date of my departure from the academy.

Fred was outraged by the letter and denied the allegations, but when pressed by the officers he openly stated that he was gay. The Navy immediately initiated discharge proceedings and transferred him from the academy to Washington, D.C. They were clearly anxious to avoid any more publicity surrounding the Naval Academy.

I could sense how devastated Fred was by what was happening, and I was one of the few people who could truly say I knew exactly what he was going through. I tried to encourage him and promised to see if there was anything we could do to help him out. In the meantime, I asked him to send me anything he felt might be useful, including a copy of the anonymous letter.

Out of curiosity, I also asked the name of the retired captain. When he told me, I felt a cold chill go down my spine. I knew that Sandy had received several calls and a letter from the same person, offering to help us on our lawsuit. He had also expressed interest in meeting me on my next trip to Annapolis. Fortunately, Sandy had declined his offer.

When I received the copy of the anonymous letter, I immediately compared it to the letter that Sandy had received from the captain. Both letters were computer generated, and I immediately recognized from my work with computers that they had both been printed on the same particular model of laser printer. I also knew that it was not a printer used at the Naval Academy.

The captain had been very tricky, but he had missed one thing. In the letter he sent to Sandy, he had carefully used a completely different typeface than the one used on the anonymous letter. However, he had forgotten to alter the page-numbering typeface. In both letters, the page numbers matched exactly—identical typeface, size, and position on the page. Along with all the other evidence, there wasn't much question as to who the "anonymous midshipman" was.

Unfortunately, that knowledge could not help Fred. The damage was already done. It absolutely sickened me that anyone could be so incredibly vicious and cruel. I could only imagine that the captain's state of mind was the result of a lifetime of self-hatred now turned inside out.

More than anything, I wanted to help Fred, but it was too late. Within a few months, he was discharged from the Navy, after almost five years of exemplary, unblemished, proud service. Fred's discharge was every bit as frustrating and outrageous as my own, but it was just one more example of what the military does nearly five times on every single day of the year.

I had recently completed my classes at NDSU, and just as Marc was joining the case I received a job offer from some friends of mine in New York City. The thought of moving from Fargo to New York was both intimidating and tempting, and although I enjoyed being back in the Midwest, I was growing increasingly restless. Although I understood the importance of our lawsuit, I realized that, lawsuit or not, I still had to make plans for the rest of my life.

But I was no longer in this arena solely for myself, and in a cardboard box in the corner of my apartment were hundreds of reasons to keep going. They were the letters, the united voices of so many people who, like Fred Steckler and me, had crossed the line between the concept and reality of discrimination. After all, I was only twenty-five years old. If I was going to do this thing, I might as well go all out. So, in what was becoming a fairly normal routine, I sold everything that wouldn't fit in my car and drove with my remaining possessions to New York City.

The lawsuit was moving along slowly, as always. The Justice Department had assumed the Navy's defense, which is normal procedure in a case like this. The first stage of the lawsuit involved the government trying to convince Judge Gasch to throw the case out of court.

In their initial papers, the Justice Department's lawyers made a number of standard claims about jurisdiction and other legal technicalities hoping to convince the judge to dismiss our case. As we had expected, they also played heavily on the question of my resignation, claiming that I had made a voluntary "choice" to leave Annapolis. In making that choice, they argued, I had forfeited my right to sue for reinstatement.

Marc countered in our own papers by explaining that it really made no difference whether I had resigned or been discharged. It was irrelevant. The military's policy, he explained, had created the entire situation in which I was forced to choose between resignation and discharge. If the policy itself was unconstitutional, as we were suing to prove, then I should never have been put in that situation. In other words, the government had no right to defend the policy with its own results.

Additionally, Marc argued that there was nothing "voluntary" about my resignation. The academic board had sealed my fate with its discharge recommendation, and Major Funk had assured me that an appeal to the Secretary of the Navy would have been futile. In fact, the policy's own wording required the discharge of service members who stated that they are homosexual. The Secretary of the Navy could not have kept me even if he wanted to. The choice wasn't whether or not I wanted to be discharged from the academy, but rather, how long I wanted it to take. Either way, the result would be the same. We had also finally received a response to the letter I had sent to the Secretary of the Navy, firmly denying my request for reinstatement. If nothing else, that response gave us the ammunition we needed against the military's arguments.

Despite the strength of our position, we were concerned about how Judge Gasch felt about the issues surrounding homosexuality. In his research, Marc discovered that Judge Gasch had recently decided in favor of the military in a military case involving homosexual conduct. Although ours was not a conduct case, we questioned whether he would appreciate the difference between homosexual status and homosexual conduct. This distinction could well determine his entire approach to the case.

Our hopes were not enhanced by the discovery that the eighty-four-year-old judge had previously served as an officer in the Army—as a military lawyer. He was also the chairman of the Judges' Prayer Breakfast Association. His personal moral and religious feelings would undoubtedly play some role in his decision-making process. It seemed the more we learned about Judge Gasch, the more we began to worry about our chances for success.

After we and the government had finished filing our written arguments, or "briefs," the next stage in the case was a face-to-face meeting with the government lawyers before Judge Gasch in Washington. This process, "oral argument," is the final chance for each side to make its points and answer questions from the judge before he prepares his decision. At this point, we hadn't even started discussing the constitutionality of the military's policy. We were simply in the pre-trial stage, trying to convince the judge that we had the grounds to sue. His decision would only be on whether or not to let the case continue.

Oral argument was held in Washington, D.C., on June 13, 1989, almost six months after the filing of our original complaint. The argument provided few surprises. The Justice Department lawyers restated their arguments and Marc explained our responses. Judge Gasch didn't give many clues as to his leanings, and we were left with little more than before in hoping for a positive outcome. Now it was just a matter of waiting for his decision. In a few weeks, we would know whether our efforts had been in vain.

During this time, I was still in the process of getting accustomed to New York. Life in the city bore little resemblance to anything I had experienced before, especially in Fargo. It seemed to be a distillation of everything in America—a concentrated sampling of the spectrum between opulence and desperate poverty, both extremes existing side by side. I had never been exposed to real poverty before, and was particularly affected by the homeless people begging for change on practically every street corner. They are a reality to which every New Yorker becomes accustomed, at least as much as one can. These people stood as a constant reminder that despite our advancement, our strength as a nation, our technology, we are still unable to care for everyone.

I was working in SoHo, the area in Manhattan south of Houston Street known for its many artists and art galleries. Lambda's offices were only a few blocks away, so Sandy and I had lunch together whenever we could. Although much of our time was spent discussing the lawsuit, our conversations inevitably wandered through a realm of topics related to civil rights, AIDS, and the political and social direction of the country.

Sandy is a woman whose unique background and experience have given her a remarkable gift of insight and understanding. Her father, a man of African American, Cuban, and Chinese descent, had served as a member of the Communist party during the late thirties and early forties. Although he fought in Spain during the Spanish Civil War, he refused service during World War II in protest over the military's policies of racial segregation. He spent a year in prison for his failure to enlist. He and his wife later became union organizers, and Sandy was raised in New York's Greenwich Village in a home where race and workers' rights were the primary topic of dinner conversation.

She literally grew up on the picket lines with her mother, and became involved in the earliest stages of the civil rights movement during the 1960s, as well as the growing protest movement against the Vietnam War. Years later, after a marriage in which she had raised two children, she finally came to terms with her own homosexuality. At the age of thirty-seven, she started college, later going on to finish law school. After a

year as a public defender in Philadelphia, she began work at
Lambda—only one month before we filed our lawsuit.

As she told me herself, "I'm a Jewish, black, Cuban, Chinese lesbian mother of two. I grew up a regular Jewish colored
girl in the Village. I'm about as much a minority as you can get,
and everything I know about discrimination and hatred I know
from my own personal experience. I know it from my life and
from the streets, and it's something I've spent my entire life
fighting against."

Regardless of the issue, she had an uncanny ability to cut
straight through to the underlying core. I learned a great deal
from my conversations with her, but perhaps most important,
about how prejudice, racism, and homophobia are closely in-
terrelated. They are all, in essence, the result of ignorance and of
long-ingrained stereotypes.

About a month after our oral argument in Washington, I
received an excited call from Sandy. Judge Gasch had released
his decision that morning, and he had denied the government's
motion to dismiss our case. He had rejected their arguments
about my resignation, and the case was free to continue. We had
overcome a significant obstacle, and now the government had to
take us seriously.

Although it was a small victory, we all breathed a huge sigh
of relief. We were over the first significant hurdle, and concerns
that had plagued us from the beginning. What had been Lambda's greatest worry, the resignation issue, was now laid to rest,
thanks significantly to Sandy's idea to submit the resignation-
withdrawal letter over seven months earlier.

I thought, also, that we might have mistaken Judge Gasch.
His decision seemed contrary to his conservative background,
and I was hopeful that we might have misjudged him. I would
discover soon enough, however, that we had not. His presence
would become the greatest stumbling block in our case.

As I had expected, moving to New York had greatly increased my day-to-day involvement in the case and the broader
issue of gays in the military. As a media center, New York
allowed me to be far more accessible, and Howard Bragman,
our PR specialist, was doing an excellent job of educating the
press about our case and the military's discriminatory policy.

With television or radio appearances only a cab ride away, I found myself doing more and more of them. I was also becoming increasingly active as a public speaker, bringing my experiences and the issues of gays in the military to universities and civic organizations around the country. I also participated in fund-raising events for Lambda and other civil rights organizations in which I had become involved, including the Human Rights Campaign Fund, the country's largest gay and lesbian political action committee.

In only a short time, Howard, Marc, Sandy, and I had become a well-coordinated and effective team, not only in dealing with our lawsuit, but also concerning the whole issue of gays in the military. Despite the cyclical nature of the lawsuit and its media attention, we were constantly working on new leads and ideas to challenge the military policy. Hardly a day went by when we didn't talk to each other on the phone. As new information came to light, from important documents to other cases of military discrimination, we would discuss their legal significance and their media potential. It seemed that every new legal development spawned more intense media attention to our case and the issue of gays in the military. In turn, this attention inevitably helped to dredge up new information that we could use in our lawsuit.

Since Judge Gasch's decision to let the case continue, the government had vehemently avoided Marc's attempts to undertake "discovery," the gathering of documents and evidence used as the basis for arguments in the case. Marc had submitted numerous requests for documents and scheduled depositions with military officials so that they could explain the basis of their policy.

During the course of our document requests, Sandy learned through congressional sources that the Department of Defense had recently completed a major study about the suitability of gays for military service. The military was apparently trying to cover up the report because its findings were in conflict with the policy banning gays. When the government refused Marc's requests to disclose the document, we began working with Congressman Gerry Studds and his executive assistant, Kate Dyer, in an attempt to track down a copy. This association would prove to be one of our greatest assets in the fight against the military's policy. With the support of Congressman Studds and Kate's incredible dedication and skill, we would achieve some of our most important victories.

Although the Justice Department produced a few of the other documents that Marc had requested, they refused to schedule any of the depositions we had requested. Instead, they demanded that I be made available for a deposition. When Marc asked what they expected to learn that was not already in the record, they made it clear that they wanted to determine if I had ever been involved in any homosexual conduct. They claimed that any conduct I might have been involved in would allow them to refuse my reinstatement.

This request violated many principles of administrative law, not the least of which was the fact that my entire discharge was based on a statement. I had never even been accused of being involved in homosexual conduct, and the government could not expect to use the pretext of discovery to dredge up entirely new grounds to shore up a discharge that had already occurred. Marc made it very clear that he would direct me to not answer any questions relating to sexual conduct. When the government said it still wanted to depose me, Marc said that deposition would be held only if the government responded to our many outstanding document and deposition requests. But neither side was willing to give in, and we finally scheduled a "status conference" in front of Judge Gasch to iron out the discovery disputes.

From the start of the hearing, Judge Gasch's demeanor was decidedly less equitable than during our earlier appearance. Although he had agreed with our prior arguments, it was clear that he could not understand why we needed to probe the military's justifications for its policy. When Marc insisted that it was necessary to examine the reasoning behind the policy, Judge Gasch responded, "It ought to be obvious to you why they need such a regulation." It would have been an ignorant comment coming from anyone, but from the person responsible for the fair adjudication of our lawsuit, it was chilling. Judge Gasch then ordered Marc to allow the government to depose me.

Marc responded, "Your Honor, let me just be clear about

one thing. They're trying to turn a status case into a conduct case. In the administrative proceeding that they initiated, they discharged my client on the basis of his status. If he is asked at a deposition, 'Have you ever engaged in conduct?' I'm going to direct him not to answer."

Judge Gasch snapped back, "And I'll direct him to answer."

"And we will then see where we are," Marc answered.

"You know where you are right now," Gasch said sternly. "You've got to answer it or I'll dismiss your case. When are you going to have his deposition?"

Realizing that it was senseless to continue arguing with the judge, Marc agreed to schedule the deposition for the upcoming Saturday. He knew his objections to the questions were justified, and he would not allow me to answer them. If the judge wanted to dismiss the case after the deposition, he was welcome to do so. Marc was more than ready to take an appeal on this issue.

The prospect of being grilled by the Justice Department lawyers didn't particularly thrill me, but there was nothing at this point we could do to avoid it. On the day before leaving for Washington, Marc and I spent part of the afternoon preparing for the deposition. He explained the format, and discussed areas of questioning that would probably be raised.

The deposition started at eleven-thirty Saturday morning in a conference room at the Justice Department building in Washington. Marc, Sandy, and a young associate from Wachtell Lipton sat with me opposite Kenneth Kohl, the Justice Department attorney, and two uniformed military lawyers. A court reporter was present to take down a transcript of the proceedings. Despite a certain polite formality, the tension in the room was clearly high as I was sworn in and the questioning began.

Kohl started by asking lengthy series of questions about numerous topics, like where I had lived after leaving Annapolis and who my roommates had been. He then surprised us with a series of medical questions, introducing copies of my medical records from Annapolis. He asked, line by line, if any of the answers to my medical questionnaires had changed since my discharge. Marc objected to the relevance of the questions, but allowed me to continue answering. The line of questioning seemed benign enough, but I got an uneasy feeling that Kohl was leading up to something.

Sure enough, a few minutes later, Kohl asked, "Do you have any reason to believe that you might test positive for HTVL-3 [HIV] antibody if you were tested prior to your re-enlistment?" What a tricky bastard, I thought. He's trying to come at the conduct question from behind.

Marc looked at me and said, "Subject to my continuing reservation, you can answer the question."

I answered, "No."

"Have you ever been tested since August 13, 1986?" Kohl asked. That had been the date of my last medical examination at Annapolis.

"He can answer the question subject to my continuing reservation and rights," Marc interjected.

"I have been tested," I responded.

"And what were the results?"

"They were negative."

"How many times have you been tested?"

"Three."

"What prompted you to get those tests?" he finally asked.

At this point, Marc objected, restating his objections as to the relevance of the questions. "I'm going to direct him not to answer," he said to Kohl, "unless you give me some understanding of what the relevance is."

"Here is the reason I'm asking," Kohl answered. "I'll be very direct. He might have gotten these tests because he was required by his employer. He might have gotten these tests because he's involved sexually and participated in sexual conduct. I want to know which it is."

"Why don't you just ask the question?" Marc asked. "There are no secrets here."

Marc and Kohl continued to argue, Kohl finally restating, "The question is, Mr. Steffan, what was the reason you obtained these three examinations?"

"I'm directing him not to answer that question," Marc interjected.

"Was the reason you obtained these three tests that we've

referred to related at all to any sexual conduct that you are involved in?" Kohl asked.

This time Marc knew that Kohl had crossed the line. Objecting again, he directed me not to answer the question and launched into a long explanation for the record, stating all the legal reasons he was using as the basis for our refusal to answer the questions.

When Kohl tried to claim that the questions were relevant, Marc simply said, "I appreciate your position, and it's something we are prepared to litigate."

About an hour and a half had passed since the beginning of the deposition, so we took a short break. When we returned to continue the questioning, Kohl got right back into the conduct issue. This time, he asked about a dozen questions, using time frames from before, during, and after the academy, as to whether I had ever been involved in homosexual conduct. After each question, Marc simply repeated our objection and directed me not to answer.

Kohl spent the remainder of the afternoon questioning me about nearly every aspect of my time at the academy, from plebe year, through acceptance of my sexuality, all the way through to my discharge. The whole process was extremely slow and tiring. Marc handled the deposition expertly, maintaining total control despite Kohl's underhanded efforts to get at the conduct issue. By five o'clock, we were all exhausted and tempers were pretty hot on both sides. Kohl was especially upset, having spent nearly six hours questioning me with nothing to show for it.

Just when I thought we might finally be done, Kohl returned to the conduct issue, asking almost desperately, "Mr. Steffan, have you ever had a homosexual relationship?"

Marc repeated his objections and refused to allow me to answer the question.

"Did you ever have any friends that you believed were homosexual?" Kohl asked.

Marc stopped the court reporter. "Just one second—off the record."

He looked straight at Kohl and asked, "Do you really want to get into this?"

"Get into what?" Kohl responded.

"Get into asking him about other people, asking him to name names so you can gratuitously discharge innocent people who are otherwise pursuing successful careers? Is that really what you want?"

Kohl said flatly, "That's exactly what we want. We believe in the policy."

Marc stared blankly back at him. He would later explain to me that, in this moment, he first understood exactly the kind of mentality we were up against. "I guess it's just a job to you," he finally said scornfully, "and I wish that was on the record."

We went back on the record and Kohl continued his line of questioning, asking, "Since you left the academy, have you ever been in contact with any midshipmen at the academy who are homosexual?"

Marc interrupted, "I'm directing him not to answer on the basis that I previously stated. You can get another witness if you want to conduct some sort of witch-hunt—OK? And that is on the record."

Finally, Kohl introduced into evidence a newspaper article in which I had stated that the cost of my training at Annapolis had been $110,000. He asked, "If you had resigned from the Naval Academy during your sophomore year when your self-identification as a homosexual had culminated, couldn't you have saved the Naval Academy a heck of a lot of money?"

It was the most enraging question of the day. My face went hot with anger as I responded, "What do you mean by 'saved'?"

"What I mean by that," Kohl answered coldly, "is instead of having to spend $110,000 on you for four years of education, they would have had to spend only approximately half that, because you could have resigned."

I was so enraged that I couldn't even respond. I felt like reaching across the table to strangle him. Marc addressed Kohl: "You can save that for a brief. If the Navy hadn't discharged him, it would have a fine soldier. That is our position. Your position is that you wasted money. Our position is that you threw away money by throwing away a fine soldier. OK? Save it for a brief."

After a few more gratuitous sexual-conduct questions that we declined to answer, Kohl finally gave up. "We have no further questions, and we're done, and it's not even six o'clock," he remarked facetiously.

Nothing I had experienced since my discharge had been as upsetting or arduous as this deposition. We had already spent nearly a year in the courts and had not even begun to address the underlying question of the constitutionality of the military's policy. Now, with Judge Gasch likely to dismiss the case, we were even further from that goal. I had been warned that a lawsuit of this nature could take years, but I was only beginning to realize how much time, effort, and frustration would fill those years.

The deposition left me with an enhanced sense of urgency. If Judge Gasch dismissed us and we lost our appeal, our case could be over for good. Now, more than ever, we needed a boost, some way to focus more national attention on the issue.

The most promising hope seemed to be the suppressed military study we had learned about earlier that year. All we were able to discover so far was that the report, entitled "Nonconforming Sexual Orientations and Military Suitability," had been prepared by a Defense Department subsidiary known as the Defense Personnel Security Research and Education Center, or PERSEREC, located in Monterey, California.

Kate Dyer had been trying diligently, through Gerry Studds and Congresswoman Pat Schroeder's offices, to get the report from official government sources. She called everywhere at the Pentagon and other military and government facilities and was given a whole range of excuses as to why the report couldn't be released. Some of the officials she spoke with claimed the report simply didn't exist. Others claimed it was classified, or that they could not locate it without first knowing its report number. They knew, of course, that without a copy of the report, she was unlikely to know its report number.

I had also mentioned our search for the study to Frank Wilkinson, a reporter who was preparing an in-depth story about our lawsuit for *The Village Voice*. He had fared somewhat better, managing to track down and speak with one of the report's authors, Dr. Theodore Sarbin. In a conversation with Frank, Dr. Sarbin discussed the content and findings of the report, confirming our information that its findings contradicted the military's homosexual-exclusion policy. Unfortunately, Sarbin was unwilling to give Frank a copy of the report.

Marc was eventually successful in obtaining a small part of the report from the Justice Department, but they would only release the cover and a few worthless appendices stating policy information we already had. They withheld the remainder of the report under the "deliberative process privilege," claiming that the report represented internal discussion on policy matters and was therefore not subject to public review. This privilege, however, did not apply to factual information and data contained in the study. Despite this fact, the government refused to release the bibliography of documents used to create the report. Furthermore, they maintained that a "reasonable search" had found no additional documents related to the policy.

Marc sent copies of what little he had received of the report to Kate in Washington. Not really expecting to find anything important, she glanced through the material. Then she noticed something on the upper left-hand corner of the cover—the report number, PERS-TR-89-002. She thought that if she called back some of her government sources and requested the report by its report number, they might send it without checking to see what it was about. She immediately placed several calls, requesting report number PERS-TR-89-002, and was assured that a copy of the report would be sent immediately. Within a few hours, however, she had been called back by each office. The report could not be released, they explained, because it was "still under review."

The more we learned, the more obvious it seemed that the military was covering up a study whose results they simply didn't want to accept. Since beginning our search earlier in the year, we had become discouraged about our chances of getting the report and, over the past few months, had nearly given up trying. Since our discouraging status conference with Judge Gasch, we sensed a new urgency, and both Kate and Howard had been exhausting their sources in an effort to track down the report.

Kate decided to set up a meeting in Washington for September 18 between Gerry Studds, Pat Schroeder, Dr. Sarbin, and Maynard Anderson, the assistant deputy undersecretary of defense for security issues. Anderson had been at the core of the Defense Department's resistance in releasing the report. Hopefully a little direct congressional pressure might break down that resistance.

Finally, on the day before the scheduled meeting, Kate's efforts paid off. She received a complete copy of the report, along with some related memoranda, through an unofficial congressional source. The source was so concerned about the Defense Department using photocopy analysis to trace the report back that Kate was directed to copy it on at least five different photocopiers and destroy each prior copy.

On the night before their scheduled meeting, Gerry Studds and Pat Schroeder read the study with growing astonishment. What Maynard Anderson had characterized as a flawed and useless report was clearly an expertly written, painstakingly researched study of exemplary quality. The study's authors, Dr. Sarbin and Captain Kenneth Karols, a Navy flight surgeon and Ph.D. psychologist, were praised in the Department of Defense memoranda dated prior to the document's release for their "expert qualifications in research and military medicine."

It was the report's conclusions that exposed the real reasons for the military's unwillingness to release it. After careful scrutiny of numerous scientific studies and shifting social and judicial trends regarding homosexuality, Doctors Sarbin and Karols stated, "Our studied conclusion is that the military services will soon be asked by the courts or the Congress to reexamine their policies and practices regarding the recruitment and retention of men and women whose sexual interests deviate from the customary."

In regard to those polices, they went on to say, "Studies of homosexual veterans make clear that having a same-gender or an opposite-gender orientation is unrelated to job performance in the same way as being left- or right-handed." Through analysis of recent, significant changes in social attitude and scientific understanding of homosexuality, they finally concluded, "The lessons of history tell us that the legitimacy of our behaviors, customs, and laws is not permanently resistant to change. Custom and law change with the times, sometimes with amazing rapidity. The military cannot indefinitely isolate itself from the changes occurring in the wider society, of which it is an integral part."

Although the report had been completed in 1988, the accompanying memoranda showed that the Department of Defense had rejected it, demanding findings more in keeping with present policies. In a memo to PERSEREC's director, Deputy Undersecretary of Defense Craig Alderman, Jr., stated bluntly that Sarbin and Karols had "missed the target." He demanded that PERSEREC abide by an earlier guidance memorandum that discouraged the analysis of job performance and suggested focusing on homosexual conduct and laws which criminalize sodomy.

They were specifically ordered to ignore the findings of the American Psychological Association and any "adherents to its general approach concerning homosexuality." The APA had worked since the mid-seventies to dispel misconceptions that homosexuality is a mental disorder. Alderman ended his memo with a subtle but clear threat: "All of us want PERSEREC to succeed. The key to success is to ensure that materials are produced which are relevant, useful, and timely."

Without Undersecretary Anderson's or the military's knowledge of the disclosure, Gerry Studds, Pat Schroeder, and Kate Dyer entered their meeting the following afternoon armed with the complete report. Two military officers accompanied Dr. Sarbin and Anderson.

Congressman Studds began, "Undersecretary Anderson, how would you characterize the study in question?"

Anderson, seated right next to Dr. Sarbin, launched into a vicious attack of the "flawed and useless" study, calling it a "feeble, unreadable waste of the taxpayers money, containing absolutely nothing of value whatsoever." Gerry, Pat, and Kate smiled politely as Anderson wove his tale completely unaware that Gerry was holding the report among the papers on his lap.

When he had finally finished his harangue, Gerry looked at him, placed his hand on the papers he was holding and said, "I think you should know that I have the complete report right here, and I've read it."

Kate would later describe to me the "look of complete shock that crossed Anderson's face at that moment as he stared back at us. His face went as white as a sheet, and after a long pause, he simply looked down and said, 'Oh.' "

The meeting continued as both Gerry and Pat commended Dr. Sarbin on his "wonderful, well-written, and illuminating report."

"I guess nothing in your report surprises me," Gerry said. "I'm simply impressed that you had the guts to actually say it. It's an extremely important document that certainly deserves public scrutiny. We're all looking forward to sharing it."

Within days, the story of the long-awaited PERSEREC report hit the front page of The New York Times, as well as every major paper in the country. Howard was inundated with information requests, and Sandy, Marc, Kate, and I spent most of the next few days talking with reporters about the report we had all worked so hard to unearth. With even the military's own research advocating change, the contradictions in its policy had never seemed clearer.

After examining the report's bibliography, Marc understood why the government had withheld it even though it was not covered by the deliberative-process privilege. Among the sixty-eight bibliographical entries and within the report's text were numerous references to military studies and other documents related to the policy that the government had failed to produce or even identify in their earlier document response. As Marc later wrote in a motion to Judge Gasch, "It is thus manifest that defendants' 'reasonable search' for responsive documents was neither reasonable nor complete."

Several days after the PERSEREC report hit the press, Kate Dyer arrived for work at Congressman Studds's office in the Cannon House Office Building near the Capitol. On her desk was a manila envelope that had been shoved under the office door during the night. She was shocked to find that the envelope contained another report on homosexuality prepared by PER-SEREC. Until now, this second report's existence had been completely unknown to us.

Entitled "Preservice Adjustment of Homosexual and Heterosexual Military Accessions: Implications for Security Clearance Suitability," the study had been prepared a year after the first report and examined the question of gays as security risks.

By comparing background information on heterosexual soldiers
with that of soldiers discharged for homosexuality, the study
sought to determine how these groups differed in regard to their
suitability for positions involving security clearances.

The findings were every bit as dramatic as those of the first
PERSEREC report. Michael A. McDaniel, the study's author,
wrote, "The preponderance of the evidence presented indicates
that homosexuals show preservice suitability-related adjustment
that is as good as or better than the average heterosexual." In
other words, homosexuals, based on the military's own predic-
tors, are less likely to be security risks than heterosexuals. In
fact, of all the sexuality/gender combinations, the study found
heterosexual males to be the worst potential security risks.

The second PERSEREC report was among the documents
referenced in the first PERSEREC report's bibliography—all
the more reason to support our contention that the Justice Department lawyers had deliberately withheld it in an attempt to
cover up the existence of relevant documents. The second report
spawned another, even larger, wave of media attention, focusing
more pressure than ever on the military's contradictions. If we
could keep up this kind of pressure, sooner or later the policy
was going to crack.

Within a few weeks of my deposition, we were back in
Washington in front of Judge Gasch. The government had filed
a motion to dismiss the case because of our refusal to answer their
conduct questions, which was certainly no surprise. In the short
discussion before the judge, Marc reiterated our objections to the
questions. When Judge Gasch repeated his threat to dismiss the
case, Marc responded, "Fine. Then I would ask Your Honor to
enter an order of dismissal and we will take our appeal."

"All right," Gasch replied.

The entire proceeding lasted exactly ten minutes. The process was beginning to remind me more and more of my hearings
at Annapolis, with startlingly similar results.

After Judge Gasch entered his dismissal, Marc filed our
appeal to the United States Court of Appeals for the District of
Columbia, which is one level below the Supreme Court. Nearly
a full year would pass before we would have an opportunity to
make our arguments before the three-judge appellate panel.

Despite our dismissal, we were all riding high after the release of the PERSEREC reports. They marked a major victory, not simply because of their content and importance, but also because the experience proved that by working together, we had real power. Through determined effort and organization, we had managed to discover, release, publicize, and bring to the national public forum important studies that, without our effort, might have been suppressed for years or even decades.

With this sense of enhanced confidence, we felt ready to take on the military. We were ready for the next challenge and the next opportunity. In our discussions following the PERSEREC release, Howard, Marc, Sandy, Kate, and I each expressed the incredible feeling of momentum we could feel this issue gaining. Enough people were aware of and interested in this policy that the pressure surrounding it would continue to grow. We were confident that "critical mass" had been achieved.

Shortly after the dismissal of our case, a completely unexpected development occurred in the Midwest, a development that would prove as important as anything that had occurred to date. Students at the University of Wisconsin in Madison had begun protesting against their campus ROTC program for violating the university's nondiscrimination policy, which prohibits discrimination on the basis of sexual orientation. The ROTC program, which utilized campus facilities and granted college credit for military-science courses, abided by the military's policy banning homosexuals. Although, technically, any student was allowed to take ROTC courses, openly gay students could not receive ROTC scholarships and were not eligible for military commissions upon graduation. These limitations effectively precluded openly gay students from receiving any of the real benefits provided by the program.

The Wisconsin protests generated interest across the country over ROTC programs violating university nondiscrimination policies, most of which specifically protected sexual orientation. Several other campuses began organizing similar protests against the ROTC discrimination.

Just as the Wisconsin protests were building, Jim Holobaugh, a senior ROTC cadet at Washington University in St. Louis, was being discharged for homosexuality. Holobaugh, the second-highest ranking cadet in the university's program, had also appeared in posters for a national ROTC recruiting campaign. Having come to terms with his sexuality during college and concerned about the military's policy banning gays, Jim came out to his commanding officer. He explained his fears of being subject to discharge once he graduated and accepted his commission as an officer in the Army. Although the officer had promised Jim confidentiality, he later reneged, demanding that Jim either resign or face discharge proceedings for homosexuality. Under these threats, Jim resigned from the ROTC program.

That probably would have been the end of Jim's story, except that the military, in what would become a series of disastrous blunders, decided that discharging Jim Holobaugh just wasn't enough. Several weeks after Jim's resignation was accepted, he received a $45,000 invoice from the military demanding that he pay back the full value of his ROTC scholarship. Already upset and disappointed by his discharge, and completely unable to pay back the scholarship, Jim decided to fight the repayment order.

After spending hundreds of dollars on a lawyer in St. Louis, Jim realized he would never be able to afford the cost of litigation. He had heard about our lawsuit and managed to get in touch with Marc Wolinsky. Marc eventually put him in contact with Bill Rubenstein, a lawyer from the American Civil Liberties Union in New York City. The ACLU's strategy was not to file a lawsuit but, rather, to publicize Jim's story and work to create public pressure to reverse the repayment order.

Before making the final decision to go public with his case, Marc asked me to speak with Jim about my own experiences and what he could expect once his story hit the press. I was open about the negatives—the public scrutiny, the inconveniences, and frustrations. But I also explained the incredible feeling of satisfaction that came from being a part of change, of giving a part of yourself to help the people without an opportunity to fight back. Jim was also feeling the stress of dealing with his family and their reaction to what was happening. Although he had come out to them before his discharge, they were not excited about the prospect of a public battle. In the end, I told him he had to make his own decision. "You're the one that has to

live with this," I said, "and only you have the right to decide
whether or not to pursue it."

Jim made that decision, and a few days later his story was
covered in *The New York Times*. The military's decision to
demand repayment of his scholarship was like a bucket of gas-
oline on the already smoldering ROTC issue. The outrage boiled
even more furiously when two cadets from the ROTC program
shared by Harvard and MIT came out, were discharged, and
were sent similar scholarship repayment bills.

Jim and I were asked to speak at Harvard and MIT and,
later, at a number of schools in the Midwest, including the
University of Wisconsin. On the day of the Wisconsin event,
over thirty college campuses around the country participated in
simultaneous protests and news conferences to voice their outrage over the military policy banning gays. In only a few short
weeks, an idea initiated at a single university, something that
none of us working on the national level had even envisioned,
had grown to become one of the largest coordinated student
protest movements since the end of the Vietnam War. Ironically, this generation of students was now fighting for the right
to get *into* the military.

Perhaps most surprising and encouraging to me was the
large, often majority, participation by nongay students and faculty members who joined in opposing the policy. Student and
faculty senates began debating the issue and contemplating res-
olutions to set deadlines for a policy change. If the military
refused to change the policy, they warned, the ROTC programs
would be eliminated.

Recognizing the importance of the ROTC movement, the
ACLU began organizing a nationwide effort to assist campuses
interested in challenging the military policy. Gerry Studds
helped add to the pressure by coordinating a series of congressional letters opposing the repayment orders. The first letters,
signed by thirty-five House members, voiced outrage over the
exclusionary policy, the recent ROTC discharges, and especially the repayment orders.

Within weeks, the military finally caved in to the mounting
pressure and dropped the repayment orders issued to Holobaugh and the two other cadets. But through their own obsti-

nacy they had helped propel the ROTC issue to a much higher plateau. By the middle of the next school year, more than fifty schools had either passed deadlines or were considering the removal of ROTC, and several schools had already banned the programs.

I continued speaking about the military issue, primarily on college campuses, completing more than twenty engagements through the following year. My work on the issue had become so consuming that I eventually left my job in SoHo. I managed to eke out a living through computer consulting, part-time programming work, and whatever speaking fees were available through the schools. I was pleased with the direction and momentum of public support for a change in policy. In fact, a Gallup poll completed in the spring of 1990 had found 62 percent of the American people in favor of allowing gay men and lesbians to serve in the military. Clearly, a great deal had been accomplished in a very short time—thanks, in part, to our lawsuit and the public support it helped garner. I felt confident that no matter what the outcome of our lawsuit, the policy could not stand for much longer.

With Iraq's invasion of Kuwait and the intervention of American troops in the Persian Gulf, we began to hear stories that exposed yet another new facet to the ongoing debate.

Shortly after the decision to enter the Gulf, the Department of Defense issued a "stop-loss" policy, effectively suspending the authority to discharge soldiers for all but the most serious offenses. Kate and Sandy began receiving information about gay soldiers who had come out to their commanders before the deployment, and were told they would be sent to the Gulf anyway. The stop-loss provisions, the commanders explained, suspended the authority to discharge homosexuals.

One of those soldiers, Donna Lynn Jackson, received a similar assurance after coming out to her commanding officer. She decided to make sure her commander was correct, and sought confirmation from the next-highest authority. That authority confirmed the commanding officer's assurance, but added that after Jackson returned from the Gulf, she would be discharged for homosexuality—provided, of course, that she was still alive.

Outraged, Jackson told her story to the press and was quickly issued an honorable discharge by the Army. The military claimed that no change in policy had occurred, and the few gay soldiers who chose to make their stories public were discharged. The vast majority who did not were sent to the Persian Gulf.

Through these cases, we were able to gather some compelling documents that clearly supported our suspicions about the stop-loss directive. One Marine Corps reserve center sent letters to several gay soldiers who had come out, stating, "Claimed sexual preferences do not constitute a basis for exemption from the mobilization process." The letter went on to state that the soldiers would be mobilized, but warned that any homosexual conduct "may be subject to disciplinary action and possible discharge."

Another letter relied more on an explanation of stop-loss: "Presently, based on the declaration of partial mobilization, requests for separation cannot be considered. Once the Secretary of Defense issued the Partial Mobilization order, the services are effectively precluded from separation activity by stop-loss provisions."

Still another letter, sent to a lesbian reservist in Washington, is worth quoting in its entirety:

1. *In response to your request for discharge from the United States Air Force Reserve based on your stated homosexual orientation, we will need the following:*
   a. A marriage license and certificate of marriage listing you and your spouse indicating that both partners are female;
   b. Or, signed sworn affidavits from both you and your significant other stating your current relationship and your intent to marry.
2. *This information must reach this unit prior to your recall for active duty, which is dependent on the world situation and could be imminent.*
3. *Discharge processing can only occur when this information is received.*

This letter was particularly meaningless because homosexual marriage is not presently recognized anywhere in the United

States. But perhaps what was most remarkable about these letters was the government's sudden familiarity with terms like
"claimed sexual preferences," "homosexual orientation," and
"significant other"—terms that before the Persian Gulf had
found no usage in military correspondence.

As tensions built between the forces in the Gulf, our appellate hearing was finally held in Washington, D.C. The three-
judge panel included Judge Douglas Ginsburg, the former
Supreme Court nominee.

From the beginning of oral argument, all three judges expressed clear criticism of the Justice Department's questions
regarding sexual conduct. I felt a great sense of relief as they
repeatedly and pointedly attacked the reasoning of E. Roy
Hawkens, the Justice Department's attorney assigned to handle
the appeal. Hawkens attempted to argue with the judges, but
was shot down at every turn. After our many depressing hearings before Judge Gasch, it was reassuring to see that there were
at least a few judges out there who could see beyond prejudices
to simple principles of legal fairness. By the time the hearing was
done, Hawkens was visibly embarrassed, and I was confident
that we had scored a victory.

Just over a month later, the appellate panel issued a unan-
imous reversal of Judge Gasch's dismissal. They declared the
government's sexual-conduct questions irrelevant and ordered
Judge Gasch to reinstate the case. If the government was going
to defend the policy, it was going to have to be on the basis of
my statement and nothing else. Nearly a year had passed since
the dismissal. Now we were back in the pit with Judge Gasch,
and I could only hope that the appellate court's slap in the face
might bring him a little closer to reality.

After the ruling, Marc resurrected his ongoing discovery
requests for government documents, and about a month later
another status conference was held in Washington. We weren't
really expecting anything unusual, so I decided not to attend the
hearing. I should have known better than to miss a chance to
watch Judge Gasch in action. This would turn out to be his most
memorable performance to date.

From the beginning of the hearing, Gasch was as belligerent
as ever. Part of our discovery requests related to information

about gay service members shipped off to the Gulf conflict, and Marc pressed hard for disclosure. The government's latest attorney, David Glass, argued vehemently against releasing the documents, claiming that they would be too difficult to track down. When Marc argued that our requests were clearly not burdensome, Gasch responded, "Well, it looks overburdensome to me. You ask for an encyclopedia."

"Well, Your Honor," Marc answered, "I differ. I don't think it's particularly burdensome."

Gasch, clearly upset, shot back, "The most I would allow is what relates to this plaintiff, not every 'homo' that may be walking the face of the earth at this time."

Marc couldn't believe his ears. The judge had referred to me as a 'homo'—a clearly derogatory term—in the middle of a court hearing.

Marc continued his arguments, referring to an affidavit I had submitted about an academy policy of allowing senior midshipmen who are found uncommissionable for medical reasons to graduate. He argued that we should also have access to information relating to that policy.

"You know what it is," Gasch answered. "He's not eligible to continue as a student."

"Well, Your Honor, I contest that as a matter of fact, I'd like to—"

"On what basis do you contest it?" Gasch interjected.

"On Mr. Steffan's affidavit," Marc responded.

Gasch asked scornfully, "That he's a 'homo' and knows other 'homos'? Is that it?"

This time, Marc knew that Gasch had gone too far, but he realized that this was not the time to confront him. "No, Your Honor," he said quietly. "That is not in his affidavit."

After the hearing, Marc, Sandy, and Cal Steinmetz discussed their shock over Gasch's comments. It seemed hard to believe that a federal judge would so clearly express his bias, especially during a recorded court hearing. They all agreed that it was time to push for Judge Gasch to be removed from the case.

When Marc called to tell me what had happened, I actually started to laugh. It was almost too incredible to believe. Judge

Gasch had finally shown his true colors, and now we had a chance to be free of him.

This was also an opportunity to show people just how biased the legal system can be against minorities. In our view, Judge Gasch's use of the derogatory term 'homo' was every bit as offensive as if he had used 'nigger' to refer to an African-American. Howard Bragman leapt into action and within a week stories about the judge's comments had appeared in *The New York Times, The Wall Street Journal, The Washington Post, Los Angeles Times,* and just about everywhere in between. In the LA *Times* article, Judge Gasch gave his only public comment, saying he had no regrets about his statements. Judge Gasch's comments also earned the top spot in *Newsweek*'s "Overheard" section, a listing of the week's most outrageous and humorous quotes.

Judicial standards regarding bias are very clear. A judge must step down in a case if he is biased against one of the parties. But the law also provides a stricter standard in order to protect the public image of the court. It states that a judge must step down in any situation in which "his impartiality might reasonably be questioned." Based on this standard, it seemed clear that Gasch would have to remove himself from the case.

After Marc filed his motion to disqualify Judge Gasch, the government had the opportunity to respond, as is normal procedure. Quite remarkably, they tried to argue that "homo" is not a derogatory term, and that the judge's comments in no way expressed bias. It was interesting to note, however, that in all of the previous hearings, Judge Gasch had only used the terms "homosexual" and "gay." Only after an embarrassing remand by the appeals court and our continuing persistence for documents did he suddenly introduce his new terminology.

In our final response, Marc submitted a remarkable twelve-page affidavit from Professor John E. Boswell, the chairman of the Yale history department and a leading expert on the historical evolution of attitudes toward minority groups. His book *Christianity, Social Tolerance, and Homosexuality* is considered the definitive work regarding the development of social attitudes toward homosexuals.

In his affidavit, Professor Boswell traced the evolution of

terms used to describe homosexuals from the sixteenth century to the present. He also described the derivation and usage of the term "homo" as a derogatory epithet which came into general use in the late 1940s. After an exhaustive list of examples from current dictionaries and press reports, Boswell concluded that the term "homo," "may be slightly less vulgar than 'queer,' 'fag' or 'faggot,' but is equally a sign of antipathy. No objective person could reasonably conclude that an adult who repeatedly employs the term 'homo' in a public forum, particularly in a courtroom, is open-minded or fair on the subject of homosexual orientation."

A friend of Marc's perhaps summed it up best when she said, "If one of my kids had said what the judge said, he would have gotten his face slapped."

Judge Gasch responded to our request by issuing a decision in which he flatly refused to step down from the case. But he included an interesting twist. In the same decision, he also submitted his ruling on our outstanding discovery requests, granting us access to far more documents than we had expected. It seemed confusing, but upon reflection, the wisdom of this split decision became readily apparent. Judge Gasch knew that if we chose to appeal his decision, his actions would appear far more impartial in light of a favorable discovery ruling. By granting us generous discovery, he would take some of the force out of our allegations of bias.

The process was further complicated by Judge Gasch's announcement that he would retire at the end of the summer, only a few months away. Despite the weight of our allegations, Marc wondered whether the appellate court would remove a senior judge who had served nearly thirty years on the bench just before he was about to retire.

These complications notwithstanding, we decided to appeal the decision. Judge Gasch's comments had simply been too outrageous to be overlooked, and even if we lost the appeal, it would eat up some of the precious time before his retirement. One way or another, we would be rid of him before he could rule on the constitutionality of the military's policy. Utilizing an unusual, immediate appeal request called a petition for a writ of mandamus, we asked the appellate court to remove Judge Gasch from the case.

A new three-judge appellate panel was chosen to review the writ. Unfortunately, they turned out to be three of the most conservative judges in the appellate circuit. Much of the law is, unfortunately, the luck of the draw, and this was simply a draw that we lost. The judges refused our appeal with no more explanation than a "petition denied."

For me, it was a bitter lesson in the politics of the courts. We could have appealed the issue to the Supreme Court, but we didn't feel it was worth the effort and the wait of probably more than a year. We decided instead to get back to the core issues of the case and push ahead to the final ruling. Interestingly, after we dropped our efforts to remove Judge Gasch from the case, his office released a statement clarifying his retirement plans. The judge had decided to delay his retirement until all of the cases before him were completed.

In June of 1991, Sandy called to tell me about an interview she had just given to Michelangelo Signorile for his magazine, *OutWeek*. Signorile and *OutWeek* had recently gained notoriety after publishing a cover story posthumously outing Malcolm Forbes. This time, Signorile was working on an "outing" article with particular bearing on the issue of gays in the military. He was planning to out Pete Williams, the undersecretary of defense for public affairs, who had served as the Pentagon's chief spokesman during the Persian Gulf conflict.

I had heard rumors about Williams's sexuality from friends in Washington ever since he started appearing on television, but I had never given them much credence. In fact, the whole concept of outing made me a little uneasy. After all, I had essentially been outed by the military, and I knew what it felt like. Sandy was especially vehement in her opposition toward outing, and had expressed her position to Signorile.

Despite my feelings about outing, I could not ignore the importance of how this story could serve to highlight the blatant hypocrisy of the military's ban on gays. There was no doubt in my mind that if Pete Williams was outed, the military's policy of excluding homosexuals, based in part on security concerns, would face the most intense public scrutiny yet. Even Sandy, despite her initial opposition, eventually changed her mind and decided to support Signorile's position in regard to this particular outing.

I called friends of mine in Washington, as well as some reporters I knew, to see if I could find out more about the story. Several of them knew bits of what was happening, and by piecing them together, a clear picture came into focus. It seemed that the entire Washington press corps had known about the story for several days, and a reporter from NBC News had secured an exclusivity agreement from *OutWeek* to break the story. Michelangelo Signorile was planning to hold a press conference on the steps of the Capitol the following week to announce the upcoming *OutWeek* article on Williams.

It appeared that none of the mainstream news sources were planning to break the story before the news conference for fear of becoming embroiled in the debate over outing. Several of them were still reeling from the public outcry over disclosure of the name of the woman who had accused William Kennedy Smith of rape. It appeared clear, however, that once *OutWeek* broke the story, many of the other sources would carry it.

In the meantime, Marc uncovered a remarkable document among the papers that the military had been forced to turn over to us as a result of Judge Gasch's discovery ruling. It was a draft letter from Headquarters, Department of the Army (HQDA), and much to our shock, it outlined a future change in the military's homosexuality policy. The HQDA letter explained the significant advancement of social understanding and acceptance of homosexuality, stating, "As homosexuality gains more recognition in society at large as a viable alternative lifestyle or a valid sexual orientation, the issue of justifying regulations that prohibit the presence of persons of homosexual orientation in the military becomes a civil rights issue of discrimination against a particular segment of the American population."

The letter also admitted the invalidity of arguments that homosexuals pose a security risk: "Current research has not identified that homosexual personnel are any greater security risk than their heterosexual counterparts. Additionally, clearer distinctions are being drawn between sexual orientation and sexual behavior related to issues of degradation in good order, discipline and morale in military units." These statements were a clear reference to the PERSEREC reports.

The letter outlined a new policy regarding homosexuality,

stating: "The Army shall not discriminate in recruitment, promotion or retention practices against persons of homosexual orientation." It went on to state that sexual misconduct would be treated equally, regardless of whether it occurred between heterosexual or homosexual service members.

It was an incredible document, certainly as positive as we could have written ourselves. Although a date for the policy change was not indicated, it was clear that a change was at least being considered, and at the highest levels of the military. What was particularly interesting is that the letter used the exact reasoning that we were attempting to cite in the courts.

We immediately released the document, and it received coverage in *The Wall Street Journal,* the *Los Angeles Times,* and several other major papers. On the same day, *The Washington Post* carried a front-page story on Captain Greg Greeley, an Air Force officer who had led the Washington, D.C., gay pride parade on the last scheduled day of his military service.

Greeley's military service was scheduled to expire at midnight that evening, but he was instead dragged in by Air Force investigators for a three-hour grilling in which they tried to get him to reveal the names of other gays in the service. After his repeated refusals, they finally gave up, threatening him with a continuing investigation. Shortly thereafter, they simply granted his discharge.

David Martin from the CBS News Washington bureau decided to combine the stories, and Greg and I both appeared in a piece on gays in the military for the Tuesday CBS evening news. Although David never discussed *OutWeek*'s upcoming story on Pete Williams with me, it was clear that CBS was already positioning itself for the story. The mainstream news organizations hadn't been particularly interested in the gays-in-the-military issue of late, at least not until they heard about the upcoming Pete Williams article.

A few days later, I managed to obtain a draft copy of the *OutWeek* article. The article was well written, and I felt that it dealt effectively with the moral dilemma behind the involuntary outing of Williams. The article explained that Williams was not completely closeted, and that he was out to at least some of his friends, and certainly to Dick Cheney, for whom he had worked since Cheney was a congressman from Wyoming. Williams had been a regular at a gay bar in Washington before the Gulf crisis, and Signorile had interviewed several people who had made direct or indirect references to Williams's sexuality.

The core question was not really the outing of Williams; it was the hypocrisy of people like Cheney who were well aware of Williams's homosexuality and still publicly supported the military's contention that gay men and lesbians were an inherent security risk. Williams held one of the highest possible security clearances, and yet the Secretary of Defense and certainly the FBI were well aware of his homosexuality. How could they possibly support the discharges of thousands of military personnel with relatively little access to classified information in light of Williams's sexuality?

This was going to be a major story, and the administration's reaction could very well spell at least a partial revision of the policy. The real question was, What was Williams going to do? Was he going to resign? Would Dick Cheney back him, and if so, how would they deal with the obvious contradictions with the policy? Did they have some trick up their sleeves to kill the story? No matter what, I knew the next few weeks would be interesting.

Later that month, Marc called to inform me that *OutWeek* magazine had suddenly gone out of business—only four days before the scheduled news conference about Williams. I made a few phone calls and confirmed what Marc had heard. Although several people expressed their suspicions about the timing of the closure, it seemed too farfetched to think that the government might have been behind it.

A few days later, Signorile presented the article to *The Village Voice*. The *Voice* at first agreed to run it, but then an emergency meeting of the editors was called because of internal concern about the outing issue. After a heated debate, the editors voted to overturn the decision and reject the article. They would not support outing under any circumstances.

It was starting to look as if the story would never break. And yet, too many people knew what was going on. By now, many reporters in the Washington press corps had copies of the article, and it was circulating rapidly. If nothing else, the article was on its way to becoming the literary equivalent of the Rob Lowe videotape.

After several weeks, *The Advocate,* a leading gay magazine, agreed to publish the article as the cover story in an upcoming issue. During the same time, NBC threw its hat into the ring with a focus piece for their evening news on gays in the military, although the rumors about Williams were not mentioned.

I also learned that reporters from at least two major networks were pushing to break the Williams story on their own. To them, the story represented a clear issue of governmental hypocrisy that was newsworthy in itself. Although the network bureau chiefs had agreed, they were all overridden at the highest levels of the organizations.

When *The Advocate* finally carried the Pete Williams outing as its cover story, it led to a flurry of mainstream media coverage. Most of the stories, however, declined to print Williams's name. During a Pentagon press conference, Williams was questioned directly about the story. He responded simply, "As a government spokesman, I stand here and I talk about government policy. I am not paid to discuss my personal opinions about that policy or talk about my personal life, and I don't intend to." But the question remained clear. How could the Pentagon reconcile a gay undersecretary of defense, someone holding the highest possible security clearance, with its public policy of kicking out gay Marine Corps privates for reasons based on national security?

Shortly thereafter, under questioning from openly gay Congressman Barney Frank, Secretary of Defense Dick Cheney publicly admitted that the security argument was, in his own words, "a bit of an old chestnut." He went on to say that he had simply "inherited" the policy and hadn't spent much time on it. A few days later, he made essentially the same comments when questioned by Sam Donaldson on *This Week with David Brinkley.* He did, however, defend the policy as a means of maintaining discipline, good order, and morale. When pressed about his meaning, Cheney could only respond, "Well, I think that there are unique aspects to military service that justify a policy that takes into account the unique aspects of military service." It was hardly a ringing endorsement.

With so much attention focused on the military's stop-loss policy, the outing of Pete Williams, and Cheney's security-clearance admissions, we couldn't have hoped for a better posture going into the final phase of our case before Judge Gasch.

I was grateful for our many advances, but I was skeptical of our chances with Judge Gasch. After all we had been through with him, there was little doubt that he would rule against us. We only wondered whether his ruling would be artful enough to withstand the scrutiny of an appeal. As Marc told me, "We know that he's going to hurt us. The only real question is how badly."

10

---☆---

Full Circle

In the fall of 1991, we filed our final motions before Judge Gasch. After three years of constant battles to remain in court and struggling to obtain military documents, we were finally able to discuss the real merits of the case and directly challenge the constitutionality of the military's ban.

The process culminated in oral argument in Washington on November 7, 1991. As usual, Judge Gasch had another surprise up his sleeve. After listening to arguments on both sides of the issue, he took the unusual step of introducing his own evidence into the case record. The information was an excerpt from the 1988 final report of the Presidential Commission on the HIV Epidemic, better known as the Watkins Commission, noting that the majority of reported AIDS cases resulted from "people participating in behaviors such as homosexual sex and intravenous drug abuse." He also introduced information from the Centers for Disease Control, noting that 59 percent of all AIDS cases reported through August of 1991 were the result of male homosexual or bisexual transmission. He asked whether this information might have any relation to the military's policy or the reasoning behind it.

Those of us in the courtroom were dumbfounded by the judge's actions, and I wondered how he could introduce an argument that even the military had never tried to raise. After all, what did AIDS have to do with my discharge from Annapolis? In response to Judge Gasch's inquiry, the military's lawyer pointed out that AIDS was not a basis for the present policy. Nonetheless, Judge Gasch asked both sides to submit their comments about any possible relationship it might play in the issues of our case.

The rest of the hearing went pretty much as expected, but I was worried about Judge Gasch's comments about AIDS. It was a chilling suggestion that certain categories of people should be excluded from military service because they have disproportionately suffered from a particular disease.

His comments also showed significant ignorance about the AIDS epidemic, ignoring the reality that lesbians have the lowest incidence of infection by HIV, the virus that causes AIDS. And contrary to Judge Gasch's suggestion, AIDS is not a gay disease. It is transmitted not by categories of people but by unsafe sexual practices, and it can affect anyone. To suggest otherwise is to simply ignore reality. Although the AIDS epidemic initially struck the gay community in this country, the vast majority of HIV infection worldwide has resulted from heterosexual transmission. Heterosexuals also account for the most rapidly growing population of new AIDS cases in this country.

Even more to the point was the fact that the military tests all service members for the HIV virus, and those who test positive are not automatically discharged. They are allowed to serve for as long as they are physically able. But even if the military wanted to discriminate on the basis of HIV infection, it would be unnecessary to pry into the sexual orientations of service members. They would already have all the information they need to exclude those with HIV.

I shared my concerns with Marc and Sandy following the hearing, and they were equally surprised by Judge Gasch's comments. It was clear, however, that he would have no ground for asserting that AIDS had ever been a basis for the military's policy or any rational argument to suggest that it should be. Perhaps he was simply trying to bring up something he thought the government may have overlooked.

The following day, the government lawyers made clear to Judge Gasch that they were not attempting to rely on AIDS as a basis for the military's ban on homosexuals. In a short statement in response to his request, they stated: "Although all health-related issues are of concern to those who set military personnel policies, the Department's policy of excluding homosexuals pre-dates the current issues surrounding the AIDS crisis."

One month later, Judge Gasch released his final ruling. In the thirty-five-page opinion, Gasch denied each and every one of Marc's arguments, concluding finally, "The Department of Defense's regulations that prohibit homosexuals from serving in the Navy and other armed services establish classifications that rationally further legitimate state purposes." The ruling echoed the military's familiar arguments, previously used against the integration of blacks and women, that homosexuals pose a threat to good order, discipline, and morale. Gasch not only denied that gay men and lesbians constitute a true minority subject to constitutional protection, but even went so far as to suggest that homosexuals may simply "choose" their sexual orientations.

In a shocking coup de grace, Gasch devoted nearly one fourth of the opinion to his novel argument that the military's policy of homosexual exclusion serves to protect service members against AIDS. After noting the information he had entered into the record himself, Gasch wrote, "[T]he defendant's policy of excluding homosexuals is rational in that it is directed, in part, at preventing those who are at risk of dying of AIDS from serving in the Navy and the other armed services." Gasch failed to mention that the government had specifically denied any such intention in the policy. Ironically, Judge Gasch's ruling was issued on the same day that basketball legend Magic Johnson announced to the world that he had tested positive for the HIV virus.

Judge Gasch's opinion sparked a wave of outrage across the nation, not only for upholding the military's ban, but also because of its incredibly ignorant reasoning related to AIDS. Within weeks, editorials in newspapers across country, from *The Washington Post* to the *Chicago Tribune* to the *Los Angeles Times,* had denounced the opinion as shortsighted and ignorant.

Although Judge Gasch's decision was no surprise, it was still a disappointment. However, it could have been much worse. In writing such a controversial opinion and moving beyond even the government's own arguments, Gasch has unwittingly left himself far more vulnerable to an appeal. In fact, his outrageous conduct throughout this case has helped us in the long run by creating greater public interest in the case and helping to galvanize opposition to the military's policy.

We have already begun the process of appealing Judge Gasch's decision, and the case is likely to continue through the courts for several more years. Whether the Supreme Court will ever rule on the case remains to be seen. As yet, they have never addressed any case relating to the military's policy banning gay and lesbian service members.

There is a great deal of debate over the course of action the courts will take in regard to this issue. Traditionally, courts have provided substantial leeway to the military in running its own affairs, and there is reason to believe that deference will continue to be the general rule. But more recently, a federal appeals court in California ruled that the military should be required to actually explain the reasoning behind the policy and prove through evidence why the mere presence of homosexuals in the military is a threat to good order, discipline, and morale. If the military is required to discuss and justify this reasoning, there is a good chance it will not hold up in court.

In the debate over this policy, it is important to remember that it is not a law—it is simply a Department of Defense internal directive that could be overturned by the courts, Congress, the president, or even the Department of Defense itself. In light of the flurry of recent advancements including the PERSEREC studies, ROTC protests, the Persian Gulf stop-loss policy, and the outing of Pete Williams, pressure to overturn the policy has never been higher.

An independent poll conducted in the summer of 1991 by Penn and Schoen Associates found that 81 percent of the general public disagrees with the military's policy of discharging gay and lesbian service members. An astounding 90 percent were specifically opposed to the discharge of gay soldiers who had fought in the Persian Gulf. Polls by the Gallup organization produced similar results, showing that the number of Americans opposing the policy has steadily increased, even since the Persian Gulf War.

Despite this public opposition, the military continues to investigate and discharge more than 1,600 gay and lesbian soldiers each year. The cost of discharging these soldiers, including the lost value of their training, easily exceeds $100 million annually. Although the military spent over $100,000 training me, the cost of training a pilot or a submarine officer can easily run into the millions. Additionally, there is evidence to suggest that the actual number of discharges may be significantly higher, perhaps as many as 3,000 per year. The discrepancy is explained by the fact that many service members, especially officers, are often given the opportunity to resign, as I was, or are discharged under different categories to reduce the reportable figure.

As shown by his recent statements, even Dick Cheney seems to be backing away from the policy as it stands, and there is a growing likelihood that the president or Congress will act to strike it down. The Headquarters Army document seems to suggest that the military itself might eventually drop the policy on its own, especially if opposition continues to build.

Although each branch of government—executive, legislative, and judicial—has the power to overturn the military's policy, I believe the courts, in this situation, have a special obligation to act. We know, all too well, that a democratic process is highly effective in protecting the rights of the majority. After all, it is a system of majority rule. But the systems of government are often so overburdened with issues of majority concern that there is often little, if any, attention paid to purely minority issues. Quite simply, the political benefits to elected officials are not significant enough to warrant their investment of time and effort.

Additionally, politicians may be unsure of the ramifications of moves to protect minorities, especially if they fear any potential controversy. The military's antigay policy is a prime example. Although the polls show significant support for a change, many politicians fear a well-coordinated negative reaction from the far right.

The national gay-rights bill is another good example. Although less than a hundred members of Congress have signed on to cosponsor the bill, Congressman Gerry Studds once told me that the bill would easily win an unrecorded vote in the House of Representatives. The problem, he explained, is that conservative members would demand a recorded vote. With the tallies being recorded, he doubted that even all of the cosponsors would vote for the bill. They are simply intimidated, afraid to act even though they believe in change and expect the majority of their constituency to agree.

The courts exist, in part, as a safety valve for precisely these situations. They are an integral component in the delicate checks and balances designed to safeguard the purpose and ideals of the Constitution. A crucial part of that balance is in providing an avenue for groups who lack sufficient political power to effect change and safeguard their rights. When the political process breaks down, becomes stagnated, or chooses to simply ignore the plight of minorities, it then becomes the duty of the courts to step in and act.

A disturbing legacy of the Reagan-Bush era has been a complete denial of this judicial role. By branding this judicial obligation as "judicial activism," Presidents Reagan and Bush have managed to destroy a crucial element in the constitutional balances designed to safeguard the rights of all citizens. By appointing judges who narrowly view their role as simply interpreting the laws passed by Congress, and nothing more, they may have succeeded in cutting off constitutional protections to those unable to achieve legislative action.

However, at least as far as the issue of gays in the military is concerned, I am certain that the momentum that has been gained in the last few years simply cannot be ignored. No matter what happens in the courts, I am confident that this policy will not survive the decade. It can only be a matter of time before the overwhelming public sentiment for change is transformed into political action, in the form of either congressional or presidential intervention. A first step was achieved in November 1991 with the introduction of a House resolution by representatives Barbara Boxer and Ted Weiss and twenty-one original cosponsors. The resolution calls for the rescinding of the military's policy of discrimination and is steadily gaining support in Congress.

Regardless of how it is eventually achieved, the death of this policy will finally mark the end of a dark path in our country's history, a path of government-sanctioned policies of discrimination against minorities. From a broader perspective, this policy represents a keystone in the resistance to equal protection for gay men and lesbians. As it now stands, the policy provides a cruel example to the people of this country that it is somehow right to discriminate against us. The destruction of this policy will be the end of that example and the ignorance it embodies.

As for me, that day will mark the end of a long but exciting and educational struggle. Looking back over the past few years, it's hard to believe how much my life has changed. I could never have imagined during my years at the academy a path more removed from my expected career in the submarine service. I accept now that Annapolis will always hold some of the best and worst memories of my life. When I tried at first to ignore the bad, I discovered that I lost the good as well. They are forever intertwined, like all remembrances, and today I can face them both without regret.

Although you might expect that my experiences have left me embittered and pessimistic, I can assure you that they have not. True, it's sometimes depressing to see how far we have to go in this country. But imperfect as it sometimes is, there is nowhere I would rather be. I still believe in the idea of America, the idea of freedom. The past few years have simply opened my eyes to the reality that freedom is not a gift or an inheritance, it is a struggle that we undertake every day. Perhaps most important, I have learned to question—to question rules and authority, the fairness of our society, as well as my own beliefs and prejudices.

There was a time in this country when racial discrimination was the norm. People grew up with this reality, perhaps never stopping to think about or question it. After all, it was all they had known—it was a normal, natural part of their lives. We all seek security and stability, a sense of continuity and consistency. Perhaps that is why we fail so often to question our own beliefs or to challenge those practices in our society that seem wrong. We are afraid because these things are a part of our own history and development. To question them is to question the value of our heritage—indeed, to question ourselves.

Questioning is a process that cannot be undertaken without feelings of insecurity and vulnerability. Somehow, it seems better to know where we stand, even if we know deep down inside that we're wrong. And yet, we cannot escape the reality that our greatest advancements, both individual and societal, inevitably begin with the examination of seemingly basic beliefs.

My discharge taught me with excruciating clarity how vulnerable we all are. By feeling the sting of discrimination, no longer as a concept but as a cold reality in my own life, I was finally compelled to look long and hard at the system I had blindly defended for so long.

At the core of that examination was a growing understanding of the value of diversity, and the many ways in which we have attempted to destroy it. As a society, we try too often to simplify our lives by shoving everyone into neat, identical molds. Too much diversity makes us nervous, and the suppression of diversity is one of the great constants of history. We need look no further than the Inquisition, Hitler's attempts to "purify" society, or even the religious persecution that gave rise to our own Pilgrims.

Today our methods are becoming more subtle, but they look to the same goal. How come I was never taught anything about homosexuality when I was growing up? Why was it such a forbidden topic? The answer is because we have, by and large, given up overt suppression of diversity in exchange for passive suppression, with nearly equivalent results.

In attempting to censor the entire concept of homosexuality by cutting off information from young people, it is hoped that they will not "choose" to be homosexual. No approach could be more fundamentally flawed. Sexuality is no more a choice for gays and lesbians than it is for heterosexuals. The only result of this censorship is an enhancement of the feelings of isolation and inferiority that drive so many gay adolescents to depression and, all too often, suicide.

Unlike most other minorities, homosexuals have the option of hiding, of avoiding identification. Our society imposes a set of punishments and rewards designed to suppress gay men and lesbians from expressing their identity. The military is only one institution where being gay is fine, as long as you don't tell anyone. In fact, the military's policy does absolutely nothing to keep gays out of the military; it only forces them to stay in the closet.

The suppression of gay identity takes place in broader society as well, although it is often accomplished with subtlety. Many gay men and lesbians who come out to friends, family members, or co-workers are often told, "Well, I certainly don't mind, but I wouldn't go spreading it around. After all, it's really nobody else's business."

These statements may be offered in the best interests of the individual, but they echo an invidious logic. Why not simply say, "Some people don't like homosexuals, so you should hide the fact that you're gay." Only then can we see the underlying question driving the need for secrecy—why do some people dislike homosexuals?

The answer to this question is a simple one. Ignorance is the basis of all prejudice against minorities—ignorance that promotes stereotypical images which, in turn, give rise to fear and hatred. It is from this ignorance that everything else flows, and until it is directly challenged and destroyed, we will simply be treating the symptoms without affecting the disease.

By failing to express our identities, we only enhance a double standard in the public acceptability of sexuality. Homosexuals who express their sexuality are immediately labeled promiscuous and accused of shoving their sexuality onto everyone else. Yet the public expression of heterosexuality is such an integral and basic part of our everyday lives that it goes unrecognized. One need only watch thirty minutes of television or flip through the advertisements in a magazine and count the number of references to heterosexual relationships. If you remain unconvinced, try reading the marriage announcements printed in your local newspaper. Sexuality is an important part of our everyday lives, and it deserves expression, gay or straight. There could be nothing more natural than public validation of the value of our feelings and relationships.

Only now have I begun to realize the relationship between events in my own life and the gay community's overall struggle for equality. My own coming out was certainly a powerful and dramatic experience, but it took me months after Annapolis to understand that coming out is not a one-day event; it is an ongoing process, a daily commitment.

When I first left Annapolis, I wanted nothing more than to start getting on with my life. I had come out, and although I had paid a high price, I had affirmed my identity and self-worth. I was grateful for those who had come to my aid—the Talleys, my friends at Annapolis, and my parents, even though it took them a little while.

My mistake was in thinking that the first step was the end of the process. Now that I was out, I thought, there was no need to take it any further. I was happy with the acceptance I had received, but felt it wasn't necessary for anyone else to know. After all, I thought, it's no one else's business. I knew there were many wrongs in our society, including my own discharge, but there seemed no reason to fight against them.

I had unknowingly begun the process of "quiet assimilation," having come out just far enough to prove I could, and then stopping. Now I was ready to blend seamlessly into society in a kind of coming-out purgatory, neither affirming my sexuality nor denying it. Sure, I was out to a few friends, my parents, and my sister Cheryl, but I still hadn't told my sisters Cindy or Connie, or any but a few friends at work. Even if they hadn't figured it out, I assumed it would only be a matter of time before they did.

Quiet assimilation has been the plague of many an equality movement. After blacks were released from slavery in the 1860s, many black leaders urged an end to further efforts for equality, afraid that what had been gained might be lost. Similarly, the modern gay-rights movement in this country started with the 1969 Stonewall riots in New York City. Many gains were quickly made during the next few years and, as before, partial equality managed to satisfy many.

The gay community was happy with a little newfound freedom, the police stopped incessantly raiding gay bars, the military was eventually forced to stop giving only dishonorable discharges to gay soldiers, and everyone breathed a little easier. The result was a focus on quietly blending into society unnoticed. We would be sort-of open, and slip through much of our lives assuming people would figure it out on their own.

It wasn't until the AIDS crisis hit full force that the gay community learned how little had actually been gained through quiet assimilation. With no visibility and nothing beyond our status as victims, we expected the straight community to rush to our side out of mere pity.

But that help never arrived. Only after the epidemic had killed tens of thousands of gay men, with shockingly little concern from those in power, was the worthlessness of quiet assimilation exposed. Rather than challenging homophobia, we had given in to the subtle pressure of passive suppression and become invisible. The price of that invisibility was far too high, for in it we had left ourselves open to genocide through public and governmental apathy.

The last ten years have seen the rapid empowerment of the gay community. AIDS forced us to literally fight for our lives, and the most powerful ammunition in that battle has been education. Only by finally challenging ignorance and stereotypes have we begun to break down the barriers that have held us back for so long.

In this process of education, there is nothing more powerful than the personal examples we can provide to those around us. The impact of coming out, of honesty and pride, can never be overestimated. Everything we have ever won has been earned by one thing, and one thing alone—visibility. If we remain invisible, then we are powerless.

I have spent the last four years of my life working to educate people to the reality of the military's discrimination. But nothing I or anyone else has done will have any lasting impact unless it inspires gay men and women across the country to come out, to be open about who they are, and to educate their friends, family, co-workers, and classmates.

Individual contact is the most powerful weapon we have in the battle against homophobia, indeed, against all forms of prejudice. It is a battle that can only be won from the ground up. Simply knowing someone who is gay or lesbian, African American, Jewish, or a member of any other minority is the best way to overcome hatred. Only then can we understand, on an individual basis, how dramatically our similarities outweigh our differences. Until we can see beyond exceptions for skin color, gender, sexual orientation, and all the rest, we will struggle in vain to realize the promise of true freedom.

I was not the first to challenge the military's antigay policy, and much of what we have accomplished has been built upon a foundation laid by people like Copy Berg, Leonard Matlovich, Perry Watkins, and Miriam Ben-Shalom. They were fighting this battle long before I even heard of the Naval Academy, at a time when the risks were greater and the chances of success much slimmer.

Since I took my place in line, many more have joined us— Jim Holobaugh, Greg Greeley, Dusty Pruitt, and Margarethe Cammermeyer, to name just a few, each with stories more incredible and compelling than the last. When this policy falls, it will not be because of any one person or one story or one lawsuit. It will be a victory earned by every single person who has had the courage to stand up for the truth.

I have thought a great deal lately about what this whole experience has meant to me, but perhaps never as much as when I returned home to Minnesota this summer for a family reunion. My parents had bought a lake cabin, and for the first time in years we all spent a week together on vacation.

One night, after my six nieces and nephews had been put to bed, our whole family sat together on the porch reminiscing and laughing about the times we spent growing up in Warren. We shared stories about the tricks my sisters and I had played on each other and about the countless other memories of our childhood. I even finally told my mom where that strange recurring stain on her kitchen ceiling had come from.

On that night, I realized that my life has come full circle. Since Annapolis, my family has come to fully accept me for who I am—not in spite of my sexuality, but including it. Now we discuss it as openly and casually as anything else, and our family has never been closer. Following the events of the lawsuit and watching this issue unfold have opened their eyes to a whole new world of understanding, and they have all become friends that I can talk to about anything. Now Mom sends me newspaper clippings about gay issues, and my sisters always ask about my gay friends or the latest development in my lawsuit. Even Dad has become comfortable with my sexuality, and I guess, most of all, I am proud of him.

Although it will be years before my lawsuit is ultimately decided, the final result seems to matter less and less. We have already come so far and helped to change so much. In a way, I would be satisfied with nothing more than we have already gained.

No matter what the future holds, it has all been worth it to me. In the end, I can live knowing that in so many important ways, I have already won.

About the Author

JOSEPH STEFFAN, a native of Warren, Minnesota, was discharged for homosexuality from the United States Naval Academy in 1987. Since filing suit to overturn the military's restriction on gay and lesbian service members, he has become one of the nation's leading advocates against the military ban. Mr. Steffan is an active public speaker and presently a student at the University of Connecticut School of Law in Hartford.